T0330404

Globalization and Precarious Forms of Production and Employment

Globalization and Precarious Forms of Production and Employment

Challenges for Workers and Unions

Edited by

Carole Thornley

Senior Lecturer, Keele Management School, Keele University, UK

Steve Jefferys

Director, Working Lives Research Institute, London Metropolitan University, UK

Beatrice Appay

Senior Research Fellow, CNRS, France and Visiting Professor, University of California, USA

Edward Elgar

Cheltenham, UK • Northampton, MA, USA

© Carole Thornley, Steve Jefferys and Beatrice Appay 2010

All rights reserved. No part of this publication may be reproduced, stored in a retrieval system or transmitted in any form or by any means, electronic, mechanical or photocopying, recording, or otherwise without the prior permission of the publisher.

Published by
Edward Elgar Publishing Limited
The Lypiatts
15 Lansdown Road
Cheltenham
Glos GL50 2JA
UK

Edward Elgar Publishing, Inc.
William Pratt House
9 Dewey Court
Northampton
Massachusetts 01060
USA

A catalogue record for this book
is available from the British Library

Library of Congress Control Number: 2010925943

Mixed Sources
Product group from well-managed
forests and other controlled sources
www.fsc.org Cert no. SA-COC-1565
© 1996 Forest Stewardship Council
FSC

ISBN 978 1 84844 593 2

Printed and bound by MPG Books Group, UK

Contents

Contributors

Beatrice Appay is a work sociologist and a leading figure in the analysis of precarization. She is Senior Researcher at the Centre National de la Recherche Scientifique (CNRS) and a member of Cerlis research centre (CNRS-Université Paris Descartes). She is Visiting Professor at the University of California and currently responsible for a four-year research programme on 'Precarisation and poverty in the USA'. She authored *La dictature du succès: le paradoxe de l'autonomie contrôlée et de la précarisation* (L'Harmattan, 2005) and is editor (with Steve Jefferys) of *Restructurations, précarisation, valeurs* (Octares, 2009).

David Bailey is Professor at Coventry University Business School and is currently Chair of the Regional Studies Association – a major international learned society. He has written extensively on globalization, economic restructuring and policy responses, the auto industry, European integration, and the Japanese economy. His latest book (with Lisa De Propris) is *Industrial and Regional Policy in an Enlarging EU* (Routledge, 2009). He has been involved in several major research projects and recently led an Economic and Social Research Council project on the economic and social impact of the MG Rover closure.

Isabelle Berrebi-Hoffmann is a Centre National de la Recherche Scientifique (CNRS) Researcher at the Paris interdisciplinary research centre in economic sociology Lise (CNRS-Conservatoire National des Arts et des Metiers). Her research explores experts and elites in a knowledge economy, service multinational firms, models of organizations and knowledge workers. She has recently edited *Politiques de l'intime: des utopies sociales d'hier aux mondes du travail d'aujourd'hui* (La Découverte, 2009) and co-edited 'A quoi servent les experts' 126, *Cahiers Internationaux de Sociologie* (Presses Universitaires de France, 2009). She has taught at Wharton, University of Pennsylvania and at the HEC (Ecole des Hautes Etudes Commerciales de Paris).

Rachid Bouchareb is a work sociologist and a post-doctoral member of the Paris Genre, Travail, Mobilités research centre (Centre de Recherches Sociologiques et Politiques de Paris, Centre National de la Recherche Scientifique-Universités Paris VIII et Paris X). His research interests include work conflict, resistance and the formation of collective opposition, and international comparisons, as well as the degradation of work and company rationalizations, with a particular focus on international chain stores and the resulting new forms of small and medium-sized firms.

Iain Campbell is Senior Research Fellow at the Centre for Applied Social Research, RMIT University (Melbourne). His current research examines changing working-time patterns, precarious employment, temporary migrant labour programmes, new forms of labour regulation and trade union strategies.

Patrick Chaskiel is a Professor at Toulouse 3 University and a member of the Centre d'Etude et de Recherche Travail, Organisation, Pouvoir (Centre National de la Recherche Scientifique-Université Toulouse 2-Le Mirail). His research interests include trade unionism and industrial hazards, and more generally industrial risk as a sociological issue. His empirical research is focused on the chemical and nuclear industries, and on nanotechnologies, a new social challenge to the economic sphere. He has published widely in journals, including *Sociologie du Travail*.

Dan Coffey is Senior Lecturer in Economics at Leeds University Business School. His research interests span organization and operations in manufacturing industries, political economy and industrial sociology. He is the author of *The Myth of Japanese Efficiency: The World Car Industry in a Globalizing Age* (Edward Elgar, 2006), and (with Carole Thornley) of *Globalization and Varieties of Capitalism* (Palgrave Macmillan 2009), and editor (with Carole Thornley) of *Industrial and Labour Market Policy and Performance: Issues and Perspectives* (Routledge, 2003) and (with David Bailey and P.R. Tomlinson) of *Crisis or Recovery in Japan: State and Industrial Economy* (Edward Elgar, 2007).

Heather Connolly is Research Associate at the European Work and Employment Research Centre at the University of Manchester. She previously worked at the European Trade Union Institute in Brussels in the area of trade union interest representation. Her main research interests are comparative industrial relations and trade union revitalization. She is currently working on a research project on trade union responses to migration in Europe. Her forthcoming publications include a monograph to be published by Peter Lang based on her doctoral research at the University of Warwick on trade union renewal in France.

Sylvie Contrepois is Senior European Research Fellow at the Working Lives Research Institute of London Metropolitan University and a member of the Centre National de la Recherche Scientifique–Paris VIII and Paris X Universities research centre (Genre, Travail, Mobilités, Centre de Recherches Sociologiques et Politiques de Paris). Her research interests are concerned with understanding the dynamics of social change in European societies. In 2003 she published *Syndicats: la nouvelle donne* (Syllepse) about the evolution of French trade unionism. She is currently co-editing two forthcoming books arising out of her recent and current work: a study of the export of the French social model to Central and Eastern Europe completed in 2009, and a comparative research project Sphere examining the impact of restructuring on social identities in six European regions.

Isabel da Costa is an economist. She is a Centre National de la Recherche Scientifique (CNRS) Senior Researcher and a member of the Institutions et Dynamiques Historiques de l'Economie research centre (CNRS-Ecole Normale Supérieure) in Cachan near Paris. She also teaches industrial relations at the University of Paris-X-Nanterre. Her research interests include industrial relations theories and comparative industrial relations in Europe and North America. She is author (with Volker Telljohann and Udo Rehfeldt) of *European and International Framework Agreements: Practical Experiences and Strategic Approaches* (EU, 2009) and has also published with the International Labour Organization.

Alex de Ruyter is Professor at the Business School in the University of the West of Scotland (Paisley campus). He is interested in labour flexibility, non-standard employment and the impact of globalization through foreign direct investment and labour market adjustment. He also researches public sector workforce issues and policy. He has published numerous articles in both these areas, including single and co-authored pieces in leading international journals. He is an active member of the Regional Studies Association.

Juliana Frassa is a Lecturer in the Department of Sociology at the Universidad Nacional de La Plata, and has a doctoral scholarship from the National Commission of Scientific and Technological Investigations in the Centre of Labour Studies and Research. She specializes in the sociology of work and organizations. Her latest research interests include organizational culture and organizational change in state-owned companies. She has published in national and international journals and has participated in research projects about industry and territories, regional labour markets, and precarious and informal employment.

Steve Jefferys of the Working Lives Research Institute at London Metropolitan University is Professor of European Employment Studies.

He has authored books on the unionization of US car workers (1986), and (with Mick Carpenter) on the interrelationships of management, work and welfare in Western Europe (2000). His most recent monograph was *Liberté, Egalité and Fraternité at Work*: *Changing French Employment Relations and Management* (Palgrave Macmillan, 2003). Currently he researches how companies and trade unions mediate workplace discrimination. In 2009 he authored a 27-country report on the Racial Equality Directive for the EU's Fundamental Rights Agency. The same year (with Sylvie Contrepois) he completed a French Ministry of Labour project researching the role of French multinational companies in exporting French social values.

Michel Lallement is Professor of Sociology at the Conservatoire National des Arts et Metiers (CNAM) in Paris. His research affiliations are with the Lise research centre (Centre National de la Recherche Scientifique-CNAM). He has published extensively on work, employment and industrial relations, and is the author of *Le travail: une sociologie contemporaine* (Gallimard, 2007), *Le travail de l'utopie: Godin et le Familistère de Guise* (Les Belles Lettres, 2009) and *Le travail sous tensions* (Sciences Humaines Press, 2010).

Nelson Lichtenstein is the MacArthur Foundation Chair in History at the University of California, Santa Barbara, and Director of the Center for the Study of Work, Labor, and Democracy there. He is the author of *The Retail Revolution: How Wal-Mart Created a Brave New World of Business* (Henry Holt & Company, 2009), and editor of *American Capitalism: Social Thought and Political Economy in the Twentieth Century* (University of Pennsylvania Press, 2006) and many other books on labour and politics.

Michelle Mahdon works at The Work Foundation, London. Since joining in 2005, she has been involved in a variety of projects across the public and private sectors. She is a registered chartered psychologist, with an MSc and a PhD in Economic Psychology, and specializes in health and well-being issues in the workplace. She has been responsible for some of The Work Foundation's – and therefore the UK's – leading edge research in the field. Her recent projects include investigating the socio-economics of musculoskeletal disorders, mapping job quality of knowledge workers, following up well-being and job quality outcomes for ex-MG Rover workers and exploring the attitudes of organizations to improving job quality.

Béatrice Mésini is a Centre National de la Recherche Scientifique (CNRS) Researcher and a member of Telemme research group (CNRS-Université Aix-Marseille 1) at the Mediterranean House of the Human Sciences (MMSH) in Aix-en-Provence. Her research interests are multidisciplinary, using tools and concepts from diverse fields such as geography, law and sociology, and include labour migration and mobility of capital in Mediterranean agriculture, social forums and the dynamics of resistance, the peasant movement, local and global rural alternatives, and sustainable development. Her research on circular labour mobility is part of a joint programme of the MMSH (2009–11), entitled 'Places and territories of migration in the Mediterranean, XIXe–XXIe centuries'.

Leticia Muñiz Terra is a Researcher at the National Commission of Scientific and Technological Investigations and is working at the Institute of Research in Humanities and Social Sciences (IdICHS, Universidad National de la Plata [UNLP]), in La Plata. She is a Lecturer at the UNLP. Her research interests include life course, labour paths and company restructuring. She has published several articles in national and international reviews and has taken part in research projects in the sociology of work and poverty.

Alejandro Naclerio is Lecturer at the Faculty of Economic Sciences, Universidad Nacional de La Plata and Universidad Nacional de Quilmes. He obtained his PhD at Paris 13-University, France. His research work is connected with the specific conditions for innovation in developing countries and with development topics.

Martine Pernod-Lemattre is Lecturer at the University of Lille and member of Clersé research center (UMR 8019, Centre National de la Recherche Scientifique-Université de Lille). Her research fields include new forms of employment and working-time management, quality of work in services activities, the female labour market, gender equality policies and work–life balance. Her recent publications include a number of book chapters on these topics.

Udo Rehfeldt is a political scientist and Senior Researcher at the Institut de Recherches Economiques et Sociales employment research centre based at Noisy-le-Grand (near Paris). He also teaches comparative industrial relations at the University of Paris-X-Nanterre. His research interests include European works councils, trade unions and employee representation at the national, European and global levels. He is the author (with Volker Telljohann and Isabelle da Costa) of *European and International Framework Agreements: Practical Experiences and Strategic Approaches* (EU, 2009) and of many academic articles.

François Sarfati is Lecturer in Sociology at the Paris Est University and is a member of both the Circeft and the Lise (Conservatoire National des Arts et Metiers-Centre National de la Recherche Scientifique research centres. He is interested in processes of socialization at work and emotional labour.

Jens Thoemmes is a Centre National de la Recherche Scientifique (CNRS) Research Director and the current Director of the Centre d'Etude et de Recherche Travail, Organisation, Pouvoir research laboratory (CNRS-Université de Toulouse Le Mirail). His research interests include the sociology of work, organizations, working time, social temporalities, collective bargaining and employment. He has published in several books and in journals including the *Sociologie du Travail,* and is author of *Towards the End of Working Time?* (Presses Universitaires de France, 2000).

Carole Thornley is Senior Lecturer in Keele Management School at the University of Keele. Her research interests include globalization, employment systems and structures, industrial organization, public policy and equalities. She is widely published in books and in leading international journals. She has worked on numerous commissioned projects, and submitted evidence to many official inquiries and reviews. She is editor (with Dan Coffey) of *Industrial and Labour Market Policy and Performance: Issues and Perspectives* (Routledge, 2003) and author (with Dan Coffey) of *Globalization and Varieties of Capitalism* (Palgrave Macmillan, 2009).

1. Introduction: globalization and precarious forms of production and employment: challenges for workers and unions

Carole Thornley, Steve Jefferys and Beatrice Appay

INTRODUCTION

When the collapse of one American finance house in September 2008 can set in train a process that the International Labour Organization (ILO) forecast led to 20 million people losing their jobs within a year, it is not surprising that globalization is now attracting an intense interest. Whilst economic globalization has been a tendency throughout the era of capitalist organization, the increases in its speed and spread in the last few decades,[1] aided by forms of new technology and global deregulation, have made research in this area ever more pressing. Production has nearly everywhere become a movable feast. It can be switched off and switched on, or relocated much more easily than ever in the past. With respect to production, a deepening deindustrialization process in the mature capitalist economies has seen important shifts of manufacturing and also some service activities to the newly industrializing countries (NICs), the former command economies within the Russian sphere of influence, India and China/South East Asia. Simultaneously wholesale shifts in governmental ideologies and policies have seen sweeping privatizations in both goods and services sectors, and a blurring of the public/private boundaries more generally. As a result of these processes, both production and employment are becoming systematically more *precarious*. While the main transmission mechanisms for these changes have been finance markets and transnational corporations (TNCs),[2] the employment effects of the increasing concentration of world economic power in a few tens of thousands of huge firms have been experienced everywhere: full-time permanent jobs that were the hallmark of industrial growth in the second half of the twentieth century are in decline; the legal status of 'permanent' is being challenged in some countries, while everywhere the 'norm' is shifting towards 'flexible', part-time, fixed term, temporary or agency jobs. Much of this work is now increasingly carried out by migrant workers, whether fully documented or partially documented. Labour market segmentation is on the increase. The challenges for labour organizations – and for citizens and democratic concepts – produced by this increasing *precariousness* of production and employment, the process and politics of which can be defined as 'precarization', are the core issues addressed in this book.

This collection of research monographs brings together a series of international contributions. While the editors are based in the UK and France and speak both English and French, with two of them having lived and worked for a time in the USA, the book's contributors are based in North and South America, Europe and Australasia. One of the editors identified the shift towards precarization in the early 1990s.[3] Chapters consider, from a number of viewpoints, the rapid changes in global production and employment systems being experienced currently in different parts of the world, as well as the implications for, and responses by, workers and their representative organizations. The chapters collectively encompass: new forms of production and working methods; the role and behaviour of TNCs; flexibility, insecurity, individualized and precarious work; individual and collective responses, including the role of trade unions; and ideological dimensions. Each chapter combines reviews of key contributions in the relevant literatures, while offering new reflections and research findings. The details of illustrative example and specific case studies employed within individual chapters draw on a full range of industries and sectors (manufacture [auto industry], services, agriculture, state and private).

The book does not lay claim to providing either a 'textbook' or 'exhaustive' coverage of countries or of themes. Its main contribution is in providing a reader with cross-disciplinary, up-to-date, specialist and innovative approaches – many of these from academics and researchers working in non-English-language environments whose work we proudly introduce to a wider international audience. While global, national or individual specificities are of interest in their own right, each contribution has been picked for its potential to cross boundaries and to offer insights and meaning for other contexts. It is hoped this volume will stimulate debate and further research around the concept of 'precariousness' – and worker responses – within a burgeoning literature on globalization that has tended to neglect these aspects.[4]

THEMATIC PROGRESSION

The progression of the book as a whole, from macro (studies adopting a global perspective) through meso (studies looking at national elements and institutions impacted by the global) to micro (the micro-sociology of individuals, organizations and institutions), coincides to a degree with a passage through the above themes. But this structure is not intended to limit: some issues – most obviously, ideological dimensions of changes in production and employment – run through the whole, and at each stage individual contributions pay attention to cross-connections. In many respects, this corresponds to the intuitive: 'precariousness' may be something which is induced by global events and national actors but which may be experienced by individuals as an isolating and frightening life event. Equally, any resultant collective intervention may occur at any of these levels, and it is frequently the interaction between levels and actors which is in itself a focal point of interest for our contributors.

The book commences with a chapter by Nelson Lichtenstein (Chapter 2) which well illustrates the breadth and depth of our core theme, and brings home the vital nexus between the individual, the national and the global in experiences of precariousness. Lichtenstein explores precarious work and authoritarian management through a case study of the retail supremacy exhibited by the US-based Wal-Mart and its global supply chain, arguing that the nature of globalization has itself changed in the very recent past. For Lichtenstein, the retail giant's global supply chain is anchored by largely female workers, both in the export zones of China, Central America or South Asia, and filling the sales stores: 'In both instances, at both ends of the retail supply chain, work has become precarious: low paid, highly contingent, non-union, and with relatively few social protections.' The conditions of work for both groups of workers and high turnover rates are graphically illustrated in this chapter, which concludes with a note on the politics which underlie such supply chains and a call for 'humane and democratic' reconstruction.

The theme of democracy – and the challenges for it – is addressed in Chapter 3 by Beatrice Appay in her wide-ranging exploration of 'precarization', the process by which production, employment and social protection are becoming more precarious. It confronts the issue of flexibility as contributing to legitimize unfavourable changes for workers. Appay traces the provenance of each conceptual tool and explores linkages with global production and employment regimes (including that of 'lean production') and the degradation of workers' conditions – both 'full-time' and 'casualized'. Drawing in particular from research in the USA and France, she then analyses new forms of union response and argues that these are clearly a response to 'precarization' rather than a narrowly construed 'casualization'. For Appay, the breadth and depth offered by this former concept, which 'refers to the making of precariousness and the changing relations of power', offers to the Anglo-Saxon corpus not only a more powerful analytical tool but also a potentially important tool for mobilization and social change.

Dan Coffey and Carole Thornley in Chapter 4 further explore global concepts and practices through a reconsideration of 'production myths' (including 'lean production') and their role in ideological legitimation of production and employment regimes that are antipathetic to workers' interests. Employing case study material from the global automotive industry *inter alia*, they argue that there is little empirical support for either 'post-Fordism' or 'lean production' as these concepts are commonly used by academics, policy makers and practitioners, but that these concepts carry a powerful 'baggage' which becomes a mediating tool in the ideology of production and employment and which skews the terms of debate. Coffey and Thornley conclude that 'new' and global terminologies are ones which themselves require careful re-evaluation both for analytical reasons and to inform collective response to the increasing precariousness of production and employment.

The restructuring of TNCs in the global auto industry and collective negotiations aimed at reaching transnational agreements is then the very timely topic of Chapter 5 by Isabel da Costa and Udo Rehfeldt. After a review of the global provenance and significance of this trend to transnational agreements, the authors review the European situation, providing case study examples from Ford Europe, General Motors Europe and Daimler. They conclude that the recognition of the European and world works' councils by these three companies is in itself an achievement, as is the further negotiation of European agreements with these new institutions for worker representation: trade union strength has been a 'necessary' if not 'sufficient' condition for this, but achievements are unlikely to be replicated in other sectors where unionism is weak, and a lack of clarity in European law and the recession and associated downward spiral of concessions to protect jobs may put gains at risk.

Chapter 6 by Sylvie Contrepois and Steve Jefferys moves us towards the meso-level and also focuses on the role of multinational corporations (MNCs) and trade unions, in a study focused on Central and Eastern Europe (CEE), drawing in particular on case study research in Bulgaria, Hungary and Poland. The authors explore the complex processes behind the performances of CEE10[5] trade unions as a result of changes before, during and after EU adhesion, and the increase in precariousness in all its forms which has gone further than in the rest of Europe. Contrepois and Jefferys conclude that the evidence fully vindicates neither the 'Euro-optimists' nor the 'Euro-pessimists': 'The overall context is one where greater job security for some of those who are fortunate enough to secure employment in the "globalized" sectors of CEE economies is counterbalanced by a huge extension of precarious working in the rest of their economies', but it is early days.

Béatrice Mésini explores the experiences of migrant agricultural workers in Chapter 7. This chapter serves to act as a reminder of globally displaced labour in processes of globalization: the migrant workers here come from many different parts of the world, including CEE countries. Mésini's chapter emanates from a study with a group of trade unions and other associations offering legal support for migrant workers in Southern France, and focuses on the legal precariousness suffered by these workers, and attendant poor conditions of work and security. The author argues that such legal precariousness is 'sometimes purposely maintained' with policies which (following Morice, 2004 and Morice and Michalon, 2009) act to produce 'work without workers' as well as an 'injunction for forced mobility'.

Insecurity of employment is also the topic in Chapter 8 for Iain Campbell, who provides a detailed exploration of the rise in precarious work and union response in Australia. Campbell distinguishes two distinct but overlapping processes: the resurgence of certain forms of non-standard employment that are characterized by substandard rights and benefits; and the spread of precariousness within sections of what has usually been regarded as the core workforce, supposedly protected by a full-time 'permanent' employment contract. Research from a wide range of sectors is drawn upon to explore trade union responses, and Campbell concludes that 'None has succeeded yet in reversing or even pausing the two processes that have been identified. Nevertheless, it is possible to detect at least a few promising initiatives and a certain amount of experimental energy.'

Chapter 9, by Isabelle Berrebi-Hoffmann, Michel Lallement, Martine Pernod-Lemattre and François Sarfati, explores the concept – and realities – of 'hyper-flexibility' in the IT sector, drawing examples from their research in France. The authors argue that the specificities of flexibility of IT work can only be understood if systems and interactions between actors are analysed simultaneously: sectoral firm strategies, the dynamics of transnational markets, and national industrial relations regulation. The authors find that the sector is in fact more characterized by an increasing concentration of production than by 'start-up' activity, with cost-cutting and 'offshoring' an increasingly important concomitant of global competition accompanied by increases in spatial and temporal flexibility requirements for workers. The authors conclude that the elastic quality of professional time and working conditions – which at a time of offshoring, many employees feel are getting harsher . . . – as well as relatively uncertain and muddy career perspectives . . . oblige us to paint a landscape which decidedly has little in common with the fascinating image drawn by the advocates of out-and-out flexibility. Even if the stability of the contract is still the rule in French IT services, the trend is towards a work intensification and harsher conditions for workers.

The 'hyper-flexible' worker, in the sense of a 'master of his or her own destiny', is seen to be a myth, and precariousness is here experienced in the form of working conditions rather than the form of employment per se.

Jens Thoemmes in Chapter 10 explores working-time flexibility and the increasing use of 'market' concepts in negotiations, through a study of company-level agreements in a region of Southern France. Thoemmes traces the shift in the regulation of working time by state, employers and trade unions from a preoccupation with the 'health' of workers to a preoccupation with 'market' flexibilities. However, in a chapter which carefully documents accommodations and changes over time, Thoemmes notes that such changes have involved 'core' workers rather than a shift towards a more 'casualized' workforce, and has also involved renegotiating important elements of employment protection. He concludes that new rules were only able to be established through the 'organizing work' effectively conducted by trade unions, and that this represents a form of 'negotiated globalization'.

Juliana Frassa, Leticia Muñiz Terra and Alejandro Naclerio in Chapter 11 explore trade union responses to privatization and restructuring of production in Argentina in the 1990s through two case studies of state-owned companies: shipyards and oil. Their analysis focuses on company dynamics and environment at a time of Argentina's economic structural transformation, and on the actors' behaviour. For these authors, similarly to Thoemmes above, change here needs to be understood as a 'collective creation process' rather than as imposed by a political or economic environment. In each case, trade unions adopted different strategies to address the precariousness involved in restructuring. The authors conclude that the variables explaining the differential track records of the companies under study were the particular characteristic features of each company, the international climate of the sector, and the strategies developed by actors towards privatization policy.

Chapter 12 moves the discussion further towards the micro level. Heather Connolly draws on ethnographic research of the new French trade union SUD-Rail to analyse the ways in which some of the most vulnerable and precarious workers in the cleaning sector in France are organized and mobilized, in part through unions building on strategies conducted in other countries such as the USA. Connolly notes that the organization and management of employment are based 'on a quest for maximum flexibility in terms of variation in both employees' working schedule and wages, as well as on external flexibility – by outsourcing . . . by compressing production costs to a minimum'. In a detailed and carefully argued piece, Connolly concludes that organizing strategies have been very successful, but mobilizing strategies rather less so. However, the turn towards organizing the most marginalized workers is 'important for helping to limit the worst aspects of global capitalism'.

Rachid Bouchareb in Chapter 13 continues the exploration of the 'continuing relevance of collective response' in the face of growing power asymmetries and individualization through case studies involving interviews with individual workers and trade unionists in the small and medium enterprise (SME) sector in France: IT, retail and hotel/catering. Bouchareb notes that, despite diversity in the sectors, they have generally seen a rationalization trend in production which has produced new forms of both SMEs and precarious working. Employees are scattered and individualized in their work but there are a number of attempts at resistance and collective opposition: whilst employees are pushed towards more individualized forms of defence, such individualization does not take place 'without reference to more collective frameworks available in society'.

Chapter 14 returns us to the auto industry. Alex de Ruyter, David Bailey and Michelle Mahdon offer an unusual insight into the 'aftermath' of global restructuring: in this case the closure of MG Rover in the UK. The authors focus on precariousness and labour market adjustment as this pertains to tenure, income and union representation, utilizing the findings of a longitudinal survey of ex-MGR workers and qualitative data obtained from interviews with ex-MGR workers and trade union representatives. The authors note that an initial labour market adjustment was relatively successful. However, 'low pay and insecurity of tenure are now the norm for many in the workforce', along with a 'decline in representation security' which raises issues about union renewal: pressing issues indeed in a context of global recession.

The book concludes with another unusual chapter, Chapter 15 by Patrick Chaskiel, which brings us full circle to Nelson Lichtenstein's broader questioning of political, social and economic rationales and democracy. Chaskiel's topic is the 'politics of production' in the French nuclear industry and the divergences between workers as producers and consumers and as 'citizens', with the dilemmas consequently posed for trade unions. Whilst workers here struggle with the usual work-related dilemmas, in part a consequence of economic globalization, they are also impacted upon by the precariousness introduced by the 'globalization of ecological protests', which restricts the 'breathing space of high-risk industrial firms'. Chaskiel notes that to the extent that ecological movements have 'a general and universal claim, which abstracts from the monetary or politico-strategic requirements of the "system", no collective bargaining is possible between civil society and decision makers . . . tensions run through unionism'. In concluding that trade unionism' has focused for the main part on its traditional protection of the worker-consumer, and has left to other groups the role of citizen on environmental issues, Chaskiel notes that 'The question is how far societal values are susceptible to coverage by unionism': a vital challenge for the future.

In sum, our contributors collectively show the continued relevance and importance of collective response and broader social questioning of a rising precariousness of production and employment introduced by different forms of globalization. These crucially concern political and normative questions about democracy.

NOTES

We gratefully acknowledge the responsiveness of our contributors in the editing process. Our thanks also go to our editors at Edward Elgar for their help and patience.

1. An excellent introduction to economic globalization is provided in Dicken (2007).
2. Frequently backed or enabled by states.
3. Beatrice Appay (1997). Appay also organized with Steve Jefferys the major *Journées Internationales de Sociologie du Travail* (JIST) French-language conference in London in June 2007 on 'Restructuring, precarisation and values', from which many papers were collected in a book published by Octares in France (Appay and Jefferys, 2009).
4. There has been an increasing literature on international employment issues (varying in country coverage) – see, for example, Debrah and Smith (2001); Fairbrother and Rainnie (2005) on state and state employment; and the volume by Gazier and Bruggeman (2008). However, the thematic focus on 'precariousness' and worker response is a very distinctive feature of our contribution – its importance being also signified in the recent book by Vosko (2010) exploring the issues for international regulation.
5. The ten accession countries situated in Central and Eastern Europe.

REFERENCES

Appay, B. (1997), 'Précarisation sociale et restructurations productives', in B. Appay and A. Thébaud-Mony (eds), *Précarisation sociale, travail et santé*, Paris : CNRS-Iresco, pp. 509–53.
Appay, B. and S. Jefferys (eds) (2009), *Restructurations, precarisation, valeurs*, Toulouse: Octares.
Debrah, Y.A. and I.G. Smith (eds) (2001), *Globalization, Employment and the Workplace: Diverse Impacts*, Abingdon: Routledge.

Dicken, P. (2007), *Global Shift: Mapping the Changing Contours of the World Economy* (5th edition), London: Sage.

Fairbrother, P. and A. Rainnie (eds) (2005), *Globalisation, State and Labour*, Abingdon: Routledge.

Gazier, B. and F. Bruggeman (eds) (2008), *Restructuring Work and Employment in Europe*, Cheltenham, UK and Northampton, MA: Edward Elgar.

Morice, A. (2004), 'Le travail sans le travailleur', *Revue Plein Droit*, **16**, 2–7.

Morice, A. and B. Michalon (2009), 'Les migrants dans l'agriculture: vers une crise de main d'oeuvre?', *Revue Etudes Rurale: Travailleurs Saisonniers dans l'Agriculture Européenne*, **182**, 9–28.

Vosko, L. (2010), *Managing the Margins: Gender, Citizenship and the International Regulation of Precarious Employment*, Oxford: Oxford University Press.

2. In the age of Wal-Mart: precarious work and authoritarian management in the global supply chain

Nelson Lichtenstein

INTRODUCTION

To understand why work has become more precarious, contingent, and sweated in our time, one has to grasp the shape of twenty-first-century capitalism. A globalized world of commerce and labor has existed for centuries. But today's globalization differs radically from that of even a few decades past because of the contemporary role played by the corporate king-makers of our day, the big box retail chains that now occupy the strategic heights once so well garrisoned by the great manufacturing firms of the Fordist era. At the crux of the global supply chains stand the Wal-Marts, the Tescos, and the Carrefours of our time. They make the markets, set the prices, and determine the world-wide distribution of labor for that gigantic stream of commodities that now flows across their counters. What we once called 'deindustrialization' has entailed not just the destruction of a particular set of industries and communities, but the shift of power within the structures of world capitalism from manufacturing to a retail sector that today commands the supply chains which girdle the earth and directs the labor power of a working class, in the global North as well as the global South, whose condition replicates much that we once thought characteristic of only the most desperate, early stages of capitalist growth.

For more than a century, from roughly 1880 to 1980, the manufacturing enterprise stood at the center of the world economy's production/distribution nexus. In the USA government sometimes challenged the more egregious oligopolies, but for the most part the mass production firms administered their price schedule so as to insure continuous production. General Motors wanted a 20 percent pretax return on investment, and for most of the twentieth century it got it. US Steel, which J.P. Morgan created as the de facto price umbrella for the nation's most basic industry, used an elaborate system of freight surcharges to sustain the valuation of its capital-intensive mills and mines.[1] Even the manufacturers of food items and light consumer goods, like Hartz Mountain, Gillette, Proctor & Gamble, 3M, Hershey, Kraft, and Coca-Cola, conducted themselves in an imperious manner when they stocked the shelves of the regional grocery and drug chains that sold their wares.[2]

Today, however, the retailers stand at the apex of the world's supply chains. Indeed, the very phrase 'supply chain' did not exist until the early 1980s. Manufacturers had 'distribution channels,' wholesalers operated throughout a defined 'sales territory,' retailers had a network of jobbers and suppliers. Academic theorists such as Emmanuel Wallerstein developed the idea of a 'commodity chain' as part of a world systems schema. Others used the phrase 'commodity channels' to describe the way apparel moved from Asian and Central American suppliers to North American retailers. But in the twenty-first century 'supply chain,' with its hard linkages and sense of domination and subordination, has become the artful phrase.[3]

Thus much of the global economy is driven by the supply chains that have their nerve centers in places like Bentonville, Arkansas where Wal-Mart is headquartered, Minneapolis (Target), Troy, Michigan (K-Mart), Paris (Carrefour), and Stockholm (Ikea). The goal of these mega retailers is to procure only those goods that consumers will actually buy, not what the manufacturer finds it convenient and profitable to ship. Like Ford's first assembly line, which soon made obsolete so many traditional skills and processes in the metal-bending core of the US economy, so too have these supply-chain innovations transformed the manufacturer–distributor–retailer nexus. Using a wide variety of new information technologies, the big box retailers of our day collect point-of-sale data and relay it electronically through their supply chain to initiate replenishment orders almost instantaneously. Thus when Wal-Mart sells a tube of toothpaste in Memphis, that information flashes straight through to Bentonville, then on to the Proctor & Gamble (P&G) main computer at the company's headquarters office in Cincinnati, which immediately sends the electronic impulse directly to an offshore toothpaste factory which adjusts its production schedule accordingly. The venerable Ohio home product manufacturer had long used its market power and sophisticated research on consumer buying habits to secure an outsized share of shelf space from traditional retailers. Many drug and grocery chains considered P&G a self-aggrandizing bully, but Wal-Mart turned this power relationship on its head. The retailer's superior point-of-sale data collection system enabled Wal-Mart to know more about the consumers of P&G products than did the manufacturer, which is one reason that P&G moved a 200-person sales office to Bentonville in the late 1980s.[4]

Wal-Mart is the biggest company in the world today with 2.1 million employees and revenue of over $400 billion. It is not merely a huge retailer, but a manufacturing giant in all but name. The retailer tracks consumer behavior with meticulous care so that replenishment can begin almost immediately. This is just-in-time for retailers, or 'lean retailing.' The giant retailers of our day, Wal-Mart first among them, 'pull' production out of their far-flung network of vendors. The manufacturers no longer 'push' it onto the retailer or the consumer. Or to extend the metaphor, the nearly continuous stream of container ships which move between South China and the Long Beach/Los Angeles port complex are 'pulled' across the Pacific, not 'pushed' by the Chinese manufacturers who stuff their product into nearly half a million 40-foot containers each year. Moreover 'pull' production requires speed, predictability, and accuracy in the delivery of goods, since available inventory has been cut back. Constant and unpredictable changes in sales patterns must be met by just-in-time delivery systems. 'Supply chain management' – that is the new business school buzz phrase – is the 'science' of getting this to happen in the most efficient and cost-effective way.[5]

Let's see how this system works for the two huge, and rapidly increasing, sets of workers that anchor the global supply chain. The first are those, largely female workers, in the export zones of China, Central America, or South Asia, who have become the new proletariat for the manufacturers – or 'vendors,' in retail supply chain parlance – who send a giant river of commodities to a million big box shelves in North America and Europe. The second group, again heavily female, are the sales clerks and cashiers who now fill the job slots in all those big box stores that have come to dominate the retail sector in almost all countries of the metropolitan Atlantic. In both instances, at both ends of the retail supply chain, work has become precarious: low paid, highly contingent, non-union, and with relatively few social protections.

GUANGDONG'S SWEATSHOP UNIVERSE

Guangdong Province in coastal southern China constitutes a raw entrepreneurial engine linking a vast new proletariat to the American and European retailers who are putting billions of Chinese-made products on discount store shelves every day. With more than 40 million migrant workers, 130,000 garment factories, and new cities like Shenzhen, which has mushroomed to more than seven million people in just a quarter century, Guangdong lays an arguable claim to being the contemporary 'workshop of the world,' following in the footsteps of nineteenth-century Manchester and early twentieth-century Detroit. This was my thought when we taxied across Dongguan, a gritty, smoggy, sprawling landscape located on the north side of the Pearl River between Guangzhou (the old Canton) and skyscraper-etched Shenzhen. We drove for more than an hour late one Sunday afternoon, along broad, but heavily trafficked streets, continuously bordered by bustling stores, welding shops, warehouses, small manufacturers, and the occasional large factory complex. This is how the cities of the old American rust belt must have once looked, smelled, even vibrated.

Because of its proximity to Hong Kong and Macao, as well as its remoteness from the capital, Shenzhen was chosen by the Chinese government in Beijing as a special economic zone in 1979. A few years later the entire Pearl River Delta became a virtual free market, with low corporate taxes, few environmental or urban planning regulations, and most importantly, the free movement of capital and profits in and out of the region. The results were spectacular. Gross domestic product in the Pearl River region leaped from $8 billion in 1980 to $113 billion in 2002. Shenzhen's population rose twenty-fold. Guangdong province itself, which covers most of the Pearl River Delta, produces a third of China's total exports. And 10 percent of all that finds its way to Wal-Mart's US shelves.[6]

Although Wal-Mart owns no factories outright, its presence is unmistakable. Its world buying headquarters is now in Shenzhen, it has already put more than a dozen big stores in the province, with more to come, and Wal-Mart is feared and respected by everyone involved with any aspect of the export trade, which is why the executives at the Yantian International Container Terminal in Shenzhen, now the fourth largest port in the world, give Wal-Mart-bound cargoes top priority. 'Wal-Mart is king,' a port official told us. Managers at the huge Nike Yue-Yuan factory complex in Dongguan bragged that they could fill an order from the United States in just two months. Container ships are loaded in half the time it takes in Los Angeles.[7]

The workforce in Guangdong, like that of the other coastal provinces, is overwhelmingly composed of migrants from inland villages. The men work in construction and the women in export manufacture and commerce. Factory wages are low, but far higher than in agriculture, and they are rising fairly quickly because of the labor shortage generated by the export boom in toys, garments, shoes, and electronic devices. But as in apartheid South Africa or along the employment pathways carved by so many Mexican workers in the USA, these millions of migrants are essentially stateless. Under Chinese law the 'hukou,' or population registration system, links citizenship to birthplace, so local governments in the crowded coastal provinces have turned their backs on the needs of most migrant workers. They work and reside on the sufferance of their employer, which often holds their identity papers until they complete their labor 'contract.' This is why so many factories throw up huge dormitories, some housing eight or twelve workers to a room, where residence is dependent upon employment at the enterprise next door. Women workers who are fired or get pregnant are practically compelled to return to their home villages. Marriage is difficult because there is so little affordable housing for couples who work in manufacturing.[8]

Work in the Chinese export sector is poorly paid, highly episodic and insecure. There are two reasons for this. First, many manufacturers are modest in size, undercapitalized, and subject to a hyper-competitive market. When Wal-Mart's Shenzhen buying headquarters advertises a contract for a big production run, Chinese entrepreneurs jump at the chance to fill it. Even without Wal-Mart's infamous price squeeze, the Chinese are willing to take a loss on a first Wal-Mart contract in hopes that they will recoup their fixed costs in the long run. But given Wal-Mart's enormous appetite, and its bias toward large suppliers, the Chinese vendors must themselves subcontract, and the subcontractors also find their own sources of labor.[9] As with the early twentieth-century garment manufacture on the Lower East Side of New York, no one can effectively police the complex network of contractors, subcontractors, and family workshops, especially when it is a private company, not the state, which is trying to do the police work. 'The factory owners don't think they violate the law because they do not know the law,' said Liu Kai-Ming of the Institute for Contemporary Observation, which monitors working conditions in South China. 'Ninety percent of Wal-Mart sub-contractors and suppliers cannot meet Wal-Mart's own code of conduct.'[10]

Contributing to this price and production pressure is the telecommunications infrastructure that has so integrated the supply chain. These instantaneous links between Wal-Mart's headquarters in Bentonville and Guangdong Province are a mechanism that puts relentless pressure on the Chinese vendors to meet production and shipping deadlines. Before the rise of the bar code, the shipping container, and the satellite e-mail link, just-in-time production could only take place when the supplier firm was in close geographical proximity to the assembler or the retailer. Or conversely, overseas suppliers had to wait until the next season to jack up production on items that were in high demand by North Atlantic consumers. Without instantaneous inventory information – 'data mining,' as it is called today – it took weeks or months for the retailer to really know what products it had sold, to whom, and for how much. But today, Wal-Mart can accurately forecast its inventory needs, monitor the 'out-of-stocks,' and thereby change procurement schedules in a greatly foreshortened time frame. It expects the same kind of flexibility from its manufacturers; hence the stop-and-start nature of work in so many Chinese factories – and by extension in so many vendor operations around the world – generating heavy overtime and seven-day work-weeks, punctuated by short time, layoffs, and unpaid vacations.[11]

TRANSFORMATIONS IN RETAIL WORK

Now let's turn to the character of work in the retail sector itself, where in the United States more people labor than in all of domestic manufacturing. What is production in a retail store? In a factory, it is easy enough to count the output of cars, canned goods, and widgets, and if someone slacks off on the job, production itself declines. At Ford in the first decades of the twentieth century, foremen knew how to shout 'Hurry up!' in a dozen languages. Managers there could count the precise number of cars built each hour and how many workers it required to do so. At Wal-Mart, on the other hand, sales volume is like a river whose course can be charted, measured, and forecast, but over which store managers have little day-to-day control. The ebb and flow of customer traffic is subject to multiple causalities. An unseasonably warm winter day can generate a wave of shoppers who jam the registers, muddy the floor, and turn well-ordered shelves into a disheveled mess.

Thus retail is both an enormously labor-intensive industry and a necessarily unpredictable one. Keeping a lid on the price and volume of labor, which constitutes 65 percent of all controllable costs, is the easiest way to boost the bottom line. 'We must have cheap help or we cannot sell cheap goods,' wrote Frank W. Woolworth to his store mangers in 1892, when his chain of five and dimes had but a handful of outlets. 'When a clerk gets so good she can get better wages elsewhere, let her go . . . we cannot afford to pay good wages and sell goods as we do now, and our clerks ought to know it.'[12] Sam Walton understood this as well. As he wrote in his memoir, 'no matter how you slice it in the retail business, payroll is one of the most important parts of overhead, and overhead is one of the most crucial things you have to fight to maintain your profit margin. That was true then, and it is still true today.' By his own admission Walton was a 'chintzy' employer. When in 1955 Charlie Baum, the manager of one of Walton's first stores, gave his 'girls' a 25 cent an hour raise, Sam was immediately on the phone: 'Charlie, we don't give raises of a quarter an hour. We give them a nickel an hour.'[13]

In subsequent years Walton and his successors have devoted enormous skill and energy to the avoidance, minimization, or emasculation of almost every governmental mandate, some originating in the Progressive Era, that has sought to regulate the price and quality of the labor that Wal-Mart workers offer their company. It's as if Wal-Mart's corporate DNA, its entire management ethos and system of monetary rewards, has been constructed for a world that is allergic to the all the most familiar workplace reforms and regulations of the twentieth century: the Wagner Act, certainly, but also workmen's compensations laws, unemployment insurance, overtime pay, and the civil rights laws governing race, gender, age, marital status, and disability.

Store managers, some 4,200 of them, are the key figures responsible for making the Wal-Mart system work. Actually, the word 'manager' is a bit of a misnomer for this job, because the hyper-integration of the Wal-Mart supply chain has stripped them of so much of the discretion that once came with the job. From the increasingly lofty perspective of the Bentonville Home Office, these thousands of salaried store managers look like a regiment of foot soldiers, from whom genuine independence and entrepreneurialism are more dangerous than useful.

All this puts Wal-Mart firmly in the mainstream of American management practice. Since the days of Frederick Taylor and Alfred Sloan, business firms have sought an organizational structure that combined a decision-making 'general staff' with something close to a militarized organization in the field. In the 1980s some US corporations experimented with a degree of decentralization, delayering, and outsourcing, but this organizational flexibility was rarely contemplated by the retail, restaurant, and service industry chains that have proven so successful in these last decades. The same information technology that enables Wal-Mart to trace the global flow of sodas and soap can also cheaply and accurately control a million daily personnel decisions in thousands of dispersed workplaces. Firms like Wal-Mart, McDonalds, and Jiffy Lube succeed by endlessly reproducing, in an amoeba-like fashion, a thoroughly well-tested and standardized selling unit. Business school academics call such companies 'replicator organizations' because of their single-minded focus on uniformity, growth, and interchangeability, of both product and personnel.[14]

For the store managers they have crafted an 'electronic leash' that makes it feasible for executives at Bentonville and elsewhere to monitor hundreds of real-time activities at every store location: how many hours did the clerks work in hardware, have the assistant managers filled out all of their performance reviews, what is the turnover rate for cashiers with less than one year on the job? Wal-Mart managers therefore occupy the social role of the factory foreman of old, the 'man in the middle,' who was squeezed from above by top management's demand for production and cost savings, and harassed from below by a seemingly unreliable work-force whose engagement in the enterprise demands a skillful combination of seduction, discipline, and artifice.[15]

Because of the tight labor budget on which they must operate their store, all Wal-Mart managers use minor promotions and variations in the hours of employment as among their most important individual tools designed to maintain discipline and enforce efficiency. Getting a regular day shift is a prize that all Wal-Mart workers seek. And so too is 'full-time' work at the store, defined by Wal-Mart as 34 hours per week, which makes associates eligible to purchase company health insurance and participate in various bonus and profit-sharing programs. Managers can purchase loyalty and hard work if they satisfy these mundanities.

Money is therefore not the most important thing for many Wal-Mart workers, especially if they live in small-town America. For single moms, and other caregivers, assignment to a desirable shift is far more crucial, and becoming more so as Wal-Mart and the rest of the service sector run on a 24-hour, seven-day-a-week schedule. And if two or three members of the same family can find work in the same Wal-Mart, or one nearby, then household income rises accordingly even if the wages and benefits remain paltry. Indeed, such intergenerational work and income sharing represents a return to the survival strategies of the nineteenth- and early twentieth-century family, when children joined their parents to labor in the textile mill villages of the New South, or in the canneries, bonanza farms, and coal mines of that same era, thereby piecing together an income sufficient to pay the rent and stock the pantry.

Wal-Mart executives advertise the fact that three-quarters of all company managers rose from the hourly ranks. But from the perspective of a cashier or overnight stocker, the Wal-Mart managerial hierarchy still looks impossibly difficult to enter. A typical discount store has about 250 employees, and some Supercenters have 700 associates on the payroll. But salaried managers number but five or ten. There are dozens of department heads – the men and women who are in charge of jewelry, sporting goods, clothing, fresh produce, hardware, and other departments. They may supervise several people, but they are still hourly employees making just two or three dollars more than a fresh-faced teenager. Unlike most office work, where a high proportion of the white-collar employees are on salary, or even a modern factory, where up to 20 percent of the jobs involve a good deal of well-paid skill, the Wal-Mart pay hierarchy is very flat, which means that for most employees an hourly post is the end of the line.

Although a minority find a comfortable niche, for many other Wal-Mart 'associates' an awkward shift, frustrated expectations, and conflict with their manager leads to dismissal or a huffy goodbye within two or three years. Hence Wal-Mart's chronic high turnover, which has averaged between 40 and 50 percent overall, in recent years, and far higher for those newly hired.[16] This employment pattern, characteristic of the entire retail and service sector, now constitutes a new normality for millions, but it is actually a radical break from the managerial practice and state social policy that was the norm, or at least the ideal, during most of the twentieth century. When the great mass production factories and assembly lines were built a century ago, turnover seemed the subversive handmaiden to inefficiency and social unrest. 'Just as quicksand cannot be kneaded in the hands into a solid lump,' wrote one personnel executive in 1916, 'so also will it be difficult to take hold of an ever-changing mass of employees and transform it into a homogeneous, intelligent, contented body.'[17] World War I, and the era of labor radicalism that followed, seemed to confirm that judgment. High labor turnover was economically inefficient and socially dangerous. An entire profession, that of personnel management, and an entire corporate outlook, welfare capitalism, were designed to promote a linkage between workers and the companies for which they worked. In the 1920s 'progressive' firms like General Electric, Metropolitan Life, and National Cash Register all invested heavily in what would later be called corporate 'human relations.'[18]

The Great Depression proved that this was beyond the capacity of any individual company. In the USA we remember the Social Security Act of 1935 for the pension system it put on the books, but that law was also designed to stabilize employment, and workers' income, by establishing a national system of unemployment insurance and by putting in place a corporate tax system designed to encourage managers to provide steady employment and avoid layoffs. At that time cyclical employment in manufacturing seemed the great problem: retail trade, with its largely part-time and female workforce, remained uncovered by the law or unaffected by it.

Today, retail stands far closer to the core of the economy, with a workforce larger than that of manufacturing itself. But during the last half-century, turnover rates in the retail sector have advanced decade by decade, largely because of the eclipse of the traditional department store and the rise of the discount chain. Only those who work in construction, entertainment, and restaurants come and go with greater frequency. But virtually all of these employment separations in the new retail sector are defined as 'voluntary,' and therefore not subject to government regulation.[19] When Wal-Mart or one of the other big firms wants to reduce the

size of its workforce, the company avoids a formal layoff and the unemployment compensation costs that come with it. Instead, it just slows its
hiring for a while and waits for normal turnover to reduce the labor force.
Or the big retailers slash hours, which immediately reduces their labor cost
and soon generates a wave of pseudo-voluntary goodbyes. If a manager
seeks to get rid of a particular employee, but can't find an excuse to actually fire her 'for cause,' he just assigns the worker to an awkward shift
or slots her into a lowly job. Thus, of the half-million workers who cycle
through Wal-Mart each year, the proportion who actually end up with an
unemployment check is miniscule.[20]

It costs $3,000 to hire and fire an employee, but the price is cheap. Wal-
Mart, like other retailers, has been loath to acknowledge the bottom-line
advantages of high turnover, but Michael Bergdahl, a former personnel
executive, let the cat out of the bag in his 2004 memoir-cum-advice-book,
What I Learned from Sam Walton.

> It's hard to believe, but turnover drops millions of dollars to the bottom line
> in cost savings for the company. When an experienced associate leaves the
> company he or she is replaced by an entry-level associate at a lower wage.
> Turnover of associates, for this reason, actually appears, from an expense
> standpoint, to be a competitive advantage.

The rule of thumb in retail, points out Bergdahl, is summed up by the
'30/60/120/240' formula. Translated, that means that on average, store
mangers turn over at the rate of 30 percent a year, assistant managers at
the rate of 60 percent, full-time sales workers at 120 percent, and part-time
or seasonal sales at 240 percent.[21]

Thus the work culture at Wal-Mart stands in opposition to much of the
labor legislation put in place during the twentieth century. The 40-hour
work-week, which was codified in the 1930s and made a social norm in the
1950s, no longer exists. Hourly employees at almost all retail stores work an
unpredictable work-week that varies with the season. Meanwhile, a huge
proportion of all American workers, perhaps 30 percent, are now defined
as employees 'exempt' from the US wage and hour laws. Professionals,
consultants, subcontractors, the self-employed, managers making as little
as $23,000 a year are no longer covered by either the minimum wage or the
overtime penalty. Add to this a corporate culture that celebrates the long
work-days characteristic of high tech, finance, law, and health care, and
one gets a virtual evisceration of the eight-hour day and the 40-hour week
for tens of millions of working Americans. At Wal-Mart assistant managers routinely work 60 hours per week, while the standard work-week for
Home Office personnel is five and a half days, so the company has eviscer-
ated the weekend for tens of thousands of salaried workers.[22]

At both ends of the retail supply chain, new technologies, new organizational structures, and new work cultures have generated a world of precarious work. But we cannot ignore the politics that also underlies these global supply chains, either in the making of this new working class or in its potential transformation. In China the disintegration of Maoism set the stage for the rebirth of laissez-faire capitalism under conditions of authoritarian governance that has deprived a vast new proletariat of a voice and a vision. In the United States and much of Europe, the erosion of the regulatory structures and working-class institutions long associated with mid-twentieth-century social democracy opened the door to the hyper-growth of a retail sector that depended on a vast pool of cheap and contingent labor. But supply chains, like workers' chains, can be both forged and broken. Our task is to provide the historical and sociological tools to reconstruct them on a humane and democratic basis.

NOTES

1. Chandler (1962, pp. 158–99; passim); Galambos and Pratt (1988, pp. 167–9).
2. See Tedlow (1990) for studies of Coca-Cola, Sears, A & P, and the automobile companies.
3. For an overview see Bair (2005; Abernathy et al. (1999); Gereffi (1994); Appelbaum and Gereffi (1994); and Ross (2006, pp. 24–31).
4. 'Wal-Mart, P&G Link up for Efficiency,' *St. Louis-Post Dispatch*, February 14, 1989, 12B; Dyer et al. (2004, pp. 311–26).
5. Bonacich with Hardie (2006).
6. Cheng (2003); Enright et al. (2005); Studwell (2005).
7. Author's interviews with officials at Nike Yue-Yeun and Yantian International Container Terminal, September 2005.
8. Ngai (2005a, pp. 46–48); authors' interview with Pun Ngai, September 15, 2005, Hong Kong.
9. Author's interview with Tom Mitchell, *South China Morning Post*, September 17, 2005, Hong Kong.
10. Authors' interview with Liu Kai-ming, September 14, 2005, Shenzhen.
11. Author's interview with Brent Berry, formerly Vice-President, Wal-Mart World Wide Procurement, May 21, 2007, Roger, Arkansas. See also Ngai (2005b, pp. 17–18).
12. Strasser (2006, p. 31).
13. Walton with Huey (1992, pp. 62–3).
14. Levine and Lewin (2006).
15. Author's telephone interview with David Levine, May 22, 2006. Levine teaches in the Haas School of Business, University of California, Berkeley.
16. Peterson (2005); Shuit (2004).
17. Higbie (2003, p. 8).
18. Jacoby (1997); Klein (2003).
19. Bluestone et al. (1981, pp. 84–5).
20. 'Declaration of Joseph D. Hawkins,' *Barnett v. Wal-Mart*, January 23, 2004.
21. Bergdahl (2004, p. 126).
22. 'Manager, Bentonville, 6/1998–11/2005' and 'Network Administrator, Bentonville,

1/1999–8/2002,' both in Wal-Mart Workplace Surveys, at www.vault.com/companies (accessed March 2006).

REFERENCES

Abernathy, Frederick H., John T. Dunlop, Janice H. Hammond, and David Weil (1999), *A Stitch in Time: Lean Retailing and the Transformation of Manufacturing – Lessons from the Apparel and Textile Industries*, New York: Oxford University Press.

Appelbaum, Richard P. and Gary Gereffi (1994), 'Power and profits in the apparel commodity chain', in Edna Bonacich, Lucie Cheng, Norma Chinchilla, Norma Hamilton, and Paul Ong (eds), *Global Production: The Apparel Industry in the Pacific Rim*, Philadelphia, PA: Temple University Press, pp. 42–62.

Bair, Jennifer (2005), 'Global capitalism and commodity chains: looking back, going forward', *Competition and Change*, **9** (2), 129–56.

Bergdahl, Michel (2004), *What I Learned from Sam Walton: How to Compete and Thrive in a Wal-Mart World*, New York: John Wiley & Sons.

Bluestone, Barry, Patricia Hanna, Sarah Kuhn, and Laura Moore (1981), *The Retail Revolution: Market Transformation, Investment, and Labor in the Modern Department Store*, Boston: Auburn House.

Bonacich, Edna with Khaleelah Hardie (2006), 'Wal-Mart and the logistics revolution', in Nelson Lichtenstein (ed.), *Wal-Mart: The Face of Twenty-First-Century Capitalism*, New York: New Press, pp. 163–88.

Chandler, Alfred, Jr (1962), *Strategy and Structure: Chapters in the History of American Industrial Enterprise*, Garden City: Doubleday.

Cheng, Joseph Y.S. (2003), *Guangdong: Preparing for the WTO Challenge*, Hong Kong: Chinese University Press.

Dyer, Davis, Frederick Dalzell, and Rowena Olegario (2004), *Rising Tide: Lessons from 165 Years of Brand Building at Proctor & Gamble*, Boston: Harvard Business School.

Enright, Michael, Edith Scott, and Ka-mun Chang (2005), *Regional Powerhouse: The Greater Pearl River Delta and the Rise of China*, Singapore: John Wiley & Sons.

Galambos, Louis and Joseph Pratt (1988), *The Rise of the Corporate Commonwealth*, New York: Basic Books.

Gereffi, Gary (1994), 'The organization of buyer-driven global commodity chains: how US retailers shape overseas production networks', in Gary Gereffi and Miguel Korzeniewicz (eds), *Commodity Chains and Global Capitalism*, Westport, CT: Praeger, pp. 95–122.

Higbie, Frank Tobias (2003), *Indispensable Outcasts: Hobo Workers and Community in the American Midwest, 1880–1930*, Urbana: University of Illinois Press.

Jacoby, Sanford (1997), *Modern Manors: Welfare Capitalism Since the New Deal*, Princeton: Princeton University Press.

Klein, Jennifer (2003), *For all These Rights: Business, Labor, and the Shaping of America's Public–Private Welfare State*, Princeton: Princeton University Press.

Levine, David and David Lewin (2006), 'The new "managerial misclassification" challenge to old wage & hour law or what is managerial work?', unpublished paper in author's possession.

Ngai, Pun (2005a), *Made in China: Women Factory Workers in a Global Workplace*, Durham, NC: Duke University Press.

Ngai, Pun (2005b), 'Global production and corporate business ethnics: company codes of conduct implementation and its implication on labour rights in China', *China Journal*, July, pp. 17–18.

Peterson, Coleman (2005), 'Employee retention: the secrets behind Wal-Mart's successful hiring policies', *Human Resource Management*, Spring, pp. 85–8.

Ross, Andrew (2006), *Fast Boat to China: Corporate Flight and the Consequences of Free Trade*, New York: Pantheon Books.

Shuit, Douglas (2004), 'People problems on every aisle', *Workforce Management*, February, pp. 31–3.

Strasser, Susan (2006), 'Woolworth to Wal-Mart: mass merchandising and the changing culture of consumption', in Nelson Lichtenstein (ed.), *Wal-Mart: The Face of Twenty-First-Century Capitalism*, New York: New Press, pp. 31–56.

Studwell, Joe (2005), *The China Dream*, London: Profile Books.

Tedlow, Richard S. (1990), *New and Improved: The Story of Mass Marketing in America*, New York: Basic Books.

Walton, Sam with John Huey (1992), *Made in America: My Story*, New York: Bantam Books.

3. 'Precarization' and flexibility in the labour process: a question of legitimacy and a major challenge for democracy

Beatrice Appay

INTRODUCTION

In France 'precarization' has become a common term and everyone knows what it means nowadays, even if only approximately: increased job insecurity, unemployment, jeopardized social protection. Some argue that the concept is too vague, diffuse, even confusing. Because it has gained in popularity, has it also declined in meaning? Some have sought to invalidate the thesis of precarization by stating that there was 'nothing new under the sun of capitalism' and that precarity is of no interest for social scientific analysis due to its lack of novelty, the post-war period having been just a digression in the history of capitalism. One can argue, on the contrary, that the 'Glorious Thirty Years' (the 30-year-long post-war boom) are anything but a parenthesis in history: they are the result of social and democratic struggles to build a fairer society based on political and social rights. Precarization is a concept that was built to describe a contemporary trend in the history of so-called 'advanced' societies, a trend that is in contradiction to the progress of the social state and democracy. Beyond the academic field, the term has acquired a mobilizing power and an undeniable political force, in particular to question the established idea that economic growth and social progress go hand in hand. In other words, because of the realities it refers to and the societal trends it highlights, the concept of precarization puts into perspective socio-economic and political dynamics that go against the democratic ideals of contemporary societies. What are the different meanings of the concept today for the sociology of work? What exactly is precarization? How does it differentiate from its English equivalent, 'casualization', and why import it into the Anglo-Saxon vocabulary?

FLEXIBILITY AND PRECARIZATION: THE BATTLE OF IDEAS

Precarization has become a central issue in France and a recurrent theme in the media. Starting from this observation, Stéphane Beaud and Marie Cartier (2006) wonder what the social sciences can add to the domain. In their opinion, it can add consistency in analysing micro-observable changes in the field, in relation to a larger sociological perspective, as Robert Castel (1995) did when he analysed the downgrading of the wage-earning society. In proposing to the scientific community of sociologists of work that it meet for the first time in its history on the issue of precariza-tion, was the London JIST 2007 conference on 'Restructuring, precarisa-tion and values' just the result of a bandwagon effect? This would not be a flattering conclusion for sociologists in general and for the sociology of work in particular, but above all it would disregard the history of the concept and the associated conflict of ideas.

To begin with, the social scientific origins of the concept of precarization must be clarified. Although the term appeared in the late 1970s, it is not until the beginning of the 1990s that it emerged as a concept and frame-work of analysis. The World Congress of Sociology in Bielefeld in 1994 was an important landmark in its genesis, with the sessions: 'Precarisation and counter powers in the labour process' and 'Precarisation as a social process: which counter-powers?' The word 'precarization' at that time was still infrequently used, many people, including academics, being unaware of its meaning, existence and use.

As shown by Lelay (2009), in the academic field the concepts of precari-zation and more particularly of 'social precarization' are the result of col-lective research based on empirical studies and international comparisons, discussed during a series of academic workshops in 1995, 'Précarisation sociale, travail et santé' (see Appay and Thébaud-Mony, 1997). These scientific meetings mobilized a network of over 200 researchers and practi-tioners. We should also recall here the seminal input of practitioners such as work inspectors, trade unionists and occupational doctors, who were highly concerned (in their daily practice) about the destructive effects of rising precarity at work on employees' health (Huez, 1994). In the aca-demic field, it is thus simultaneously at both national and international levels, from observations collected from different industries and sectors of activity, that the analysis of precarization was initiated in strong opposi-tion to the dominant paradigm of positive flexibility.

These academic meetings contributed to defining a field of research focused on the analysis of the processes by which precarity is being imple-mented. From the beginning, as at Bielefeld, this problem was considered

as inseparable from the analysis of the counter-powers that precarization dismantles or enhances in the labour and social movements. This
dual approach – analysis of the precarization process and analysis of its
counter-powers – is based on the idea that precarization is a major trend of
contemporary capitalism, but certainly not an inexorable one, in so far as
democratic struggles and social battles for social rights are not lost before
they are fought. This approach relies on the understanding that social
scientists have a responsibility in the battle of ideas, that they contribute
actively or passively to the development of dominant paradigms and thus
validate or invalidate the ways that thought and consequently action
are organized in a given society. In direct relation to a new organization
of work implemented in the name of competitiveness and international
competition, the precarization process results from converging public and
managerial policies designed to implement flexibility, from a large-scale
ideological transformation and from intensive work carried out by many
experts in order to legitimize the rule of markets over that of the welfare
state. Although frequently described as part of the neo-liberal ideology,
these outcomes result from political forces which are not exclusively
derived from this.

The academic work is part of this social process, both to establish the
diagnoses that direct political action and, in some cases, to guarantee the
legitimacy of the ideas that guide them. In the then-emerging paradigm of
positive flexibility, the diagnosis contained in itself the solution. The crisis,
unemployment, lack of competitiveness, sluggish growth all had one and
the same cause: the rigidity of production systems and of labour markets,
which themselves were blocked by the rigidity of employment regulations,
and in particular that of full-time employment with social rights attached
to it. Once the diagnosis of rigidity was established, the solution came
by itself: stop being rigid and become flexible. The term 'flexibility' has
positive connotations and is now found in many combinations: market
flexibility, flexible technology, flexible organization, wage flexibility, functional flexibility, temporal flexibility, etc. Each term also has a positive
connotation. 'Who can be against flexibility? Who can proclaim "Long
live rigidity!"?' Rigidity, and even stability, are often regarded as the opposite of flexibility and as such, they constitute something negative (Furåker
et al., 2007).

Flexibility is a concept that has mobilized economists since the late
1970s. 'To economists, flexibility first evokes the constraints faced by firms
or the production system, i.e. market constraints and responses addressing these constraints. A company, a production system must be flexible'
(Michon, 2008). Many economists tend to assume that any regulation of
the market produces rigidity and that freeing the market will improve the

situation, provided of course one does not look too closely at the social consequences in terms of increased precarity. By doing so, they do not address the problem but leave it to sociologists. In other words, 'flexibility' can be considered as a positive phenomenon and flexibilization as a positive strategy only if they are disconnected from their negative effects on society. What are the reasons for this separation that occurred in the 1990s between precarity and flexibility, which used to be tightly linked? With reason, economists used to consider that precarity and insecurity were direct and inevitable results of flexibility. How did the complete dissociation of the two terms happen, to such an extent that today the combination of flexibility and security is envisaged as in the concept of 'flexicurity'? To explore this issue let us go back to the history of ideas.

RIGIDITY, FLEXIBILITY AND PRECARITY

The regulation school gave a particular form to the concept of Fordist employment relations (*rapport salarial fordiste*) to characterize the organization of work and a type of economic regulation that prevailed during the 'Glorious Thirty Years', a form of monopoly regulation which allowed the transposition of productivity gains into rising wages, increased benefits and social security. But this very same employment relation was also characterized by and at the same time criticized for its rigidity, which was largely due to the rise of the welfare state and powerful labour movements that led to wage gains and increased protections for employees, in particular in the larger companies. This rigidity was soon identified as largely responsible for 'the' crisis, the root of slower growth, lower profit margins and high unemployment. With this type of diagnosis, 'the' solution was not too difficult to find: the search for flexibility became the watchword, the only key capable of ensuring the return of economic growth and social prosperity – see for instance Robert Boyer's plea for flexibility in Europe (Boyer, 1986). Policies to boost growth and employment were deployed systematically to accompany measures implementing employment flexibility in France and in Europe, in accordance with Jacques Delors's European Union White Paper (1993). It was then possible to observe this strange paradox by which, in order to fight against unemployment, public policies have increasingly implemented employment flexibility.

This is an example of how a theory which cannot be labelled as 'neo-liberal' led to a diagnosis which spread out and orientated public action for over two decades at both national and international levels. Such flexibility as promoted by economists of the French regulation school reached an international audience and became the basis of a new paradigm.

The concept of flexibility first appeared in 1985 in the Organisation for Economic Co-operation and Development (OECD) documents joining in the neo-liberal plea for labour force malleability as initially promoted by the Thatcher government in the UK.

Flexibility is a concept that has been extensively used by economists since the mid 1980s, and particularly so by segmentationists. Nearly 15 years after Piore and Doeringer (1971) laid the foundation for an analysis of labour market segmentation, Atkinson (1985) proposed his model of the flexible firm, with a core workforce enjoying employment security, while others such as part-timers, temporary workers and trainees experienced numerical flexibility and 'peripheralization'. This model partly converges with that of flexible specialization presented by Piore and Sabel in 1984, itself based on the work of Italian economists on local production systems that offer territorial flexibility between companies. For economists, flexibility is a paradigmatic question and searching for flexibility is above all searching for a way to transform fixed costs into variable costs. Enhancing flexible employment precisely comes back to avoiding fixed costs and adjusting employment to the variability of production. This kind of analysis is developed from a managerial point of view and, from that perspective, flexibility is the means by which employment is adjusted to market uncertainties, changes in products, technology, skills and volume of labour.

Researchers analysing precarity in relation to the transformation of work adopt another point of view. For them, precarity entails insecurity for workers, uncertainty, expropriation of time, hindrance from accumulating wealth, and obstacles to valorizing other forms of capital (cultural, social).

A major difference, therefore, between flexibility and precarity is that flexibility refers to the constraints of the markets, to management strategies of transferring risks to workers, whilst precarity refers to the resulting situation for the workers. Has flexibility become a concept for economists and precarity one for sociologists? This dissociation is a little too easy to make and cannot be taken for granted. But at least it should make one question academic specialization and the fragmentation of research fields. It should make one question the social scientific role of social knowledge and expertise and their political outcomes, in particular when they tend to legitimize dominant trends and discredit the will to deal with problems as a whole.

The history of ideas shows that we have gone from an almost total identification between precarity and flexibility to a quasi-disjunction between the two. In the 1980s, segmentationists focused their discussions on labour force mobility and job instability. They talked about precarity, but it was not central to their thinking: precarity was just an inevitable consequence of flexibility. What was important to them was that precarity exists for some and not for others. In other words, according to segmentationists, precarity exists for some because others are protected, and the result is a segmented labour market, with areas of security and protection in the centre, and areas of precarity at the periphery. For one of the founders of the theories of labour market segmentation, Piore, the capitalist regime reports the effects of market uncertainty on the workforce and segmentation begins when a fraction of the workforce manages to protect itself from the effects of uncertainty. Precarity ultimately exists because some have no bargaining power, no power to protect themselves, and cannot properly negotiate the conditions of their employment. In this perspective, the 'Glorious Thirty Years' were not stability or rigidity for all; they were stability for some and insecurity for others. However, by focusing on the opposition between stable and precarious employment, there is a tendency to over-stress the division between stable and precarious workers as if they were 'enemies', diverting the attention from the very centre of the problem: how the corporations reorganize themselves, consolidate and enhance the concentration process whilst fragmenting the companies, promote controlled autonomy and divide the workforce, transform their management strategies and implement anti-union policies, evade their social responsibilities and undermine welfare.

By 1979, even though the issue of precarity was beginning to emerge as an important phenomenon that was intrinsically linked to the development of flexibility, there also appeared a political will to erase the concept of precarity itself as much as possible from the field of work analysis.[1] An example of this political determination can be found in the making of new terminologies. For instance, as Michon recalls, precarious jobs were promptly renamed 'specific forms of employment' (*formes particulières d'emploi*, FPE) by the French Higher Council of Statistics he then chaired. FPE became the official term to refer to precarious employment (Michon, 2008). In doing so, the Council was shadowing 'FPE' negative traits, masking precarity behind a positive terminology. This was reinforced in 1994, for example, when the French Ministry of Labour implemented the appellation 'new forms of employment' (NFE), dressing up the same bleak realities behind the same kind of positive attire. With such terminology it was then possible to keep promoting official campaigns for the 'new flexible forms of employment'. It would have been obviously difficult and politically incorrect to encourage the development of precarious employment. In the field of work, the terms 'precarious employment' and 'precarity' were censored during the 1990s and replaced by the other, more amenable ones. Officially adopted by the Institut National de la Statistique et des Etudes Economiques (INSEE), the expression 'specific forms of employment' includes all employment statuses that are not full-time and/ or short-term, such as part-time, temporary work, short-term contracts, apprenticeships and subsidized contracts.

Today, at a time of weaker, protected markets and rising precarity, it is becoming increasingly difficult to hide precarity behind flattering words, especially after such social movements as the anti-CPE one in France.[2] This can only provoke more anger from those who feel cheated, and the main issue remains that of economists in the late 1970s and early 1980s: how time is controlled and workload plans implemented, how work is reorganized and therefore intensity, quality and productivity increased; how trade unions have been disorganized and are reorganizing; how earnings and costs are being reduced. To analyse precarization means to focus on the many dimensions of the making of precarity.

'Divide and conquer, externalize and outsource' has become the motto of leading employers who use precarization to impose their law (Marchington et al., 2004). The model of the flexible firm with a stable core and a casualized periphery is close to that of the 'neo-liberal enterprise' developed by Thomas Coutrot (Coutrot, 1998). The analysis of precarization, however, relies on a related and somewhat different model, which focuses on flexibility not only inside the firms but amongst them: the 'labile firm' tends to develop a smaller core and an extended periphery through the development of 'cascading subcontracting'. With the implementation of the 'controlled autonomy model', the 'brain company' organized around its central computing system has become a major part of the central nervous system of the globalized economy (Appay, 1997, 2005). This model highlights a simultaneous process of concentration and fragmentation, through a pyramidal network of pyramidal organizations, with the main contractors at the top of the pyramids and different ranks and types of subcontractors at the intermediate and lower levels. This type of organization is now well known. Over a dozen ranks of subcontractors have been identified in certain industries. First and second subcontractor ranks are usually large firms themselves, but further down in the hierarchy SMEs and individual contractors, self-employed and even domestic workers can be identified.

If the new organization of work has been extensively described, it has been so mainly in terms of networks with a pronounced tendency to highlight cooperation and autonomy rather than the new relations of power and hierarchical forms of constraint that are implemented through market rules, international competition and contractual forms of autonomy. The controlled autonomy model associates permanent restructuring and constant change; it implements insecurity as a structural trait of the new model of production, a sword of Damocles threatening most employees, even if in different ways and to different degrees.

Indeed, precarization does not only concern subcontractors and companies at the lower ranks of the subcontracting cascade. It concerns the large corporations themselves and their workforce. In the lean production (Womack et al., 1990) and lean distribution models (Abernathy et al., 1999) the authors highlight the performance of the lean corporation and its efficient management of the workforce, which is supposed to become as 'lean' as possible itself and free from trade unions. This new model of the large corporation is close to the labile/brain-firm model based on controlled autonomy (the paradox of more autonomy and more control), which reduces the core workforce and its social benefits, except for its very top management and some strategic executives; a system which pumps up added value along the supply chain towards the very top. This system is structurally an anti-union organization and it has massively weakened the unions since the beginning of the 1980s. Benefiting from this weakening, other corporations have openly developed anti-union policies. Wal-Mart, with its nearly two million non-unionized employees, is a famous example of this anti-union strategy. Nelson Lichtenstein, Edna Bonacich and Richard Appelbaum among others have shown the destructive effects of this new mode of production (Bonacich and Appelbaum, 2000; Lichtenstein, 2006), the direct cause of the increasing numbers of working poor in the USA (Appelbaum et al., 2003) and of the deterioration of living and working conditions (Ehrenreich, 2001), which does not spare core employees (Uchitelle, 2006), management or, more widely, the middle class (Sennett, 1998; Ehrenreich, 2006). It generates a large increase in inequalities and the soaring of the highest incomes (Piketty and Saez, 2006), a phenomenon that continues to be heavily gendered.

Katherine Stone (2004) rightly points out that while many firms have entered the digital age, 'the new psychological contract' is embedded in this new organization, a new deal at work. In this new contract, the assumption of a long-term attachment between an employee and a single company is broken. Employees must now expect to change jobs frequently and firms encourage employees not to expect a career based on long-term employment. Some sectors, including the public sector, are still organized in the traditional fashion with an internal labour market typical of the industrial era. However, the public sector is also outsourcing and privatizing services along the guidelines of public–private partnership strategies (Grimshaw and Hebson, 2005), and externalizes many of its activities. The loss of a job is invariably at a high personal cost to the individual concerned. But the waves of layoffs 'dot.com', those of the net economy, unlike the dismissals of the 1980s and 1990s, do not generate the enormous anger and bitterness that such waves used to, at least among the young. Being dismissed is accepted as an unfortunate but predictable fact of life. Currently the new waves of layoffs reinforce the credo of 'no long-term' (Sennett, 1998), which dominated the first decade of the 2000s. In addition to the instability of employment, contract work includes the insecurity of social protection. If the employee is not permanently attached to an employer who provides good benefits and social protection plans, he or she loses that safety net and often the opportunity to benefit from it (Stone, 2004).

What characterizes a precarious job is not so much the length of working time as how power relations and legal responsibility are being reorganized in the triangular relationship between the employee, the subcontractor and the main contractor. Quadrangular relationships and even more complex work relations are formed when there are several layers of subcontracting workers and temporary workers working on the same premises. Microsoft has organized an internal precarious workforce, such as the now famous 'permatemps': these workers are hired on a clear understanding that their status is not permanent. They are termed 'temporary' although they perform the same tasks, often during several years, as and alongside 'permanent' workers. They sign a declaration in which they accept the status of self-employed, although performing the same functions as their permanent counterparts. Recruited on the basis of an explicit understanding that their status is indeed temporary, permatemps do not receive stock options and are not allowed to use the facilities of the company (Van Jaarsveld, 2004; Stone, 2004). But in the case of *Vizcaino v. Microsoft*, a federal court imposed employee status for permatemps with payment of the arrears of charges to the state and access to pension funds (Kesselman, 2007). However, this statute does not protect one from future dismissal.

Precarization obviously concerns the development of precarious employment within the core and subcontractors' workforces, but it also concerns an underlying transformation of full-time and permanent employment status, in particular towards more freedom for the employer to adjust the workforce to the variability of production. The USA is 'ahead' of other 'developed and advanced' countries in this matter: full-time and permanent employment is largely influenced by the rule of employment 'at will'. Under this rule, the employer can – except when company agreements exist – dismiss an employee at any moment, with or without cause and without any obligation of notice or severance pay. The only way to challenge this is to prove discrimination. The doctrine of employment at will asserts that a contract of employment may be terminated at any time by either party for any reason or no reason at all. Recent limitations have hardly affected unskilled labour (Autor, 2003) and according to recent estimates available from the Bureau of Labor Statistics (BLS), fewer than 25 per cent of employees being made redundant receive severance pay (OECD, 2004; Parsons, 2005). As stressed by Sébastien Chauvin in his analysis of day labour in Chicago, beyond employment contracts themselves, what matters the most are the rights attached to each of these contracts (Chauvin, 2007). Thus, the concealed and undergoing hollowing out of social rights attached to permanent employment is part and parcel of the precarization process. This is what is happening in France, where labour laws have been continually modified since the beginning of the 1980s in order to implement greater flexibility for the employers to restore their prerogatives. The idea of the '*contrat unique*' that Nicolas Sarkozy wanted to introduce when becoming President in 2007 goes in the same direction as the American 'employment at will' doctrine, whose purpose is to facilitate dismissal with few compensatory rights and social protection, decreased responsibility of the state and employers, and increased uncertainty for workers. The *Contrat Nouvelle Embauche* (CNE, or Contract for New Employment)[3] and *Contrat Première Embauche* (CPE, or First Employment Contract) were prototypes of the *contrat unique* with a two-year probation period. Both have since been abandoned, the first one in June 2008[4] as a result of legal actions at national and international levels after its two main features (the 'two years probation' and 'fire at will' without cause) were declared contradictory to international law by the ILO in November 2007.[5] The second bill was withdrawn, as already mentioned, under the pressure of street protests. It ignited one of the most important social movements in recent years and the government had to step back. In other words, precarization can occur by multiplying short-term contracts, derogatory forms of employment and contracting out employment, but it can also happen by changing the rules and laws of 'permanent' employment and by diminishing the social rights and protection attached to it.

THE REVIVAL OF THE LABOUR MOVEMENT AND THE RISE OF THE PRECARIAT

The analysis of precarization departs from analyses which tend to classify the poor, the unemployed and the precarious by naturalizing or even criminalizing them, emphasizing their 'fragility', weaknesses and other negative traits, downplaying their combativeness, capabilities, organizational resistance and resilience. It can be considered that it is through such a paradigm shift that the revival of the American labour movement is taking place, when the watchword is 'Change to win' with the aim of 'organizing the unorganized' – particularly undocumented immigrant workers, women, and employees among the poorest and most vulnerable. This union revival shows, if it is needed, that 'these' people amongst the most precarious are not only organizable, but can organize and take responsibilities in the trade union movement, despite the magnitude of the threats they are exposed to (Milkman, 2006).

It is from a radical change in perception of the most exploited workers that this fundamental change in the American trade union history is taking place. Not only did they find a voice, logistic support and capacity for action in this particular segment of the trade union movement, but they have also proved that they can become a driving force of the new trade union struggles. Kim Voss and Rachel Sherman consider that a sense of crisis and a desire for change in response to the devastating effects of casualization and restructuring are among the preconditions of this revitalization of the trade union movement (Voss and Sherman, 2000). From my own observations in Los Angeles in 2007, I would add the existence of a 'milieu of innovation' characterized by geographical concentration and convergence, globally and locally, between university and trade union research centres, lawyers and activists, and financial and organizational support from different sources, all creating dynamics of intense exchange of knowledge and experience. It is important to notice that a number of employers are supporting this renewal, because they want to escape the spiral of the lowest bidder and of deregulated competition that forces them to act in ways inconsistent with their values and their conception of what good work means. One can consider that Obama's election as president in 2009 is the result of a shared understanding that the United States has gone too far in the precarization process at the expense of social protections and social rights.

There is a growing understanding of a situation that no longer necessarily opposes insiders and outsiders, the rise of a common condition beyond fragmentation, opposition and differentiation. 'The precarious' are becoming a political force and they are no longer strictly equivalent to what used to be portrayed as 'the poor,' in particular in terms of cultural capital and skills. The young receive higher education but find themselves in long-term unemployment, as is often the case in France. Highly skilled young people, even in advanced industries and cutting-edge areas, suffer from precarious employment and low wages. Those who thought they were among the privileged and protected find themselves in the turmoil of restructuring; they may be dismissed or pushed out of their homes, as is currently happening in the States due to the subprime crisis.

In France, since the social movements of 1995 and in particular the anti-CPE movement in 2006, as well as in today's social movements, the terms 'the precarious' (*les précaires*) and 'precarity' (*précarité*) have come to play an important role in social struggles. 'Precarity' serves as the rallying banner of 'the no's' (*les sans*) – no job, no documents, no home – together with all the other people/groups fighting precariousness, among which are the 'Precarious Generation' (Collectif Génération Précaire, 2006) and the now famous '*intermittents du spectacle*' movement (the French precarious cultural workers' movement), or Euromayday. They form what is now called in Europe the 'precariat', a collective political subject in formation (Revelli, 1999). The 'precariat' emanates from a contraction of the words 'precarious' and 'proletariat'. It regroups the unemployed and the precarious (manual and intellectual) workers in struggle in all sectors of activity. The terminology has been used recently in France by Evelyne Perrin and Robert Castel (Perrin, 2004; Castel, 2007), but it emanates from the social movement itself. Precariousness increasingly defines the conditions under which people work in all different sectors of activity, and yet it is not only work but also living conditions that have become precarious for more and more extensive portions of the population of the 'advanced societies'. According to Alex Foti (Scheuer, 2006), one of the founders of Euromayday, the precariat is to the post-industrial society what the proletariat used to be to the industrial society.

WHY USE THE CONCEPT OF PRECARIZATION IN ENGLISH?

Why should the French concept of *precarisation* be imported into English? The terms 'precarious', 'precarity' or 'precariousness' do exist in English, while the term 'precarisation', or 'precarization', does not exist as such. If it has started circulating, it is not yet at all widespread.

In relation to work, its nearest equivalent is casualization, which comes from the Latin *casualis* (*casus*: case, event) with three main meanings: (1) what happens by chance, without premeditation, what is occasional and appears at irregular intervals (casual work); (2) what is without formality, without ceremony, relaxed, informal (casual clothes); (3) which is neither serious nor deep, but rather superficial (casual conversation). In 'casual', there is no undertone of danger as there is in 'precarious'.

The etymological origin of 'precarious' is very different: the word comes from the Latin *precare* (to pray), and what is obtained by praying or begging depends on the will, pleasure or favour of another, if not of the 'Almighty'. In 'precarious' there is a notion of danger due to a lack of security or stability, a loss of control over one's own life. It is easy to understand that although the terms 'casualization' in English and 'precarization' in French are supposed to reflect the same realities related to current changes in working conditions, employment and social protection, their meaning and semantic fields are substantially different. Precarization refers to the making of precariousness and the changing relations of power. It identifies an important trend that constructs a helpless and unprotected individual, instead of what can be expected in a democratic society: the making of a stronger individual protected by well-established and guaranteed social rights obtained through ongoing battles for better working conditions and pay.

After the World Congress of Sociology in Bielefeld in 1994, we tried to translate the French concept of *précarisation* with our English colleagues, but to no avail. The organization of the eleventh JIST conference in London in 2007, and this book emanating from the conference, offers the possibility of importing the concept into the Anglo-Saxon corpus.

Before concluding this chapter, we should mention Judith Butler, for whom the recognition of precarious lives through struggle is an act that interrupts the violence it incorporates and whose standards can be legitimized only on condition of making these standards imperceptible (Butler, 2004). To paraphrase her, we can say that the recognition of precariousness and even more so the recognition of the precarization process itself is an act that confronts and interrupts – by the analysis and through the battle of ideas – the economic and social violence it incorporates and whose standards can be legitimized only on condition of making these standards invisible and unreadable in their function of exclusion and domination. Finally we can conclude with Zigmund Bauman's assertion that 'if political rights are necessary to set social rights in place, social rights are indispensable to keep political rights in operation. The two rights need each other for their survival; that survival can only be their joint achievement' (Bauman, 2007, p. 62).

CONCLUSION

The number of studies analysing precariousness has considerably increased since the late 1990s. Despite the diversity of situations examined, a set of strikingly similar observations has emerged. These studies clearly demonstrate that the conditions of work and employment are systematically becoming more precarious – a phenomenon both consistent with and predicted by the broader concept of precarization.

To summarize briefly the state of the debate in the sociology of work: some scholars nevertheless deny the very existence of precarization, others take it for granted, and in between these polar positions lie many possible intermediate ones. Despite the diversity of analyses, there is a clear and fundamental opposition between, on the one hand, proponents of a critical analysis that identifies and highlights problems in the ways production and work are being reorganized at world and local levels, and, on the other hand, proponents of ever growing levels of flexibility. Those who view increasing flexibility in a positive light have occupied the dominant place in the sociology of work since the mid 1980s. For them, increasing flexibility is 'the' way towards a better future. But the magnitude and negative consequences of precarization are such that this prevailing position, which constitutes what can be called the 'positive flexibility paradigm', is no longer realistically tenable. Its proponents can maintain their position only because they refuse to recognize the demonstrated precarious outcomes of 'flexibilization'.

To ensure clarity in this debate, a distinction must be made between the concept of 'precariousness' and that of 'precarization'. The concept of precariousness/precarity helps the researcher identify a specific situation or condition but it does not imply the existence of a larger trend: an active process by which precariousness is implemented. The concept of precarization identifies and highlights such a trend. It opens the way towards a field of research on the *making* of precariousness, particularly in the ways work and production are being reorganized globally and locally. It focuses on the social and economic dynamics (1) in the organization of work and modes of production, in the transformation of labour markets and management strategies, and (2) in legislation regulating work, employment and welfare systems.

The process of precarization can be defined as the institutionalization of precariousness. It has been enabled by an important ideological shift in the way the individual, the state, work and society are comprehended. Within this new paradigm, the individual, his or her accountability and (supposed) empowerment, become the central focus of attention to the exclusion of larger and more destructive processes at work in the global economy. Individuals are imagined to be empowered by these processes, when in reality they are increasingly powerless to improve their circumstances, yet are held responsible for their own condition and own future.

This thesis defines the precarization process as a major trend in modern capitalist societies, a trend whose epicentre lies in the reorganization of work and production systems. Ironically, many authors continue to view the rise of precariousness as a phenomenon which affects only those at the margins of society. In fact, the precarization process is a central and key phenomenon in contemporary economies. It destabilizes the labour force as a whole, even those perceived as enjoying permanent and stable employment. Like a sword of Damocles, its threat exacerbates competition, increases insecurity and creates a sense of ever-present danger. It compels stable workers to cling to their jobs even more tightly than ever, accepting, often in silence, degraded conditions of work, wages and welfare. Although precarization affects society as a whole, it does not produce an equalizing effect. Instead it provokes divisions, accentuates differentiations and increases inequality. It disproportionately affects the most vulnerable populations such as the working poor, and in particular women and immigrants. At its root, precarization is a profoundly powerful process that poses serious long-term problems for democracies. It needs to be recognized, thoroughly discussed and ultimately evaluated for its compatibility with accepted social values such as fairness, equality and the enhancement of collective and individual rights.

NOTES

1. This was not the case in other academic fields such as the family in relation to poverty and social exclusion.
2. The 2006 youth protests in France, which lasted from February until April, were a result of opposition to a measure intended to deregulate labour. The controversial bill 'Loi pour l'égalité des chances' created a new job contract, the Contrat Première Embauche (CPE), or First Employment Contract, approved by the French Parliament on 31 March. The CPE was ended by President Chirac on 10 April under the pressure of ongoing protest and a change in public opinion which delegitimized the reform.
3. The CNE was introduced by Prime Minister Dominique de Villepin (Union pour un Mouvement Populaire (UMP). It was implemented by ordinance on 2 August 2005.
4. Bill no. 2008-596, 25 June 2008, art. 9.
5. The ILO 'invited' the French government to take the necessary measures to give effect to Article 4 of the Termination of Employment Convention, 1982 (no. 158), by ensuring that 'contracts for new employment' can in no case be terminated in the absence of a valid reason. See http://www.ilo.org/global/What_we_do/Officialmeetings/gb/lang--en/WCMS_089230/index.htm (accessed April 2010).

REFERENCES

Abernathy, F. H., J.T. Dunlop, Janice H. Hammond and D. Weil (1999), *A Stitch in Time: Lean Retailing and the Transformation of Manufacturing. Lessons from the Apparel and Textile Industries*, Oxford: Oxford University Press.

Appay, B. (1997), 'Précarisation sociale et restructurations productives', in B. Appay and A. Thébaud-Mony, *Précarisation sociale, travail et santé*, Paris: Iresco, pp. 509–53.

Appay, B. (2005), *La dictature du succès: le paradoxe de l'autonomie contrôlée et de la précarisation*, Paris: L'Harmattan.

Appay, B. and A. Thébaud-Mony (eds) (1997), *Précarisation sociale, travail et santé*, Paris: Iresco-Cnrs.

Appelbaum, E., A. Bernhardt and R. J. Murnane (eds) (2003), *Low-Wage America: How Employers are Reshaping Opportunity in the Workplace*, New York: Russell Sage Foundation.

Atkinson, J. (1985), *Flexibility, Uncertainty and Manpower Management*, Brighton: University of Sussex, Institute for Manpower Studies.

Autor, D. (2003), 'Outsourcing at will: the contribution of unjust dismissal doctrine to the growth of employment outsourcing', *Journal of Labor Economics*, **21**, 1–42.

Bauman, Z. (2007), *Liquid Times: Living in the Age of Uncertainty*, Cambridge: Polity.

Beaud, S. and M. Cartier (2006), 'De la précarisation de l'emploi à la précarisation du travail', in S. Beaud, J. Confavreux and J. Lindgaard, *La France invisible*, Paris: La Découverte, pp. 561–73.

Bonacich, E. and R.P. Appelbaum (2000), *Behind the Label*, Berkeley and Los Angeles: University of California Press.

Boyer, R. (1986), *La flexibilité du travail en Europe*, Paris: La Découverte.

Butler, J. (2004), *Precarious Life: The Powers of Mourning and Violence*, London: Verso.

Castel, R. (1995), *Les métamorphoses de la question sociale*, Paris: Fayard.

Castel, R. (2007), 'Au-delà du salariat ou en deçà de l'emploi? L'institutionnalisation du précariat?', in S. Paugam (ed.), *Repenser la solidarité: l'apport des sciences sociales*, Paris: PUF, pp. 416–33.

Chauvin, S. (2007), 'Interim industriel et mouvement des journaliers à Chicago', PhD dissertation Paris, EHESS.

Collectif Génération Précaire (2006), *Sois stage et tais-toi!*, Paris: La Découverte.

Coutrot, T. (1998), *L'entreprise néo-libérale: nouvelle utopie capitaliste?*, Paris: La Découverte.

Delors, J. (1993), *Growth, Competitiveness, Employment: The Challenges and Ways Forward into the 21st Century*, White Paper, COM(93) 700, December, Brussels: EU Publications Office.

Ehrenreich, B. (2001), *Nickel and Dimed*, New York: Holt.

Ehrenreich, B. (2006), *Bait and Switch: The (Futile) Pursuit of the American Dream*, New York: Holt.

Furåker, B., K. Håkansson and J. Karlsson (eds) (2007), *Flexibility and Stability in Working Life*, New York: Palgrave Macmillan.

Grimshaw, D. and G. Hebson (2005), 'Public–private contracting: performance, power and change at work', in M. Marchington, D. Grimshaw, J. Rubery and H. Willmott, *Fragmenting Work: Blurring Organizational Boundaries and Disordering Hierachies*, Oxford: Oxford University Press, pp. 111–34.

Huez, D. (1994), *Souffrances et précarités au travail: paroles de médecins du travail*, Paris: Syros.

Kesselman, D. (2007), 'Travail et salariat aux États-Unis: quels droits, quelles perspectives?', *Revue française d'études américaines*, **1** (111), 6–26.

Lelay, S. (2009), 'Contribution à une approche archéologique de la précarisation sociale', in B. Appay and S. Jefferys (eds), *Restructurations, précarisation, valeurs*, Toulouse: Octares, pp. 117–28.

Lichtenstein, N. (ed.) (2006), *Wal-Mart: The Face of Twenty-First-Century Capitalism*, New York: New Press.

Marchington, M.P., D.P. Grimshaw, J. Rubery and H. Willmott (eds) (2004),

Fragmenting Work: Blurring Organisational Boundaries and Disordering Hierarchies, Oxford: Oxford University Press.

Michon, F. (2008), 'Flexibiliser avec ou sans précarité?', Seminar on 'Why and how to analyse the process of precarization', 19 May, Paris: Université Paris Descartes.

Milkman, R. (2006), *L.A. Story: Immigrant Workers and the Future of the U.S. Labor Movement*, New York: Russell Sage Foundation.

OECD (2004), 'A detailed description of employment protection regulation in force in 2003: background material for the 2004 edition of the *OECD Employment Outlook*', *OECD Employment Outlook 2004*, Paris: OECD, available at http://www.oecd.org/dataoecd/4/30/31933811/pdf (accessed April 2010).

Parsons, D.O. (2005), *Benefit Generosity in Voluntary Severance Plans: The U.S. Experience*, SSRN e library, available at http://ssrn.com/paper=877903 (accessed April 2010).

Perrin, E. (2004), *Chômeurs et précaires au coeur de la question sociale*, Paris: La Dispute.

Piketty, T. and E. Saez (2006), 'The evolution of top incomes: a historical and international perspective', *American Economic Review*, **96** (2), 200–205.

Piore, M. and P. Doeringer (1971), *Internal Labor Market and Manpower Analysis*, Lexington, MA: D.C. Heath.

Piore, M. and C. Sabel (1984), *The Second Industrial Divide: Possibilities for Prosperity*, New York: Basic Books.

Revelli, M. (1999), 'Centralité du précariat', *Vacarme*, available at http://www.vacarme.org/article1067.html (accessed April 2010).

Scheuer, François (2006), 'Qu'est-ce que le précariat?' *Politique*, October 2006, available at http://politique.eu.org/archives/2006/10/333.html (accessed December 2009).

Sennett, R. (1998), *The Corrosion of Character: The Personal Consequences of Work in the New Capitalism*, New York: W.W. Norton.

Stone, K.V.W. (2004), *From Widgets to Digits: Employment Regulation for the Changing Workplace*, Cambridge: Cambridge University Press.

Uchitelle, L. (2006), *The Disposable American: Layoffs and their Consequences*, New York: Knopf.

Van Jaarsveld, D.D. (2004), 'Collective representation among high-tech workers at Microsoft and beyond: lessons from WashTech', *Industrial Relations Journal*, **43** (2), 364–85.

Voss, K. and R. Sherman (2000), 'Breaking the iron law of oligarchy: union revitalization in the American labor movement', *American Journal of Sociology*, **106**, 303–49.

Womack, J.P., D.T. Jones and D. Ross (1990), *The Machine that Changed the World*, New York: Rawson.

4. Legitimating precarious employment: aspects of the post-Fordism and lean production debates

Dan Coffey and Carole Thornley

INTRODUCTION

At the end of what is now conventionally thought of as the 'long boom' following reconstruction after World War II, the mature capitalist economies of North America and Western Europe entered a more turbulent phase, combining rising unemployment with inflation and marked by heightened social and industrial unrest. The traumas of this period were by no means evenly distributed. In America and Britain most particularly, each experiencing in the 1970s a weak productivity performance not only in comparison with preceding decades but also in comparison with other advanced capitalist economies, the reaction – fully evident in the 1980s – was a sharp swing in economic policy towards market liberalization, including deregulated labour markets. One impact of this has been a marked change in the experience and expectation of work, not least with regard to what many social science commentaries now study under the heading of 'precarious employment'. This can be broadly construed to encompass job tenure and security, job roles and task allocations in the workplace, uncertainty in pay, status and hours, and even uncertainty as to 'employer' or place of work (as, for example, with the growing use of agency work and workers available on short call); a development, moreover, not lacking in transatlantic policy enthusiasts enamoured of market flexibilities and chary of suggestions that workers' employment rights be shored up. All of these developments have occurred within an increasingly globalized economic system.

In this chapter we consider aspects of the post-Fordism and lean production debates when viewed from a particular perspective: the legitimation of precarious work. In this connection we distinguish between the two debates, for reasons to become clear.

POST-FORDISM: FALSE HISTORIES AND NEW WORD ASSOCIATIONS

Let us begin by considering in broad outline some of the oppositional elements typically brought to bear to distinguish 'Fordist' from 'post-Fordist' production. To avoid ambiguity, we are thinking here of a literary phenomenon which took off within the humanities and social sciences, and predominantly in North America and Western Europe, from about the middle part of the 1980s; provided that we do not reduce the phenomenon in question to the retro-appraisal of a single literary artefact, an obvious marker is the appearance in print of Piore and Sabel's (1984) thesis that the end of the long boom in the advanced capitalist economies of the West which followed World War II could be understood as a crisis of Fordist mass production. In this work, the authors also speculate as to forces at work which might lead to the formation of a post-Fordist state ('flexible specialisation'), possessed of contrasting features. This marker, drawing upon a number of emerging but still largely unconnected literatures, and appearing at an auspicious moment, thus carries within its pages more than a few hints of the serial contrasts with which we are concerned.[1]

Such contrasts, our principal concern in this section, are set out in Figure 4.1. Reading from left to right, we have (initially) a series of comparative assumptions about products, processes and industrial organization – to wit, the degree of customization of final goods produced, the skills required of the workers to produce, and the organization of industries in terms of the vertical span of operations undertaken within firms. Thus represented, the post-Fordist side of the comparison, in contrast with Fordism, lies on the side of more customization, more workplace skills, and less vertical integration; and indeed, the system-wide distinction lies precisely in such pair-wise contrasts. At the same time, any dichotomizing system-wide contrast described via a list of opposing elements on two sides of a divide also implies relations between elements on each side: descriptors on *each* side of a divide are being brought *into* relationship with *each* other. We should therefore be concerned to consider not only the pair-wise vertical contrasts thus represented, but also the associations implied by dint of the cross-connections established horizontally between forms for products, skills and organization.

A further feature to consider is the imagined divide which exists for many writers willing to employ this kind of dichotomizing system-wide distinction as regards the question of unionateness, with trade unions portrayed as less immanent agencies for the marshalling of worker consciousness and the settlement of terms and conditions of employment in a post-Fordist world; and even where writers do not go so far as to propose

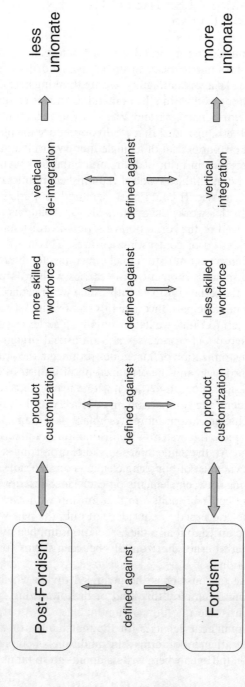

Figure 4.1   Fordism vs. Post-Fordism: oppositional contrasts and implicates

that workers are always more reluctant to join a trade union in principle, or even to participate, there is none the less a general sense that the environs of economy and society are now less amenable places. And this too is indicated in Figure 4.1. The relationship between trade union weakness and precarious work is no doubt complex, but since they are coincident phenomena in recent time and space, we hold both in mind.[2]

And our concern in this respect is that a proposition which identifies the economic traumas experienced within Western capitalism in the 1970s with the birth pangs of a new, post-Fordist type of capitalism with its own internal associations – a proposition taking this particular form, moreover, in a following decade marked by a sharp swing in economic policy in America and Britain most particularly, towards liberalization of both product and labour markets, and a state-led assault on trade unions – lends itself fairly obviously to consideration as a legitimating project vis-à-vis precariousness. On this basis, we pursue a conjecture offered in Coffey and Thornley (2009, p. 13), which is that post-Fordist analyses do not offer substantively convincing explanations for the end of the long post-war boom within Western capitalism, but are significant as a particular kind of intellectual response to subsequent economic and political trajectories.

Perhaps not surprisingly given the prominence of the Ford family name, the constituent differences distinguishing post-Fordist from Fordist production activities have been most typically illustrated (and *pace* Figure 4.1) with reference to the car industry. This is an observation of some importance from the viewpoint of appreciating both the specific character and the ideological force of the contrasts drawn up against 'Fordism'. Many writers of many viewpoints and political persuasions have made much of broader changes in the composition of production and employment in 'mature' capitalist economies; but while this is certainly evident in post-Fordist writing, the *psychological* force of the metaphor derives in the first instance from its claims to have a proven empirical footing in transformations *within* the most classically 'Fordist' of sectors – thus securing prescribed points of contrast to lay down 'rules of reading' for capitalism at large.

To this end the car industry is invoked to illustrate a capitalism characterized in the Fordist era by large-scale systems of factory (or factory-style) production, claimed in this connection to have grown to full dominance and maturity – especially in America – in the several decades immediately following the end of World War II, with the Ford River Rouge factory complex in 1920s Detroit an early if extreme progenitor; and the car industry is again invoked to show changes within this classically 'Fordist' sector, the key transition period being dated typically to the 1970s and the end of the long boom. With accounts of dramatic transitions within industries like the car industry so central to the construction of the contrasts and metaphors of post-Fordist literature, an obvious way to proceed in assessing this literature as an exercise in legitimation vis-à-vis precariousness and union avoidance is to look at the car industry – the industry of Henry Ford.

Firm and Private Consumer: The Market Interface

Suppose we commence with the question of product variety. References to a Fordist model of production, or to Fordist mass production, have been almost invariably employed over the course of the past twenty-five years to evoke systems limited in their ability to procure a range of differently speci-fied products, post-Fordism then being contrastingly defined (as per Figure 4.1) as something like an opposite. The classic example normally adduced here is the Ford Model T motor car – available, as per the much rehearsed cliché, in all colours 'black'; and the 'Fordist' label thus derived has been attached to the notional orchestration of production activities organized on a large scale for purposes of volume reproduction of more or less undif-ferentiated goods; then giving way, under pressure and not smoothly, to more flexible production methods. But bearing in mind the dates normally adduced for this development, and the assumed stamp of the characterizing forms of Fordist mass production in 1950s America, it is not at all difficult to establish the existence of very serious problems with this view. What is seemingly proposed is that factory observers in this early postwar decade, and even later, watching production unfold in the archetypal Fordist indus-try of the period, would have been impressed by the advantages of scale for producing homogenized outputs. But in that most privileged of industries for this literature – the American car industry – far from taking proper note of products varying only in some limited manner and degree, some factory observers at least were impressed by quite different potentials:

> three distinct 'makes' of automobiles, each with many models and styles . . . body is painted with one of forty-five distinct colors . . . over one hundred twenty-five separate accessory specifications . . . possible combinations are 'astronomical' . . . the schedules are so contrived as to permit each car in sequence to be preceded or followed by a car of completely different type, instead of a 'run' of similar models. (Walker et al., 1956, pp. 7–8)

Thus the enthusiastic account, published in the middle 1950s, by first-hand academic observers, of the outputs of a single American car assembly line.[3] One decade later, erstwhile historians of the same national industry would offer similar remarks. As one such put it, reflecting back on the same post-war decade:

assembly of motor vehicles has come a long way since Henry Ford's pioneer-
ing days . . . [t]he customer of the 1950s could choose among engines, body
styles, colors for both exterior and interior, and even hubcaps . . . designate . . .
accessories – radio, heater, air-conditioner, for instance – and the car combining his preferences would roll off the assembly line in company with others
representing different assortment of choices. (Rae, 1965, p. 200)

That such antecedent sentiments should even exist constitutes a severe
challenge to the intelligibility of the historical conventions of today's post-
Fordist narratives.

There is, moreover, another facet to consider. Post-Fordist literature
is noteworthy not only for omitting to acknowledge the existence of an
enormous body of antecedent commentary and evidence inconsistent with
its claims but also for a narrowing of critical precepts regarding the interface between producer and consumer, it being treated as a thing apparent
that a factory process that can assemble different components differently
must in turn imply a victory for consumer sovereignty in the market. But
as we have discussed elsewhere, an earlier generation of writers was more
apt to express diverse views – as for example Bannock (1973), writing as
ex-Manager of Advanced Programs in the Product Development Group
of Ford of Europe Inc., and decrying the introduction to Europe of the
'build your own car' marketing concept evolved in post-war America as
having presided over the simultaneous impoverishment by the 'Big Three'
of industrial design standards: for this critic, mixed-car assembly ('the
permutation of engines and interior and exterior trim and accessories, in
thousands of versions' (ibid., p. 239)) came hand in glove with accelerated
obsolescence and gradation (by price) of car-line derivatives of an increasingly conventional appearance built by oligopolists. (For further discussion of this view, see Coffey, 2006, pp. 35–8; more generally, see ibid.,
pp. 15–43.) By contrast, in the post-Fordist world, the consumer, newly
minted, is sovereign.

Firm and Private Employee: The Wage Nexus

Let us now consider 'skills' required in production and the proposition
that post-Fordism is further distinguished from Fordism in this second
critical dimension – a mass of less skilled factory operatives giving way to
the more skilled ('polyvalent'). Indeed, and following as it did hard upon
the heels of an earlier literary excitement occasioned by the publication of
Braverman's (1974) classic, and attendant 'Bravermania', contrasts were
actively drawn in the post-Fordist writing of the 1980s between the putative
new world thus emerging and the 'deskilling' process of the past, said now
to be a characteristic but particular feature of 'Fordist' mass production,

rather than endemic to capitalism. In this connection, the thrust of the contention was generally one of a positive association drawn between the range of tasks expected to be undertaken by individuals at work and the variety of products then to be produced, the first being an implicate of the second. But evidently there are problems with this view too; in the case of the emblematic car sector, for example, if auto workers in 1950s America indeed laboured under working conditions marked (*pace* Braverman) by Taylorism and deskilling, nobody thought to tell them that this was incompatible with producing a variety of differently specified cars.

What is perhaps most striking is that for this critical dimension of production the pair-wise contrast drawn to distinguish post-Fordism from Fordism should rely on functional associations posited between two of the elements on each side of the divide. In terms of our schematic representation (Figure 4.1) the second vertical contrast was (and is) to all intents justified as implied by the first – a connection running horizontally. But this assumption is striking precisely because it appears as a *new* assumption. There is no hint in Braverman (1974), for example, that 'deskilling' is a reflex of the extent to which an employing firm engages workers in producing homogenized products; indeed, for many of his examples the technical and cost implications point in other directions, as in his accounts of metal working and technical drawing, and the advent of computer-aided design and computer-aided engineering (see ibid., pp. 204–5, 243–4).[4] And while the car industry provides a contemporary case example by which to illustrate the effects of tedium in a 'boring' and 'repetitive' job – to wit, the industrial unrest and stoppages at the then (in)famous General Motors plant in Lordstown, Ohio (see ibid., pp. 33–4) – there is no suggestion that this somehow reflected a failure to differentiate the product. In fact, prior to such strikes in the 1970s academic observers researching the car industry could not only take it for granted that the assignment of workers to assembly would reflect the number of different models running on the track (Turner et al., 1967, p. 40), but were frequently at pains to emphasize flexibilities for 'non-standard' parts – and subject also to the 'almost weekly' 'changes and modifications of jobs and components' suffered by 'most' popular models 'throughout' production (ibid., p. 169) – while at the same time speculating on the continued extent of dull and routine factory work.

Defining and measuring skills is an intractable business, as too the question of locating 'representative' and 'comparable' individuals in the midst of heterogeneous aggregates; but in adjudicating on the position taken on skills-sets in the post-Fordist literature there is no need to do so, because in this literature functional associations are asserted not shown, while the internal precepts guiding construction are readily pried apart.

But we should note too how its terms are such as to imply work positively transformed.

Vertical Structures and Industrial Outsourcing

In fact we have at this stage two issues of note:

a. a marked shift in historical precepts regarding the evolving course of production in a designated exemplary industry, incorrectly asserting that the 1970s saw the first emergence of car assembly plants capable of processing varied products, combined with an asserted sovereignty of the private consumer vis-à-vis the firm, and in each case disregarding any acknowledgement of previous sentiments to the contrary;

b. a tacit assumption positing a positive functional association between product variety and the skills-sets required of individual workers employed to produce, combining with the propositions set out in (a) to assert that the 1970s also marks a border separating mass employment of less skilled assembly workers from a 'new' working experience.

What is thus proposed is a transformation in a dual-identity interface, positing changes in the doubled-up roles of two key actors, the producer-employer and consumer-worker, and it is in this context that we should next consider the vertical organization of industry, because here some of the empirical examples appear initially more 'promising': in keeping with our (predominantly) American examples so far – selected to reflect upon the status given Fordist mass production in post-war America by post-Fordist writers – we can illustrate this with regard to the union avoidance practices of the 1980s.

For example, in an instructive commentary Luria (2000) describes changing employment practices within America's manufacturing industries as a whole, as follows. Between 1980 and 1990 employment in US onshore manufacturing activity declined by some 6 per cent, with the loss of 1.2 million jobs; against this, but over the same period, the unionized workforce shrank by 2.5 million, taking union membership of the employment total from around a third of all workers to not much more than a fifth – at just 22 per cent. At the same time, the 1980s also saw the continuation of an already existing process in which manufacturing employment was redistributed from larger to smaller plants. This process was realized via corporate decisions to de-integrate vertically, 'buy not make'; and it was accompanied by deteriorating terms of employment, payrolls for employee totals falling over time for smaller sites compared with larger (ibid., pp. 166–8). And this process, which was already under way in the 1970s, combined outsourcing tendering to lowest-cost 'build-to-blueprint' workshops – a market form founded by the logic of its own construction upon precarious employment – with active de-unionization.

But when considering this last development and placing it alongside the counterfactuals and assertions on product variety and workforce skills which are the starting point for post-Fordism, it is impossible to see anything other than a legitimating device. Because we have an aggressive development (de-integration) occasioning precariousness and de-unionization represented as but one element in a package that practically compels one to see an improved deal for the consumer-worker vis-à-vis the producer-employer.

Legitimating Precarious Employment

If we date this packaging together of questions of product variety, workforce skills and industrial organization, by means of vertical pair-wise comparisons across and horizontal associations within two halves of an 'industrial divide', to the appearance of and enthusiastic reception for Piore and Sabel (1984), then our point is as much about the rapid extrusion of *this* lesson at *this* juncture as it is about this particular work. The hedges and qualifications with which individual writers might handle this package should not blind us to the rapid proliferation of studies playing variations on a theme: 'time and again', as Coates (2000) observes, the argument is subsequently advanced that the 'postwar golden age had been organized on the basis of Fordist mass production', but 'was now shifting to a new paradigm of organization variously labelled "flexible specialisation", the "new competition", "disorganized capitalism", "reflexive accumulation"' (ibid., p. 42).[5] Perhaps the most salient feature of this manner of treating events, possessed by a quality of cathexis and characterized by obeisance to the sweep of metaphor, is the hold it took in America and Britain, in the second of which at least post-Fordist themes were adopted by writers distancing themselves from the labour movement.[6] But in these countries the market metaphor was politically ascendant, with Reaganism and Thatcherism pushing strident visions of decline and renewal.

Even so, it is still striking that so much of the sociological theorizing which gathered pace from the 1980s to explain the weakening position of trade unions and organized labour movements opted for metaphors rationalizing this as post-Fordist. If we consider the industrial data from America, we have in fact evidence of a process in which work is outsourced and terms and conditions of employment degraded, overlooked by large corporations controlling this process and collectively defining the terms of autonomy allowed subordinate businesses. The associations with which post-Fordist commentary surrounded this (real) development can be readily exposed, and for the exemplary instance of the American car industry, as commencing with a counterfactual: the fiction that the 1970s saw the first appearance of factories making varied products. And this demonstration in turn undermines the linked assertion as to the nature of the new experience at work favoured by many adopting post-Fordist themes. But fictions, and the assertions mounted upon fictions, can also have (real) effects, enabling or facilitating a process by defining the precepts governing debate or comprehension. Yet if ideological forms possess, in this sense, a real force and an enabling content, what is remarkable in this instance is how easy it is to expose post-Fordism in its legitimating aspects.

In this respect, it is interesting to touch upon one more issue, namely the relationship between academics based in the social sciences and humanities and the business press, and their share of responsibilities for post-Fordist forms of understanding. We might take stock, for example, of the significance of a business researcher like W.J. Abernathy, who published one book in the late 1970s arguing that the car industry had become locked into a form of mass production based on large capital investments requiring stable markets in which to sell goods in large quantities (see Abernathy 1978), and a subsequent co-authored study in the early 1980s recanting on this position because of the revivifying effects of Japanese car manufacturing methods and philosophies, and new microprocessing technologies (see Abernathy et al., 1983). The impact of such stances on the template arguments in Piore and Sabel (1984, esp. p. 248) is obvious. But in the interim, Abernathy – in another joint study published in *Harvard Business Review* – also proposed that American business had much to learn from Europe, and with little to fear from social democracy (Hayes and Abernathy, 1980). Thus on the side of the academic business press this was a period marked by *hesitancy* as to how best to explain the weak performance of the American (and British) economy, and where to turn; and while we can certainly trace important inputs to the Piore and Sabel thesis from the side of the academic business press, the final form of their argument was their own. The point need not be amplified: post-Fordism is in large measure a construct of 'intellectuals' grounded in the social sciences and humanities, trained to be sensitive to legitimation.

It is therefore interesting in this connection to see how far the post-Fordist strand of conceptualization has spread to treatments of contemporary social activism as this occurs outside of the traditional labour movement. For example, Buechler (2000) sees 'the transition to post-Fordism' as undermining 'traditional bases of mobilization':

Fordism was especially likely to promote working class mobilization . . . and enlarged the role of the state as a legitimator of working-class organization through unions and as a mediator of the conflicts between capital and labor. Thus, under Fordism, it is not surprising that the social movement sphere was monopolized by the labor movement . . . Indeed, it was the labor movement's success in mobilizing and organizing for a higher standard of living that created one of the pressures toward a post-Fordist accumulation strategy. (ibid., pp. 123–4)

LEAN PRODUCTION: A NEW IDEOLOGICAL FORCE

Let us next consider 'lean production', a phrase coined in connection with the world-wide car assembly plant performance surveys famously reported in Womack et al. (1990). This was a best-selling management book of the 1990s focused on the car industry and reporting materials compiled under the auspices of the International Motor Vehicle Programme (IMVP) research project centred at MIT, but sponsored and funded by leading firms from the world's auto industry. 'Lean thinking', to borrow the title of Womack and Jones (1996, 2003), another best-seller, emerged from an industry-promoted research and research-dissemination programme. This is an important contrast with the early development and packaging of post-Fordism, in which academic figures in the social sciences and humanities played a primary role. Maintaining some sense of comparative dating is also important: post-Fordism, in the sense with which we are concerned, emerged in the decade before 'lean production' was coined. But since the key text in this instance is again a study of the car industry, this remains an appropriate industry to consider from the viewpoint of judging lean production as a further proposition.

Beginning with the principal claims of the lean production movement regarding resource productivity potentials in production, we next address the complex question of the interpolation of these claims into the pre-existing body of post-Fordist commentary, while at the same time offering some remarks on a topic germane to both – namely the status accorded in each to Japanese car makers, and in particular to Toyota.

Lean Production: A Revolution in Production Potentials

This last is important, because in so far as resource potentials in production are concerned the principal claim in Womack et al. (1990) is that Japanese-owned car assembly plants could be seen on the basis of careful world-wide survey data to be enjoying enormous advantages in labour productivity for reasons other than (high) automation levels. In this connection, Japanese car makers were described as 'lean', because purportedly enabled to reduce sharply the resources needed – 'half the human effort' (ibid., p. 13) – to produce any output by means of innovative production management philosophies and methods. This survey used a labour productivity measure constructed around the hours of labour actually employed in the performance of a standardized set of car assembly tasks. In retrospect, this study passed too quickly from publication to outright acceptance – as per today's lean thinkers – or outright rejection, via aggressive promotion and polemic. As we argue elsewhere, another view is to reconsider the interpretation of the original survey data, while accepting impressive aspects to the original research effort. From this perspective, we have proposed in Coffey and Thornley (2006, 2008) (and for a detailed and more formal demonstration see also Coffey, 2006, pp. 71–88) that:

a. if factories based in Europe had been put to one side, a comparison between Japanese and non-Japanese car assembly plants in the original survey would have struggled to find any evidence of labour productivity advantages in Japan, after automation;
b. while a bias factor in the original survey design, which weighted all plant employees as if they worked a single non-overtime shift regardless of actual conditions, renders even the difference between Europe and the rest of the world speculative;
c. a re-interpretation which would place the subsequent career of 'lean production' on a new footing.

Observing dissonance between claim and evidence does not of course alter the fact of a remarkable career, even a brief glance at which suffices to indicate the many constructions placed upon lean production as a legitimating device. For example, the idea of lean production was pushed hard by its leading sponsors in a context where it no doubt eased the politics of accommodations sought between giant American and Japanese corporations in the US car and auto industry in the 1980s and 1990s, glossing these with the varnish of unalloyed improvement (see Coffey, 2006, pp. 120–5). Perhaps less subtle is the fact that under the presidency of George Bush Jr the US Environmental Protection Agency (EPA) made 'lean thinking' a part of its voluntary programmes for industry, with some unsubtle hints laid down that by this means international agreements like Kyoto were rendered less pressing (see ibid., pp. 173–6) – a policy predilection still apparent some time into the Barak Obama administration. With lean production thus neatly packaged as Medicinal Compound – a 'nearly universal antidote . . . to . . . wasteful practices . . ."lean thinking"' (Hawken et al., 1999, p. 127) – it is reasonable to consider the ideological force represented in the workplace; and here a number of critics observing the role ideas play in shaping forces in complex industrial and workplace settings have identified a legitimating device for moves against unions and degrading of terms and conditions of employment, at a time when many labour movements were already at a low ebb in their recent histories, and not least in the transatlantic economies. There is now a rich body of case and historical work exploring this theme – both in recent studies such as Stewart et al. (2009) and Pulignano et al. (2008), and in earlier commentaries like the influential Jurgens et al. (1993) (and see also Bradley et al., 2000, pp. 39–48).[7]

The weight of promotion of lean production not only by corporations but also by state bodies – a pronounced feature in America, as elsewhere (and not least Britain) – combining with a previous absorption with Japanese manufacturing practices in the West, has underscored a rapid assimilation into business school canons and the lexicons of consultancy; and no doubt claims made on its behalf have been taken to heart by many managers. It is interesting therefore to observe that Luria (2000, pp. 169–76) reports that a database compiled at the Ann Arbor (Michigan) Industrial Technology Institute, comprising data updated from 1992 on more than 1,000 smaller manufacturing firms, suggests that those 'self-conscious and improvement oriented' businesses given to the deployment of what they perceive to be 'Japanese-style methods' are typically weak on 'modernity' – poor investors in hardware and software for business scheduling and quality function, and in product development and shop-floor automation (ibid., pp. 170–3) Caught within macro-industrial structures based on repeat contract bids and competitive tenders – the movement towards de-integration and de-unionization previously noted – it is no surprise to find smaller manufacturing firms chary of certain kinds of hard investment; and here we can take stock of the fact that lean production was originally sold on the basis that Japanese car makers had been demonstrated to have discovered practices involving measures *not* based on capital expenditure yet transforming labour productivity.

But one legitimating feature of lean production for 'active' managers consigned to manage shops competing on low wage costs and with little developmental activity might well also be the degree of validation of 'self-worth' and 'talent' afforded in the course of pursuing the promises enshrined within of workforce reductions at any target output. This is consistent with the finding that these firms – far more 'systematic' than mere sweats in monitoring manufacturing processes and experimenting with initiatives like 'total quality management', 'problem-solving groups' or 'just-in-time' – most usually score badly, if now similarly to less systematically managed sweats, on employment variables like wages and training, as well as on value added per employee (see Luria, 2000, p. 171).

We make this point to highlight the many-sided potentials of lean production as an ideological force and an exercise in legitimation, appealing for different complexes of reasons in different ways to different levels in the chains of production. The launch of the 'lean thinking' movement in America in the 1990s – several decades *after* the move by its large manufacturing concerns to engage in outsourcing and union avoidance – might also be considered for the licence thus permitted corporate executives, and indeed elected government officials with social and economic responsibilities in this area, not to talk about longer-term problems with this kind of macro-industrial structure.

Post-Fordism, Lean Production and Toyota

It is interesting to compare the precepts of lean production with those of post-Fordism, and in respect of each the status they accord the 'Japanese' car industry. For example, the post-Fordist literature of the 1980s is noteworthy for allotting a peculiar and particular role to Japanese car makers, crediting them with taking a lead globally in breaking away from the principles of Fordist mass production. But commentary over the past several decades has tended to date the first appearances of volume assembly lines in Japan processing a mix of model specifications to the middle 1960s – for example, the discussion in Shiomi (1995, p. 35), or the timeline in Fujimoto (1999, pp. 51–3) – and while for Western commentators absorbed in the assumptions of post-Fordism this kind of dating is usually cited as 'proof' that Western car makers must first have learned how to assemble a variety of car model specifications from the Japanese, the correct inference must in fact confirm Japanese firms as late arrivals (see Coffey, 2006, p. 19). This observation is an important one, demonstrating as it does the double-edged quality of the myth-making entailed in post-Fordist commentary – offering a faux account of comparative industrial developments both in the West *and* in Japan.

But equally it is noteworthy how little this presumption weighed in the original design of the world-wide survey of car assembly plant productivity that gave birth to the conceit of lean production, when reported and publicized in Womack et al. (1990). The principal architect of this survey – an American engineer, J.F. Krafcik (the same MIT-based researcher who coined the phrase 'lean production'; see ibid., p. 13) – made an attempt to standardize the labour productivity data obtained by means of an 'adjustment' mapping to take some account of differences in physical dimensions like car size; but he disregarded at the point of construction the relevance of model range – one would imagine partly to deal only with differences readily expressed as statistical averages over all members of a car line, but also on explicitly stated grounds that from the viewpoint of the worker on the line installing one variety of component rather than another makes little difference to the effort required – and hence was not a significant factor. Moreover, in addition to having discounted product variety as an issue for productivity measurement, the same engineer also dismissed the post-Fordist conceit, for example, that Japanese car assemblers favoured policies of mass customization, finding the opposite.[8] This, it can be safely observed, has not been much noted or discussed in writings of a post-Fordist cast, which have since absorbed 'lean' metaphors with little reflection.

But even where there are safe grounds for identifying consonant views, we are in any case still firmly rooted in a world of retro-projection and myth. There are many difficulties to the view, for instance, that American manufacturers felt compelled to outsource work in the 1970s to meet the threat of low Japanese labour costs, although this has since been a much favoured explanation, 'legitimation' once more.[9] And it is also interesting to see the extent to which both post-Fordist writers in the 1980s and lean thinkers subsequently have been apt to depict Japanese car manufacture as being highly de-integrated vertically, since the evidence here is (again) far more complex.[10]

One complicating factor here is the proactive role played in the shaping of these myths by the leading Japanese car maker, Toyota. A full study of how Toyota's status in both post-Fordist commentary and lean production has evolved would be a substantial undertaking, but a proper starting point here would be Taichii Ohno, a self-propagandist on behalf of the corporation who ended up as a Toyota executive vice-president. In a book originally written for Japanese audiences in the 1970s (Ohno, 1978, 1988), but soon to reach a Western audience, Ohno seemed to take credit on behalf of Toyota for surpassing Henry Ford by mixing model specifications on a single assembly line – a faux history from Japan about Toyota's achievements in manufacture which helped feed the myths of Western post-Fordism. How to interpret this is complex, because one is torn between considering the boast as merely inspired 'marketing' (see Coffey, 2006, p. 38) and contemplating the nuanced appeals of such unlikely claims, placed initially before a Japanese audience and in the context of a still recent occupation (ibid., p. 165). But subsequently, Toyota has fed the myth machine assiduously – promoting at every juncture the view that a distinctive Toyota production system (TPS) 'exists'.[11]

From this viewpoint, while there are certainly pronounced features of 'othering' entailed in the Anglo-American post-Fordism, the 'Orientalism' is a complex one, because the distinctiveness allowed the Japanese car giant Toyota is deemed to be positive for its transformative effects and is moreover fed by the corporation; by the same token, it is evident that Toyota plays a similar role in the lean production movement. It is interesting to observe that the status of Toyota has been unaffected by the struggles of the Japanese national economy over the course of the past several decades, reflecting perhaps not only its transnational status but also the orientation of 'lean thinkers' towards private corporations rather than national capitalisms (see Coffey, 2006, pp. 127–31).

It is also important to observe the extent to which the facts of Toyota and its actually existing practices suggested by evidence – its 'factuality' – has increasingly diverged from what lean production describes as the essence of its manufacturing model. The famous 'just-in-time' producer began to experiment with segmented car assembly lines connected by intra-process buffers in the 1990s, experiments which still continue. At the same time, as the corporation has globalized its supply chains, its reliance on inventories of parts has increased concomitantly, but with little sign of executive anxiety. By the same token, the presumption that Toyota – allegedly 'just-in-time' – would naturally prefer localized sourcing is no longer an obviously tenable proposition.[12] If we combine these with counterfactuals of much longer standing – (see Figure 4.2) – we can at this juncture begin to reconsider Toyota as beneficiary of a production fantasy. On the one hand, pertaining perhaps to post-Fordist literature, Toyota is accredited with a very extensive set of achievements (an über-fantasy) hard to sustain against the evidence: in this view, Toyota invents 'mixed' model assembly, specializes in mass customization, localizes production, and has a zero tolerance of stocks and buffers. On the other, there is the more localized but still dramatic vision of lean production, to which claims as to which car maker first mixed models on an assembly line, or the benefits of mass customization, are not essential – although other features of the Toyota myth remain so, notably those drawing on the company's account of its 'just-in-time' paradigm. The dividing line, however, is not one that should be drawn too hard or fast.

CONCLUSIONS

To conclude: in this chapter we consider two production 'myths' or 'fantasies' each of which plays a role in legitimating production and employment regimes that are antipathetic to workers' interests vis-à-vis precariousness of work. In considering the way in which post-Fordist literature legitimates precarious employment, we reject its thesis that the breakdown of

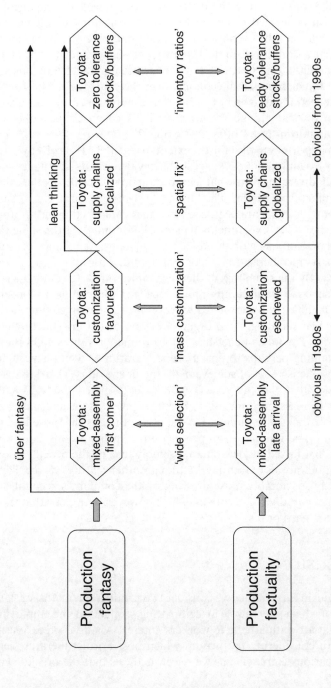

Figure 4.2   Production fantasy and production factuality: some comparisons

the post-World War II 'long boom' constituted the transitionary phase of a punctuated equilibrium, with capitalism traversing states on each side of an historic divide neatly distinguished as a series of pair-wise contrasts defined around questions of product variety, workforce skills and industrial organization. By this means, post-Fordist literature confounds real developments with fictions: it thus associates the very real fact that large corporations in the 1970s and 1980s sought to avoid unions and lower wage costs via processes of outsourcing and competitive subcontracting with an implied elevation for many consumer-workers vis-à-vis producer-employers. We propose that the narrowed precepts and historical and empirical counterfactuals of this conceit, marked by cathexis and notable for casual and uncritical reliance on metaphor, do not so much carry ideological baggage as exist as cultural mirrors to a new conservative ideology – hence the success of post-Fordist commentaries in America and Britain. It is in this context that we locate the lean production movement of the 1990s, a legitimating force of growing range and application, licensing existing corporate trajectories.

We have emphasized that these two phenomena are identical neither in point of origin nor in form, although differences and incompatibilities are little noticed – partly because neither exists to encourage critical debate or discussion, but also because post-Fordism is primarily the concept of 'intellectuals', lean production of corporations. These conceptualizations and attendant derivations require careful evaluation for reasons of positive analysis both of production forms and of production ideologies, to inform collective responses to increasing precariousness of production and employment.

NOTES

1. Given this, we should perhaps observe at the outset that while French writers adhering to the (French) 'régulation' school frequently discuss 'Fordism' and its 'history', they sometimes do so in a way not conforming to the perspectives that are the subject of criticism in our chapter. Thus, for example, while Piore and Sabel (1984, p. 309) cite Aglietta (1976 [1987]) as an influence, the differences between these two works are at least as illuminating as the similarities. In the case of the latter, a founding contribution to French régulation theory, carrying distinctively neo-Marxian elements and laced with traces of Durkheim, there is at no point a suggestion that mass production equates with 'homogenized' products (for example), the exposition being focused squarely upon explaining economic crisis by reference to wage-setting arrangements and consumption potentials within a particular organizational and technological milieu.
2. Suggestions of increased precariousness of employment for workers rash enough to join unions in previously non-union workplaces are also a well-known phenomenon, part of the 'fear stuff' mixed in with the 'sweet stuff' and 'evil stuff' documented by Roy (1980) in a classic study of the resistance of firms to trade union drives in America's post-war Southern states, a reminder that unionization has always contended with hostility in

the world's richest capitalism. Union membership naturally carries risks too even where membership is established, as shown for example in the revealing study by Addison et al. (2003) for 1990s Britain, which finds multiple plant firms closing plants most likely to choose sites with a stronger union presence.

3. The same passage is cited and discussed in Lyddon (1996, p. 83), an important paper which identifies the unreliability of 'mass production' as a linguistic measure if the appearance of this term is taken to denote simple replication of identical goods. For example, Peter Drucker, the famous managerialist, is quoted, and again in the 1950s, as arguing that 'the essence of genuine mass production' was that it created 'a greater diversity of products than any method ever devised by man', owing to the possibilities for combining parts differently to form a 'large variety' of goods (Drucker, 1955, pp. 85–7, in Lyddon, 1996, p. 82). This observation is a highly germane one.

4. Braverman saw such developments as introducing the first signs of degradation in the profession of the design engineer, with parts of what were previously personal skills being transferred to machinery, while shoring up divisions between conception and execution. There is nothing in this vision, received with plaudits in the 1970s by many of the enthusiasts for post-Fordism in the 1980s, that would be inconsistent with changes of the kind making assembly of different combinations of different parts (see n. 3) cheaper to engineer; moreover, his comments on the degrading effects of division of labour on the working life of the individual are also interesting when compared with those of Bannock (1973) on product aesthetics, scathing as to the consequences for products built from 'permutations' of 'separately' designed parts.

   This can be contrasted with subsequently popular views: '[t]he main link between properties of the product market and the organization of work and skills appears to be batch size – of products, components and parts – and strategies to translate product demand and variety into batches of components and parts' (Sorge and Streek, 1988, p. 25) – a not unrepresentative later contribution (in this respect) contrasting 'Fordism' with 'diversified' production of 'quality' goods.

5. The first of these ('flexible specialisation') is simply the thesis of Piore and Sabel, whose claim of an industrial divide is far from being rejected in these other contributions: for example, in the course of their proposal ('disorganized capitalism') that capitalism at large was now shifting from a 'more' to a 'less' organized state, a perspective also tending in any case towards a naturalizing approach to the travails of labour, Lash and Urry (1987) both endorse their approach (see ibid., pp. 198–9) and also their terminology: 'Fordism to flexibility . . . an integral part of the disorganization of contemporary capitalist societies' (ibid., p. 283).

6. Consider the précis offered in Dworkin's (2007) recent commentary on changing intellectual fashions concerning the future of 'class' politics as seen by British post-Fordists, an enthusiastic group notable for the number of decamping Marxists flocking to the banner. Thus in a section perhaps too gently entitled 'a fond farewell to Marx', and discussing *Marxism Today* and the 'New Times' project associated with writers including Stuart Hall: 'standardization, mass production, scientific management, economies of scale, and centralized and hierarchical structures of Fordism were [it was alleged] being supplanted by a post-Fordist economy', giving way to 'flexible manufacturing systems, decentralization, sophisticated forms of stock control and marketing, diverse patterns of consumer demand' (ibid., p. 73). This summary could just as readily have drawn its elements from Piore and Sabel, a key reference text, except that in this instance 'mass socialists politics' (see ibid.) is now posited as an obverse of 'Fordism'.

7. For discussion of a recent Ford car assembly plant closure event and the different ways in which 'lean production' can become an issue to consider, see also Coffey and Thornley (2009, ch. 3 esp. pp. 51–5) and Coffey and Thornley (2010, appendix).

8. The view that Japanese car making equals 'customization' via provision of generous lists of factory-fit options on car model features became a popular one amongst Western commentators in the 1980s, but is contrary to fact: Krafcik in a survey carried out towards the end of this decade established that Japanese car makers in

fact eschewed this practice (for further discussion of which see Coffey, 2006, pp. 23–8; and for Krafcik's survey, see ibid, p. 41, n. 8). In so far as the Krafcik methodology for measuring car assembly plant productivity is concerned, we might note that the assumption that the range of models being assembled is largely irrelevant to the labour required to install a particular category of part, while open to challenge, also dismisses any link between product variety and skills (see also Coffey, 2006, ch. 4).

9. As we observe elsewhere, this is not compelling, given the shape of the available empirical data: in the 1970s hourly compensation rates in American manufacture were flat, while wage bills tumbled as work was outsourced to non-union sites; but even though Japanese hourly compensation rates were rising over the same period, America's trade deficit with Japan increased (see Coffey and Thornley, 2009, p. 157, n. 14). Findings of this kind are not necessarily surprising given the complexity of trade interactions, which will reflect not only non-price variables at the product level and exchange rate determinations, but also the wider political economies of market access and market protection. But they provide little sustenance for one of the most persistent forms of justification for de-unionization, which is that international competition plus high labour costs made it 'necessary' (see ibid., pp. 18–19).

10. For a discussion of some of the complications of assuming that Japanese car manufacturers have typically been vertically de-integrated see Coffey (2006, pp. 166–8; see also Coffey and Tomlinson, 2003, pp. 123–35), describing the shifting precepts of Western discussions over the course of a period in which Western corporations were outsourcing to avoid unions.

11. This is fully reflected, for example, in the status awarded Toyota in Best (1990) (on the 'new competition') and Lash and Urry (1994) (on 'reflexive accumulation'); and it is evident too in what are now standard textbook accounts for university and college students, as for example the treatment of production and work in recent editions of Giddens' *Sociology*. It is interesting to note that these later contributions award a much higher status to Toyota than is evident in either Piore and Sabel (1984) or Lash and Urry (1987), confirming the progress of its emblematic appeal.

12. For discussion of Toyota's experiments with intra-process buffers and implications that might be drawn, see Coffey (2006, pp. 98–110) and Coffey and Thornley (2008). An important starting point, upon which these analyses build, is provided by Monden (1998). A key writer from the viewpoint of Toyota's growing reliance on inventories as it has globalized its production operations is R.J. Schonberger, whose changing views have tracked this development (compare, for example, Schonberger, 1982, with 2001, or later contributions).

REFERENCES

Abernathy, W.J. (1978), *The Productivity Dilemma*, Baltimore: Johns Hopkins University Press.

Abernathy, W.J., K.B. Clark and A.M. Kantrow (1983), *Industrial Renaissance: Producing a Competitive Future for America*, New York: Basic Books.

Addison, J.T., J.S. Heywood and X. Wei (2003), 'New evidence on unions and plant closings: Britain in the 1990s', *Southern Economic Journal*, **69** (4), 822–41.

Aglietta, M. (1976 [1987]), *Regulation et crises du capitalisme* [*A Theory of Capitalist Regulation: The US Experience*], Calmann-Levy [London and New York: Verso].

Bannock, G. (1973), *The Juggernauts: The Age of the Big Corporation*, Harmondsworth: Penguin.

Best, M.H. (1990), *The New Competition: Institutions of Industrial Restructuring*, Cambridge: Polity.

Bradley, H., M. Erickson, C. Stephenson and S. Williams (2000), *Myths at Work*, Cambridge: Polity.

Braverman, H. (1974), *Labour and Monopoly Capitalism: The Degradation of Work in the 20th Century*, New York: Monthly Review Press.

Buechler, S.M. (2000), *Social Movements in Advanced Capitalism: The Political Economy and Cultural Construction of Social Activism*, Oxford and New York: Oxford University Press.

Coates, D. (2000), *Models of Capitalism: Growth and Stagnation in the Modern Era*, Cambridge: Polity.

Coffey, D. (2006), *The Myth of Japanese Efficiency: The World Car Industry in a Globalizing Age*, Cheltenham, UK and Northampton, MA: Edward Elgar.

Coffey, D. and C. Thornley (2006), 'Automotive assembly: automation, motivation and lean production reconsidered', *Assembly Automation: The International Journal of Assembly Technology and Management*, **26** (2), 98–103.

Coffey, D. and C. Thornley (2008), 'Lean production: the original myth reconsidered', in V. Pulignano, P. Stewart, A. Danford and A.M. Richardson (eds), *Flexibility at Work: Developments in the International Automobile Industry*, Basingstoke and New York: Palgrave Macmillan, pp. 83–103.

Coffey, D. and C. Thornley (2009), *Globalisation and Varieties of Capitalism: New Labour, Economic Policy and the Abject State*, Basingstoke and New York: Palgrave Macmillan.

Coffey, D. and C. Thornley (2010), 'Swing plants or punishments: a study of a Ford closure decision', *International Journal of Automotive Technology and Management*, **10** (2/3), 252–69.

Coffey, D. and P.R. Tomlinson (2003), 'Globalization, vertical relations, and the J-mode firm', *Journal of Post Keynesian Economics*, **26** (1), 117–44.

Drucker, P. (1955), *The Practice of Management*, London: Heinemann.

Dworkin, D. (2007), *Class Struggles*, Harlow: Pearson Education.

Fujimoto, T. (1999), *The Evolution of a Manufacturing System at Toyota*, Oxford and New York: Oxford University Press.

Hawken, P., A.B. Lovins and L. Hunter-Lovins (1999), *Natural Capitalism: The Next Industrial Revolution*, London: Earthscan.

Hayes, R.H. and W.J. Abernathy (1980), 'Managing our way to economic decline', *Harvard Business Review*, 58 (4), 67–77.

Jurgens, U., T. Malsch and K. Dohse (1993), *Breaking from Taylorism: Changing Forms of Work in the Automobile Industry*, Cambridge: Cambridge University Press.

Lash, S. and J. Urry (1987), *The End of Organized Capitalism*, Cambridge: Polity.

Lash, S. and J. Urry (1994), *Economies of Signs and Space*, London: Sage.

Luria, D. (2000), 'A high road policy for U.S. manufacturing', in C. Howes and A. Singh (eds), *Competitiveness Matters: Industry and Economic Performance in the U.S.*, Ann Arbor: University of Michigan Press, pp. 165–79.

Lyddon, D. (1996), 'The myth of mass production and the mass production of myth', *Historical Studies in Industrial Relations*, **1**, 77–105.

Monden, Y. (1998), *Toyota Production System: An Integrated Approach to Just-in-Time* (3rd edition), Norcross, GA: Engineering and Management Press.

Ohno, T. (1978), *Toyota Seisan Hoshiki: Datsu Kibo no Keiei wo Mezashite* [The Toyota Production Method: How Can We Overcome the Managament Philosophy of Scale Economies], Tokyo: Diamond Sha.

Ohno, T. (1988), *Toyota Production System: Beyond Large Scale Production*, Cambridge, MA: Productivity Press.

Piore, M.J. and C.F. Sabel (1984), *The Second Industrial Divide: Policies for Prosperity*, New York: Basic Books.

Pulignano, V., P. Stewart, A. Danford and A.M. Richardson (eds) (2008), *Flexibility at Work: Developments in the International Automobile Industry*, Basingstoke and New York: Palgrave Macmillan.

Rae, J.B. (1965), *The American Automobile: A Brief History*, Chicago and London: University of Chicago Press.

Roy, D. (1980), 'Fear stuff, sweet stuff and evil stuff: management's defenses against unionization in the South', in T. Nichols (ed.), *Capital and Labour: A Marxist Primer*, Glasgow: Fontana, pp. 395–415.

Schonberger, R.J. (1982), *Japanese Manufacturing Techniques: Nine Hidden Lessons in Simplicity*, New York: Free Press and Macmillan.

Schonberger, R.J. (2001), *Let's Fix It!*, New York: Free Press.

Shiomi, H. (1995), 'The formation of assembler networks in the automobile industry: the case of Toyota Motor Company (1966–1980)', in H. Shiomi and K. Wada (eds), *Fordism Transformed: The Development of Production Methods in the Automobile Industry*, Oxford: Oxford University Press, pp. 28–48.

Sorge, A. and W. Streeck (1988), 'Industrial relations and technical change: the case for an extended perspective', in R. Hyman and W. Streeck (eds), *New Technology and Industrial Relations*, Oxford and New York: Blackwell, pp. 19–47.

Stewart, P., K. Murphy, A. Danford, T. Richardson, M. Richardson and V. Wass (2009), *We Sell Our Time No More: Workers' Struggles Against Lean Production in the British Car Industry*, London and New York: Pluto Press.

Turner, H.A., G. Clack and G. Roberts (1967), *Labour Relations in the Motor Industry: A Study of International Unrest and an International Comparison*, London: George Allen & Unwin Ltd.

Walker, C., R. Guest and A. Turner (1956), *The Foreman on the Assembly Line*, Cambridge, MA: Harvard University Press.

Womack, J. and D.T. Jones (1996), *Lean Thinking: Banish Waste and Create Wealth in Your Corporation*, Bath: Simon and Schuster.

Womack, J. and D.T. Jones (2003), *Lean Thinking: Banish Waste and Create Wealth in Your Corporation* (2nd edition), Bath: Simon and Schuster.

Womack, J., D.T. Jones and D. Roos (1990), *The Machine that Changed the World*, New York: HarperCollins.

5. Global restructuring of transnational companies: negotiations in the auto industry

Isabel da Costa and Udo Rehfeldt

INTRODUCTION

The internationalization of the economy has, from the beginning, represented a challenge for workers and unions. The labour movement tried to address this challenge as early as 1864 with the creation of the International Working Men's Association. The latest form of economic internationalization is generally referred to as 'globalization'. As many chapters of this book show, one of its dimensions is the development of precarious forms of production and employment, including 'atypical' forms of work, but globalization also has an impact on 'full-time core work', particularly through restructuring.

We will here address one of the aspects of global restructuring, the emergence of transnational negotiations with multinational or transnational companies (TNCs). Transnational collective bargaining (TCB) with TNCs is relatively recent since most of the agreements were signed after 2000. By TCB we mean collective bargaining practices between employer and employee representatives aiming at reaching transnational agreements (global, European or other regional) whose content can range from symbolic to far-reaching. At the global level, TCB between TNCs and global union federations (GUFs) has led to the signature of international framework agreements (IFAs), which so far have been primarily concerned with core labour standards and corporate social responsibility (CSR). In Europe, there is no legal framework for TCB at the transnational company level, but this level of bargaining has none the less been emerging. If we exclude the agreements to set up European works councils (EWCs), restructuring is the major issue for TCB at the company level in Europe (European Commission, 2008; Telljohann et al., 2009; da Costa and Rehfeldt, 2010).

This paper is based on our fieldwork about TCB in automobile companies in Europe (da Costa and Rehfeldt, 2006, 2007). We chose the auto industry because it pioneered two of the most striking developments in industrial relations at the European level: the evolution of the role of some EWCs from the mere practice of information and consultation rights towards collective bargaining with management in order to prevent plant closures and to save jobs in Europe; and the tendency to expand the representation of workers beyond the frontiers of the European economic space, by creating world works councils (WWCs) which have co-signed IFAs together with GUFs. We will start with a brief recall of the first world councils and the developments at the European level fostering TCB. We will then concentrate on the dynamics of the transnational agreements aimed at saving jobs in the auto industry.

INTERNATIONAL UNION CO-ORDINATION IN HISTORICAL PERSPECTIVE

The international trade secretariats (ITSs) of the metal-working, chemical and food sectors, which were particularly affected by the process of inter-nationalization, started to encourage the creation of 'world councils' in the 1960s to co-ordinate union action within TNCs. By the 1990s, this strategy had evolved into the signing of IFAs by the GUFs, the new denomination of ITSs since 2002. Meanwhile, transnational union action towards TNCs had developed at the European level aiming at obtaining information and consultation rights, particularly in cases of restructuring. These develop-ments would not only set the infrastructure leading to TCB in Europe but also reinforce TCB at the global level.

Charles Levinson, successively Assistant General Secretary of the International Metalworkers' Federation (IMF) and General Secretary of the International Federation of Chemical and General Workers' Unions (ICF), was a key figure in the diffusion of the idea of TCB with TNCs, through both his activities and his debated writings. According to Levinson's theory (Levinson, 1972) the evolution of transnational union action should parallel that of the multinational character of companies and follow three stages: the first consists in the organization of interna-tional solidarity with a union involved in a conflict at a TNC subsidiary; the second includes the co-ordination of simultaneous collective bargain-ing at different subsidiaries of the same company in several countries; the final stage is integrated bargaining with the management of the TNC on the basis of common demands previously defined by the different national unions (Rehfeldt, 1993; da Costa and Rehfeldt, 2008).

In the 1970s there was widespread concern about TNCs becoming out of control of the nation states. TNC strategies of job relocation were perceived as a threat to employment in many European countries, all the more so since the economic downturn was resulting in increased unemployment rates in many labour markets. Besides regulation by different national governments there were attempts at regulating TNCs at the international level as well. The OECD *Guidelines for Multinational Enterprises* were adopted in 1976 (and revised in 2000), soon followed by the ILO's *Tripartite Declaration of Principles concerning Multinational Enterprises and Social Policy* in 1977 (revised in 2000 and 2006), and there were ongoing negotiations in New York to establish a United Nations Code of Conduct for Multinational Enterprises. The international labour movement favoured these attempts by international institutions to regulate TNCs and also pushed for the adoption of codes of conduct, although criticizing these instruments because of their lack of sanctions and legal means for enforcement.

The European Commission had, since the 1960s, undertaken a series of initiatives to promote workers' representation in European transnational companies (Didry and Mias, 2005; da Costa and Rehfeldt, 2008). In 1980 the Commission presented a proposal for a directive about information and consultation in multinational enterprises, known as the 'Vredeling directive', which entailed compulsory consultation and the possibility of negotiations in cases of total or partial closure of subsidiaries. This project was intensely debated and strongly opposed by the employers. The European Commission presented in July 1983 a modified version of the Vredeling directive, aimed at getting the employers' approval of it. The reaction of the multinationals and of the European employers' organization UNICE remained extremely negative. Some multinationals, including prominent American TNCs, had led an extensive lobbying campaign against the directive. For UNICE, the OECD guidelines were quite sufficient and there was no need for an extra piece of European legislation. This position had the support of the British government of Margaret Thatcher. Its threat of using its right of veto at the European Council of Ministers was enough to prevent the adoption of the directive, at least until 1990 when the European Commission submitted a new proposal, introducing the idea of EWCs, which was finally adopted by the European Council of Ministers in 1994, under the qualified majority rule, a new procedure made possible by the change in the European Treaties that had taken place at Maastricht in 1992. The directive on EWCs went into effect on 22 September 1996. Unlike the Vredeling proposal, it does not include mandatory bargaining in cases of restructuring, but rather mandatory bargaining for the constitution of a body of employee representatives for the purposes of information and consultation in all TNCs employing at least 1,000 employees within the European Economic Area (EU plus Norway, Iceland and Liechtenstein) and at least 150 in more than one member country.

Until the 1990s, no TNC had agreed to recognize a world council as representative for its workforce, or an ITS as bargaining partner to negotiate a transnational agreement. International union strategy was hindered by the strong ideological divisions that existed at the international confederate level, particularly during the Cold War period, as well as at the regional and industry levels. The situation started to evolve in the 1970s and the 1980s with the creation of the European Trade Union Confederation (ETUC) in 1973 and the debates about the adoption of European legislation on worker participation. The existence at the European regional level of a political will to adopt a form of social legislation and of a united confederation with its united industry federations – which progressively integrated unions coming from different ideological traditions – played an important role in the development of transnational strategies and co-ordinated union actions within TNCs (Rehfeldt, 1993; da Costa and Rehfeldt, 2008). In addition, the creation of a new institution for worker representation at the European level, based on European social legislation, gave a new impetus to transnational union strategies towards TNCs. As Turner (1996) pointed out, structure came before action in Europe. With time, significant forms of union co-ordination and action have emerged. However, the tension Turner emphasized between transnationally co-ordinated responses and national protest against the effects of internationalization is still here and is even increasing with the financial and economic crisis that hit Europe towards the last quarter of 2008.

EWCs today exist in most large companies. They vary widely in their functioning. Most often the information procedures do not allow for truly informed debate let alone real means to influence strategic decisions. Most EWCs have a limited impact on company decisions, many of which the EWCs are merely informed of, and not always in due time (Rehfeldt, 2004; Kerckhofs, 2006; Waddington, 2006). In a small but increasing number of cases, however, particularly concerning restructuring, and notably in the automobile industry, EWCs have started to play a more significant role. Some of the EWCs set up in the automobile sector became the actors in two important innovations in industrial relations in Europe: on the one hand, TCB on restructuring at the European level at Ford, General Motors (GM) and Daimler; on the other hand, the setting up of a new type of world works council at Volkswagen, DaimlerChrysler and Renault, which thereafter negotiated IFAs on CSR and core labour standards. This evolution is all the more remarkable since nothing in the European legislation forced the management of these companies to go beyond the periodic informating and consultation of their EWCs. It is an autonomous initiative of the social partners. We will here focus on TCB on restructuring at Ford, GM and Daimler.

FORD EUROPE

Ford's EWC was created on 16 September, 1996 – just six days before the entry into force of the EWC directive – and it includes three trade union officers as experts. In January 2000 it was the first EWC to sign an agreement in the auto industry at the European level, the 'Visteon agreement'. This agreement came about on the occasion of the reorganization of Ford with the externalization of part of its production. The company's restructuring strategy actually started in 1997, when all the equipment suppliers belonging to Ford on a world level had been gathered within a group called APO (Automotive Product Operation), which later became Visteon. The Visteon spin-off brought about negotiations aiming at protecting the ex-Ford workers transferred to the new company. This was done by the United Auto Works (UAW) for the USA and by the EWC for Europe. The protection obtained in Europe is quite similar to that contained in the UAW Ford 1999 Agreement which was negotiated just before.

All the ex-Ford workers transferred to Visteon during the spin-off were to benefit in their new work contracts from the same employment conditions as before, including seniority and pension rights; for the duration of their employment at Visteon they were to have a lifetime guarantee that their wages, benefits and other conditions would be equivalent to those of Ford's workers in their countries (including discounts for auto purchases, for instance); before final separation, they could ask to return to Ford (flow-backs), and would reintegrate according to job availability and a series of other criteria within five years maximum (their right to reintegration ceased after two job refusals); after the final separation they could apply for jobs open to external recruitment at Ford, and have priority for recruitment at equal levels of competence. A working group, composed of Ford management and the select committee of the EWC of Ford, was put in charge of the application and the follow-up of the agreement. The agreement also contained commercial and subcontracting clauses between Ford and Visteon so that the latter would be able to ensure these terms of employment for the workers covered during the following two product cycles. Subsequently employment security would be dependent on the efficiency and competitiveness of each facility. The problems that occurred during the first years of the implementation of the Visteon agreement were partially solved by the negotiation of an annex signed by both the Ford and the Visteon EWCs. The agreement was renegotiated in 2003 on the occasion of Visteon's 'Plan for Growth'.

The Visteon agreement was the first substantial agreement negotiated with a multinational corporation at the European level. There were a few previous agreements considered as 'substantive' in the literature, including two on restructuring: Danone in 1997 and Deutsche Bank in 1999 (Carley, 2001). But whereas these two only set up a number of principles and provided for future dialogue at local levels, Ford's Visteon agreement was the first one to deal in a specific way with a particular case of restructuring and to lay down constraining and detailed rules to be applied at local levels, which furthermore concerned both employment and production. The agreement was considered as successful by the EWC and the unions because, despite employment reductions, there had been no plant closures among the sites transferred to Visteon in the period when we conducted our interviews, that is, before 2008.

The experience, also judged in a positive way by the management, paved the way to other agreements signed by the same parties at the European level: the GFT (Getrag Ford Transmissions) agreement of 2000 and the IOS (International Operations Synergies) agreement of 2004 protect the personnel concerned during restructuring along the lines of the Visteon agreement; the 'Memorandum of Understanding' in 2000 and the revision of the EWC internal rules in 2002 clarify the conditions for bargaining at the European and national levels. Finally, in 2003, the vice-president of Ford Europe in charge of human resources and the president of the European works council of Ford also signed an agreement on 'Social Rights and Social Responsibility'. The agreement is similar to the IFAs sponsored by the IMF but is not signed by the latter, or by a national or European trade union organization. The scope of application of the agreement is not global; it applies only to the European operations of the company.

These agreements were not formally negotiated in cooperation with the European Metalworkers' Federation (EMF). The Ford EWC functions on the basis of an internal mandate given by the local and national representatives of the employees. The 'external' trade union organizations intervene only as national experts (German and British). The fact that the German expert is also the co-ordinator between the EMF and the EWC is never put forward, and the EMF, as such, did not sign the agreements and does not have a responsibility in their implementation. Yet a key factor in the conclusion of the Visteon agreement was the high level of transnational co-ordination between employee representatives, both within Europe, and between Europe and the USA (Carley, 2001, p. 37). Indeed, the EWC and the UAW had met and decided to co-ordinate their bargaining strategies, with the UAW signing first and the EWC obtaining equivalent conditions in Europe.

Taken as a whole, the agreements between the management of Ford Europe and the Ford EWC represent a high degree of development of common rules. They deal not only with political principles or broad and general procedures, but rather with concrete and substantive questions such as job security and working conditions. They were signed without industrial conflict and testify to the interest of the two parties in this type of procedure. The recent crisis, however, put a serious strain on the follow-up of the Visteon agreement, bringing to the fore its shortcomings in a critical situation of major restructuring and triggering shop-floor industrial action on the part of laid-off Visteon workers in the UK.

Indeed, as Visteon filed for bankruptcy and was put under administration in the UK, the administrators, KPMG, immediately moved to close down all three Visteon UK facilities. On 31 March 2009, with no advance notice, the 610 workers – of whom about 510 were ex-Ford employees, according to the union Unite's press – were told in short meetings at the end of the shift that they were made redundant and had to leave the premises. No guarantees were given as to redundancy pay (only the statutory minimum was offered) or pension rights. As a reaction, the workers spontaneously occupied the plant in Belfast (Northern Ireland). The Basildon (Essex) and Enfield (north London) plants were occupied the next day. After several weeks of sit-ins, with strong popular support for their cause, and a campaign led by Unite, an important improved settlement was reached with Ford and Visteon in early May. It included notice pay, a lump sum, and full Ford redundancy entitlements. Additionally, the ex-Ford employees received a 5.25 per cent pay increase awarded to Ford workers since November but not yet implemented at Visteon. The legally complex pensions issue, however, remains unresolved at the time of writing. Some 3,000 employees have paid into the Visteon (ex-Ford) pension fund and could lose up to 40 per cent of their pensions and more if they have to go into the national Pensions Protection Fund. Unite has asked the government's pensions regulator to investigate the handling of the fund and has launched a campaign demanding pensions justice for the laid-off UK Visteon workers.

GENERAL MOTORS EUROPE (GME)

The agreements signed at GME in March 2001, October 2001, December 2004, April 2008 and January 2009 are the most significant restructuring agreements signed with a TNC at the European level, since they theoretically protect all the company employees in Europe. They are the result of a co-ordinated strategy. For years, GM restructuring and reorganizations had been negotiated at the local level with plants being pitted against each other. Progressively the GM EWC adopted a European-level strategy (Herber and Schäfer-Klug, 2002; Kotthoff, 2006) of transnational solidarity – sometimes referred to as 'sharing the pain' – based on three principles:

- no plant closures;
- no forced redundancies;
- systematic search for negotiated and socially responsible alternatives.

The EWC of GME, officially called 'GM European Employee Forum', in order to avoid the nomination 'works council', was created on 16 September 1996 – that is, as in Ford, six days before the entry into force of the EWC directive. It also has two external trade union officers as experts: a German one from IG Metall and a British substitute from the TGWU (now Unite).

The first European agreement between the GM EWC and the management of GME was signed in May 2000, and had been negotiated in cooperation with IG Metall, on behalf of the EMF, and after co-ordination with the Fiat EWC. It protected GM employees transferred to joint ventures of GM and Fiat. Existing collective agreements remained in force and there were to be no economic redundancies until 2010. In the case of the failure of the GM–Fiat alliance, which actually took place in 2005, employees kept the right to return to their former employer.

In March 2001 the EWC signed a second agreement on the reorganization of GME, the 'Luton agreement'. It introduced two important developments. First, it protected all GME employees and not just those concerned with a specific operation (as in Ford–Visteon spin-off or the GM–Fiat joint venture). Secondly, it was signed after co-ordinated collective action including a strike at the European level. The agreement came about after the announcement by GM management in December 2000 of a restructuring plan with the reduction of 10,000 jobs world-wide, of which 6,000 were to go in Europe, including the closing down of the GM Vauxhall plant in Luton (UK) – which represented 2,000 jobs. Previous cases of job reductions had led to competing national employment security agreements, but this time the EWC refused the whipsawing logic of local negotiations, and its select committee adopted a strategy of transnational solidarity including both European-wide mobilization and transnational negotiation. The employee representatives together with the EMF organized a

'European action day'. On 25 January 2001 the employees of nearly all the European GM plants participated in a common strike and/or 'action day' against plant closures. This put pressure on the negotiations that were taking place in Zurich between the EWC and the management of GME. Management agreed to work with local employee representatives to avoid forced redundancies. Negotiated alternatives included part-time work, 'voluntary severance' and early retirement, as well as transfers to other GM locations. Vehicle production (though not car production) was to be maintained in Luton. The terms of this European framework agreement were to be reproduced through collective bargaining at all the national levels, in order to make it legally binding.

A few months later, after the announcement in August 2001 of further job cuts, known as the 'Olympia plan', a third framework agreement between GM management and the EWC was signed in October 2001. The plan included reducing capacities in the GM Opel, Vauxhall and Saab plants, and threatened the Astra production sites at Antwerp (Belgium) and Bochum (Germany), as well as the Corsa production sites in Saragossa (Spain) and Eisenach (Germany). GME management and the EWC reached a 'common understanding of important principles', which meant that the EWC accepted the objectives of the Olympia plan – including measures to improve productivity levels to 'world-class benchmark standards', as well as the generalization of 'best practices' – but that management committed itself to implementing the capacity adjustments with no plant closures, with no forced redundancies and in a 'socially responsible' manner.

Yet, in September 2004, GM management again announced its intention to close a production site and, in October, its further intention to cut 12,000 jobs in Europe. This time the EMF called a meeting of its affiliates and established a 'European trade union co-ordination group' – composed of members of the EMF secretariat, representatives of the national unions involved, as well as members of the GM EWC – which adopted a common action programme and called for a European day of action to take place on 19 October. Throughout the sites in Europe, 50,000 GM workers participated in it. An agreement was signed in December by the management of GME, the EMF, the national unions and the GM EWC. While recognizing the economic problems faced by GM and its need to reduce costs and jobs, the agreement reaffirmed the 'no forced redundancies' and 'no plant closures' principles of the previous agreements.

In June 2006, however, GM management announced the closure of the Azambuja plant in Portugal. As a response, the worker representatives organized a series of co-ordinated actions in all the European plants. The management of GME agreed to negotiate a new European agreement before closing the plant, but it actually never did so. This evolution shows the strength of a union strategy co-ordinated at the European level, but also the fragility of these agreements in the absence of a legal status for transnational collective bargaining at the company level in Europe.

These difficulties reinforced the determination of the unions and the EWC to fight against any other plant closure. In order to avoid just reacting to management's announcements of restructuring and job reductions, the unions and the EWC sought to have an input in the choice of production sites for future investment. Even before GME organized the competition between five plants for the next Astra/Zafira production, a Joint Delta Working Group was organized to negotiate a fair distribution of car volumes allowing for the survival of all the plants (Bartmann and Blum-Geenen 2006, 2007). The EWC, the national unions and the local representatives of the Delta Group plants signed a 'European Solidarity Pledge' which demanded a European agreement providing for fair capacity utilization with no plant closures and no forced redundancies. According to the pledge no local agreements would be signed until such an agreement safeguarded all the plants. The work of the Delta Group and the European solidarity pledge paid off. In April 2008, management, the EWC and the unions of GME signed a European framework agreement for the next generation of the Astra/Zafira model which excluded forced redundancies and guaranteed production in the GM plants of Ellesmere Port (UK), Bochum (Germany), Trollhättan (Sweden) and Gliwice (Poland) for the lifecycle of the new models. The plant in Antwerp (Belgium), which had not been chosen for the next-generation Astra, was to be safeguarded after the run-out of the current Astra production by two models of a new-generation vehicle. In addition, GME signed another European agreement guaranteeing for the first time an information and consultation process on outsourcing and that transfers of employees to suppliers could only happen on a voluntary basis. The affected employees were to be treated as if they continued to be employed by GM for a minimum period of five years. In the event that the company contract with the supplier expired, the right to return was guaranteed for a minimum of five years also.

With the car sales crisis of autumn 2008, the EWC of GME signed yet another new agreement on 12 January 2009. It set common rules to reduce the working time by resorting to short-time working (partial unemployment) in all the sites of the group in Europe to avoid economic redundancies and plant closures. Once again, the unions and the EWC were thus able to achieve their core demands in the negotiations: no plant closures and no forced redundancies. This is all the more remarkable given the world-wide GM situation. It will remain an outstanding example of how transnational solidarity pushing for socially responsible restructuring can be achieved, regardless of what the future of GME might be. At the time of writing, the latest restructuring plan includes, among other measures, the closing down of the Antwerp plant despite the efforts of the EWC and the fight of the Belgian workers to save those jobs.

DAIMLER

A 'European committee of the employee representatives', limited to the network of the dealers, was constituted at Daimler-Benz as early as 1992. The Daimler-Benz group was initially hostile to the constitution of a European works council. One month before the entry into force of the European directive, however, it signed a 'voluntary' agreement for the establishment of the EWC. After the merger with Chrysler in 1998, a WWC was also set up, on an informal basis. It was definitively institutionalized, by an agreement signed on 18 July 2002, under the name 'World Employee Committee'. The same year it negotiated and signed an IFA on basic labour standards and industrial relations, co-signed by the IMF. This agreement is often considered as one of the best examples of monitoring and follow-up of an IFA. Almost all the cases that have been brought to management's attention under the agreement have found a solution.

Only 6 per cent of Daimler employees in Europe worked outside of Germany. This structural element explains the absence of negotiations at the European level. Before the separation of Daimler and Chrysler in 2006, the transatlantic links were more important than the European ones. Since then, three European framework agreements have been signed. Faced with restructuring, the Daimler EWC also took the road of transnational negotiation to protect jobs at the European level (Metz, 2008). In 2006, two European framework agreements were signed, the first on information and consultation and the other on the adjustment of the levels of employment. The latter came after the announcement by management that there would be a reduction in the number of jobs which particularly touched white-collar workers. In Germany, the level of employment was protected by an agreement signed in 2004 which prohibited any dismissals before 2012. The aim of the European framework agreement was to prevent dismissals at the European level, by seeking alternative measures for the reduction of employment. In 2007, another European agreement was signed on the adaptation of the organization of the sales in Europe after the separation of Daimler and Chrysler. About 400 employees were transferred to other companies of the group, avoiding non-voluntary transfers. The employees concerned received a 'welcome bonus'. Thanks to the agreement negotiated by the EWC, this bonus now applies not only to Germany but also at the European level.

The European agreements at Ford, GM and Daimler required a delegation of the capacity to negotiate from the national to the European level and at least three types of co-ordination: between the national level and the European level; between the national trade unions involved and the EWC; and between the EWC and the EMF. This type of co-ordination legitimates and reinforces the transnational collective bargaining on the TNC level. The co-ordination has also evolved. All three EWCs have more than ten years of experience and there have been many meetings, particularly between the members of the select committees. Personal contacts and trust relations have been built progressively, facilitating the emergence of solidarity and strategic bargaining at the European level.

The European agreements negotiated by the Ford, GM and Daimler EWCs go beyond the framework agreements signed in other industries and deal with substantive rules and issues. The significant number of agreements shows the relevance of the procedure for the parties involved. The European agreements at Ford, GM and Daimler differ, however, in scope and style of industrial relations, which have been more conflictual at GM. The union involvement is also stronger in GM, with the EMF now being recognized as a partner in European-level negotiations and having signed the latest agreements. It subsequently also did so at Daimler.

CONCLUSION

The recognition of the European works councils by these three companies, which all opposed the EWC directive before it was adopted, is in itself an achievement, as is the further negotiation of European agreements with these new institutions for worker representation, since the EWC directive only gives these new bodies rights to information and consultation, not to collective bargaining. Our analysis of the negotiations led by these EWCs on restructuring outlines the extent of the evolution of the trade unions' and employers' attitudes. The fact that two of these companies have headquarters in the United States facilitated the evolution towards TCB, but so did the strong concentration of the employment in Germany within all three companies.

The automobile sector in many countries was, and still is, a trade union stronghold. The automobile sector has strong mechanisms of employee representation used by strong trade unions at the national as well as at the European level. The EWCs in the three cases analysed are exclusively made up of trade union members. This facilitated the emergence of strategies co-ordinated at the European transnational level. It has been noted that other auto companies with strong union presence have not evolved into European collective bargaining at the company level (Fetzer, 2008). This is true, but we think that while a strong union presence might not be a sufficient condition for transnational collective bargaining to emerge, it is certainly a necessary condition, without which the legitimacy of strategic collective action at the European level and the European transnational solidarity entailed will be difficult to achieve.

The EWC directive is now over ten years old and so are these EWCs. There has been an evolution in the attitude of the national trade unions, whose European co-ordination has developed, giving the EMF an increased role. The EMF played an important part in the negotiations for the creation of the EWCs which it co-ordinates in the automobile sector. It initially created a European network of 'European trade union co-ordinators'. For each EWC, an EMF co-ordinator was appointed, generally a full-time officer from a national union of the TNC's headquarters. The EMF has developed a wide range of transnational activities in Europe and has been increasingly involved in elaborating a union response to TNC restructuring, including TCB. The GM agreement of 2004 inspired a document adopted by the EMF in June 2005 on socially responsible restructuring (EMF, 2005) to be implemented through an early warning system resting on the EMF co-ordinators in the EWCs. In the event of even an informal transnational restructuring within a European TNC, the EMF co-ordinator, with the EMF Secretariat, is to set up a European trade union co-ordination group consisting of EWC representatives and one trade union officer for each national union involved. This group will try to negotiate a European framework agreement on job security, prior to any national negotiations (EMF, 2006, p. 15). The EMF has also elaborated internal rules concerning mandates for TCB and the adoption and signing of European agreements. The EMF experience in turn has inspired other European industry federations. However, the example of Forest, the Belgian subsidiary of Volkswagen, in 2006 shows that the principles adopted by the EMF are not always applied by its national associates, since neither the Volkswagen EWC nor the German trade unionists informed the EMF and their Belgian colleagues of the restructuring plan which threatened them and which was finally settled locally without prior European negotiation.

Concerning TCB at the company level in Europe, at least two major issues remain open. The first is the legal status of these agreements in the absence of European legislation on the matter. The European Commission is considering the possibility of adopting an 'optional framework' for TCB at the company level and has included its preparation in the 2005–10 Social Agenda. As long as there is no European legislation, the implementation of these agreements depends on their reproduction at all the national levels involved and on the strength of the signing parties. But, as we have seen, even in the highly unionized auto industry, and in companies where a strong co-ordination of transnational collective action has been successfully elaborated, this is not unproblematic. The second major issue is the clarification of the respective roles of the EWCs, the unions and the European federations which sign these agreements. The recent revision of the EWC directive, adopted by the European Parliament and Council of Ministers on May 2009 (da Costa and Rehfeldt, 2009), however, has left these issues unaddressed.

The institutional and union characteristics of the automobile sector make the diffusion of this type of transnational bargaining on restructuring towards sectors and companies where the trade unions are weak and in which the EWCs have little influence unlikely, unless the management of the TNC is interested in this type of negotiation. With the current recession, restructuring has increasingly become a major issue globally and at the European level. TCB could conceivably constitute a high road to a search for collectively negotiated and socially responsible ways out of the crisis. Industrial relations, however, essentially continue to take place within national contexts with the risk of rising protectionism and a downward spiral of concessions to save jobs.

REFERENCES

Bartmann, Martin and Sabine Blum-Geenen (2006), 'General Motors Europe: the challenge of the solidarity pledge', *Mitbestimmung*, international edition.

Bartmann, Martin and Sabine Blum-Geenen (2007), 'Where to relocate production?', *Mitbestimmung*, international edition.

Carley, Mark (2001), *Bargaining at the European Level? Joint Texts Negotiated by European Works Councils*, Luxembourg: Office for Official Publications of the European Communities.

da Costa, Isabel and Udo Rehfeldt (2006), 'La négociation collective transnationale européenne chez Ford et General Motors', *Connaissance de l'emploi* (Centre d'Etudes de l'Emploi), **35**.

da Costa, Isabel and Udo Rehfeldt (2007), 'European works councils and transnational bargaining about restructuring in the auto industry', *Transfer*, **2**.

da Costa, Isabel and Udo Rehfeldt (2008), 'Transnational collective bargaining at company level: historical developments', in Kostantinos Papadakis (ed.), *Cross-Border Social Dialogue and Agreements: An Emerging Global Industrial Relations Framework?*, Geneva: International Institute for Labour Studies/ International Labour Office.

da Costa, Isabel and Udo Rehfeldt (2009), 'Les CEE et la négociation collective transnationale: les accords européens et mondiaux dans l'automobile', *La Revue de l'IRES*, **61-2009** (2).

da Costa, Isabel and Udo Rehfeldt (2010), 'Restructurations et comités d'entreprise européens: dynamique de la négociation transnationale', in C. Didry and A. Jobert (eds), *L'entreprise en restructuration, dynamiques institutionnelles et mobilisations collectives*, Rennes: PUR.

Didry, Claude and Arnaud Mias (2005), *Le moment Delors: les syndicats au cœur de l'Europe sociale*, Brussells: PIE and Peter Lang.

EMF (2005), 'GME restructuring and framework agreements: an example of EMF European company policy', *EMF Focus*, **1**.

EMF (2006), *Handbook on How to Deal with Transnational Company Restructuring*, Brussels: EMF.

European Commission (2008), *Mapping of Transnational Texts Negotiated on Corporate Level*, Brussels (EMPL F2 EP/bp2008).

Fetzer, Thomas (2008), 'European works councils as risk communities: the case of General Motors', *European Journal of Industrial Relations*, **3**.

Herber, Armin and Wolfgang Schäfer-Klug (2002), 'How a European works council learned to negotiate', *Mitbestimmung*, international edition.

ILO (1977 [2000, 2006]), *Tripartite Declaration of Principles concerning Multinational Enterprises and Social Policy*, Geneva: ILO, available at: http://www.ilo.org/public/english/employment/multi/ download/english.pdf.

Kerckhofs, P. (2006), *European Works Councils: Facts and Figures 2006*, Brussels: ETUI-REHS.

Kotthoff, Hermann (2006), *Ten Years General Motors European Employee Forum (EEF)*, Düsseldorf: Hans-Böckler-Stiftung.

Levinson, Charles (1972), *International Trade Unionism*, London: Allen & Unwin.

Metz, Thomas (2008), 'Le comité d'entreprise européen vu d'Allemagne: l'exemple de Daimler-Chrysler', in Europe et Société (ed), 'Les négociations transnationales en Europe' in *Les Cahiers de la Fondation*, **69–70**.

OECD (1976 [2000]), *Guidelines for Multinational Enterprises*, Paris: OECD, available at: http://www.oecd.org/dataoecd/56/36/1922428.pdf.

Rehfeldt, Udo (1993), 'Les syndicats européens face à la transnationalisation des entreprises', *Le Mouvement Social*, **162**.

Rehfeldt, Udo (2004), 'European works councils and international restructuring: a perspective for European collective bargaining', in Elsie Charron and Paul Stewart (eds), *Work and Employment Relations in the Automobile Industry*, London: Palgrave Macmillan.

Telljohann, V., I. da Costa, T. Müller, U. Rehfeldt and R. Zimmer (2009), *European and International Framework Agreements: Practical Experiences and Strategic Approaches*, Luxembourg: Office for Official Publications of the European Communities.

Turner, Lowell (1996), 'The Europeanization of labour: structure before action', *European Journal of Industrial Relations*, **2** (3).

Waddington, J. (2006), 'Revision of the EWC Directive: how EWC members see it', *Mitbestimmung*, **8**.

6. Trade unions facing uncertainty in Central and Eastern Europe

Sylvie Contrepois and Steve Jefferys

INTRODUCTION

The global power of employers has increased dramatically since 1989. Their reach has been extended to nearly every corner of the world; and in those Western countries where once their power was constrained by countervailing trade union or social democratic or Communist opposition, these universalistic oppositions are everywhere significantly weaker. But if trade unionism has had a hard time globally, trade unionism in the transition states of Central and Eastern Europe has had a really hard time. From playing major institutional roles in managing labour in the command economy and in the political sphere, CEE unions have nearly everywhere been marginalized, losing their mass memberships in downward spirals of decline and fragmentation. The political systems they operate in have generally stopped offering workers and their organizations special protection and privileges. Privatizations have swept away state-run industries and services. The economies they operated in have been restructured away from heavy industry, often in circumstances where vast injections of foreign and often highly mobile capital have permitted a few hundred multinational companies to capture considerable economic power.

More recently, in 2004 and 2007, the 'market-making' aspect of the European Economic Community led to the enlargement of the European Union to include ten of these former Russian satellite states. Yet enlargement also imposed EU social policy, including directives which inserted or reinforced both social dialogue procedures and tripartism into existing labour codes, industrial relations systems and employment-related political decision-making processes. The intent of the wave of social directives was to use 'legal enactment', to borrow the Webbs' (1897) term, to provide general principles to ensure that improving market efficiencies would not have the result of leading to a race to the bottom in terms of hard-fought-for wages and working conditions. These principles were embodied in what has been described as the 'market-regulating' aspects of EU social policy.

What impact have EU membership and its associated employment policies had on trade unionism? Can we agree with the 'Euro-optimists' that the 1994 Directive instituting EWCs 'creates for the first time a transnational system of industrial relations based on European legislation' (Schulten, 1996, p. 303)? The EWC Directive clearly fuelled hopes that EWCs would be an important step towards a European industrial relations system (Marginson and Sisson, 1994).

The 'optimists' argue that EU social policy as a whole has also enabled what is best described as 'soft' forms of transnational employment regulation: human resource (HR) policies and procedures on non-wage issues are discussed and possibly modified in the absence of formal collective bargaining and written and signed agreements. More broadly, Iankova and Turner (2004) suggest that 'tripartism' has made progress in Central and Eastern Europe. They see this as a special emergent form of neo-corporatism where negotiating structures are multi-level, where negotiations are largely political rather than purely on economic and social issues, and where the involvement of civic groups goes beyond the representation of labour, business and the state.

Yet perhaps we should be more pessimistic? The assessment that CEE 'tripartism' played a positive role is, for example, challenged by Martin and Cristescu-Martin (2004). These authors argued that reliance upon tripartite social partnerships and the state have generally failed to bring industrial relations in CEE closer to European norms and that there has been very little development of 'shared values' among different actors. They suggested that:

> With the low levels of trust in organisation, and the particularly low levels of trust in employment relations organisations, it is evident that shared values were unlikely to form the basis for sustaining integrated national systems of employment relations. (Martin and Cristescu-Martin, 2004, p. 635)

They saw tripartism as largely 'window-dressing', with very little impact on economic performance – although they conceded that it enhanced 'regime legitimacy' and reduced 'the threat of social conflict' (2004, p. 633).

'Euro-optimism' has also been challenged by those who argued that the EWC Directive was too weak to support such a development, and who queried whether social change could be institutionally imposed 'from above' (Streeck, 1997). It was further queried by those who argued that enlargement to countries without strongly embedded trade unions and effective employment regulation could weaken the whole European social model (Vaughan-Whitehead, 2003). In addition, given the known weaknesses of trade union representation in CEE, concerns were expressed that the presence of non-union employees from these countries on EWCs could undermine trade union influence on these and reduce their independence from the employer.

This chapter explores the complex processes behind the performances of CEE10 trade unions as a result of the changes before, during and after EU adhesion. It first sketches the huge economic and political challenges facing trade unions within these new member states. In these economies, where before the transition nearly everyone had a permanent job, uncertainty in employment has become nearly universal. Precarity in all its forms is increasing still more rapidly than in the pre-enlargement EU member states. The next section provides a brief summary of the general characteristics of the CEE10 trade union movements before narrowing the focus to report on the trade union experience in just three of these countries: Poland, Hungary and Bulgaria.[1] Finally, the chapter presents a conclusion arguing that neither the Euro-optimists nor the Euro-pessimists are fully vindicated by the trade union experience of CEE unions since their adhesion to the EU.

THE ECONOMIC CHALLENGES

Three major economic changes – the liberalization of financial markets, the commercialization of product and service markets and the privatization of many publicly owned service or commodity supplier organizations – took place across the whole of Europe in the 1980s and 1990s. Within the EU15 (pre-2004 member states) they occurred over an extended period and in a context of democratic debate in which trade unions often exercised the considerable employee voice they had acquired over the previous three decades. Unions were often able to slow down or stop the process and give the economy and their members more time to adapt.

In Central and Eastern Europe, in contrast, liberalization, commercialization and privatization occurred virtually simultaneously, essentially in the ten years from 1995,[2] and in circumstances where the officially recognized pre-transition trade unions had lost much of their credibility as representatives of employee voice.[3] Foreign direct investment knocked down doors and totally reconfigured the host economies. The period after their initial 'velvet revolutions' of 1989–91 constituted a highly dramatic period of change.

The transition to 'political democracy' after two or more generations without experience of it thus occurred in a context where the CEE economies faced very major adjustment problems in refocusing away from being selected producers for Russia to engaging with Western Europe and other world markets. Tensions appeared between those seeking to retain many of the benefits and structures of the pre-transition system, and those wishing to sweep all of those away as rapidly as possible in order to achieve the promise of full integration into a much more wealthy global economy.

From the trade union perspective the biggest challenges were: the huge rise in unemployment that accompanied a significant restructuring to services away from heavy industry (where the unions were most strongly implanted); the privatization of much of the service sector and of the most productive parts of manufacturing; dealing with the large number of sophisticated foreign multinationals that began to invest in CEE; the establishment of negotiating relations with genuinely representative employers at local, sector or national-levels; and the loss of much remaining popular credibility for the unions as well as national-level political influence in the shift towards parliamentary rather than single-party government.

Accompanying these processes was a form of economic segmentation. Martin (2006) argues that FDI by MNCs also helped create a more 'segmented' business system and national economic and employment model than existed in the EU15. He suggests (pp. 1353–4) 'capitalism in Central and Eastern Europe is segmented into three types . . . managerial capitalism, in the privatized and about to be privatized state sectors; entrepreneurial capitalism, in the *ab initio* private sector; and international capitalism'. Martin (p. 1355) describes the huge swathe of 'managerial capitalism' within CEE countries as where 'managers determine enterprise strategies without serious challenge'. 'Entrepreneurial capitalism' he characterizes as the domination of firms by 'owner-managers with highly personal management styles'. In both these two segments the openings for independent employee voice through the trade unions are highly limited. By contrast, in the MNC sector Martin believes: 'Corporate international human resource strategies determine employment relations, with high earnings, relative to national employers, in exchange for high effort and high commitment' (ibid.). He goes on to argue that 'each form of capitalism has its characteristic pattern of employment relations'. This 'segmented' social model is common across CEE and should be regarded less, he maintains, as temporary or transitory, and more as rooted in a core dualism: influences 'governed by inheritance from the socialist past' in tension with 'aspirations for a free-market future'. Recognizing that social model pluralism occurs in most capitalist societies, Martin argues the 'degree of structural and ideological differentiation is greater in CEE' (2006, p. 1355).

What have been the impacts on people's working conditions of the processes of industrial restructuring, privatization and economic segmentation? Prior to their EU accession a detailed study of labour markets in CEE found many key differences between working conditions there and in the EU15. Ladã (2002) argued that there were several common features across CEE candidate countries that distinguished them from the EU15. First of all, employment rates were lower and unemployment rates were often higher. Workers tended to be older and more workers worked in very small organizations. Women made up a larger proportion of the labour force and women were more likely to be employed in managerial occupations. Another gender difference was that women were not so disproportionately affected by part-time work as in Western Europe, but in CEE part-time and limited-duration employment was less common in general. There was also less employment in the services sector and more in agriculture. As a consequence, work organization was more traditional and industrial, and less service-oriented.

Working conditions were generally much less favourable. Working hours were appreciably longer, as well as being more unsocial; pay was also considerably lower than in the EU15, although rates were increasing at a faster rate; and workers received less training from their employers. Finally, if we turn to industrial relations, Ladã shows that worker information and consultation over organizational change were rare. Staff representatives in Central and Eastern Europe were generally less likely to be informed across a wide range of issues.

Reviewing the changes that took place between 2000 and 2005, Eyraud and Vaughan-Whitehead (2007) use Labour Force Survey data to show a range of ways in which working conditions have become more precarious in the 2004 EU enlargement member states of CEE. In particular they note an increasing use of fixed term contracts; the introduction of temporary agency work; growing 'involuntary' part-time work; sharp increases in the numbers of 'self-employed' workers; and the persistence of somewhat higher levels of weekend working than in the EU15. In the face of these challenges to workers' jobs and working conditions, how effective are the different countries' trade union movements?

TRADE UNIONS IN CENTRAL AND EASTERN EUROPE

The concern that enlargement to the new member states might be used as a way of enabling 'social dumping' – a downward worsening shift of working conditions and in employee voice – is brought out graphically in two figures provided in an EU Commission report on contemporary European industrial relations (EU, 2009, p. 20). One shows that the total numbers of trade union members remained generally stable over the decade from 1995 to 2005 in the EU15 at around 37–8 million. However, when membership for the whole EU27 (post-2007 member states) is calculated for the same period, the aggregate figure is pulled down primarily by a falling membership in CEE countries: from some 52 million to 42.3 million.

The second figure from this same DG Employment report on industrial relations depicts the data in terms of trade union density: union members in paid employment as a proportion of the wage-earning population showing more stability among the EU15 member states, but a dramatic collapse in membership in the ten countries that acceded to the EU in 2004. The report concludes that the downward density trend across all EU members has been 'spectacularly' aggravated by the membership decline in the new member states.

The concern for the trade union movements that still have considerable national-level influence is that the decline across the whole EU27 to a membership proportion of 25.1 per cent in 2005 from 30 per cent ten years earlier presages an associated decline in European-wide political influence. At face value the evidence is that the top-down transposition of EU social directives on to the CEE10[4] provided little benefit to the trade unions.

Yet the strengths and weaknesses of trade unions and the varying roles they play in different industrial relations systems are notoriously difficult to assess. Among the indicators that are often used to help make meaningful comparisons are trade union density among the total country employment base, the degree of trade union structural fragmentation, the extent of strike activity and the coverage of collective bargaining agreements. All the CEE10 countries have statutory minimum wages and labour codes that establish legal frameworks for employer–employee relations, and all have tripartite social dialogue institutions at national levels, either predating the 1989 transition or introduced in preparation for EU accession. Yet the presence of formal structures does not necessarily lead to effective dialogue. An important indicator of trade union influence is whether in the post-EU accession period the structures in place have led to effective national social partner, bipartite or tripartite agreements. Table 6.1 provides some data on these five characteristics to attempt to allow a certain degree of comparison and permit a limited level of generalisation.

We have ranked the CEE10 countries in Table 6.1 in terms of their latest reported (or estimated) levels of trade union density, running from the lowest to the highest. As can be seen, there are significant differences between them: in Estonia and Lithuania the density levels are around one in ten workers while Romania and Slovenia both report one in three

Table 6.1   Characteristics of CEE10 trade unionisms, 2007–2008

	Pop. (m)	Trade union membership density % (latest year)	No. of peak trade unions	No. of striker- days per 1000	% formally covered by collective agreements	Recent social dialogue agreements
Estonia	1.34	9	2	n.a.	25	No
Lithuania	3.34	10–12	3	1.6	10	No
Poland	38.1	14	3	3.5	40	No
Latvia	2.26	15	1	0.6	24	No
Hungary	10.0	17	6	3.5	25	No
Slovakia	5.41	17	2	0.01	35	Yes
Bulgaria	7.6	20	2	n.a.	36	Yes
Czech Republic	10.5	21	2	n.a.	26	Yes
Romania	21.5	30–5	4	31.5	53	Yes
Slovenia	2.0	44	6	n.a.	96	Yes

Notes: n.a. = Not available

Sources: 2009 population data from: http://epp.eurostat.ec.europa.eu/tgm/.
   Trade union density from: OECD (2009) *Statistical Extracts*, European Trade Union Institute (ETUI) National Industrial Relations country reports or expert communications from Laas in Estonia; Lulle in Latvia; Woolfson in Lithuania; Cziria in Slovakia; Pop and Stoian in Romania; and Poje in Slovenia.
   Peak trade unions are the state-recognized national union confederations; Numbers provided by ETUI National Industrial Relations country reports or national experts in private communications as above.
   Average annual striker-days per 1,000 employees (2000–2007) from OECD (2009) *Statistical Extracts* except for Slovakia, where the data is just for 2005 with a 0 response for all other years.
   Collective bargaining coverage data from: ETUI National Industrial Relations country reports or expert communications (as above); for Bulgaria, Skarby (2006); for Poland, Gault (2005).
   Recent social dialogue agreements from: *EIROnline* and expert communications (as above).

or more of the workforce belonging to a trade union; the other six trade union movements report density of levels somewhere between one in seven and one in five workers.

As far as the coverage of collective bargaining agreements goes, there is more uniformity. Six of the CEE10 report formal coverage of from one in four to one in three of their workforce.[5] Only Lithuania with just 10 per cent coverage at the low end and, again, Romania (half the workforce) and Slovenia (virtually the whole workforce covered) at the high end appear as outliers.

Considering national social dialogue, only in Bulgaria, the Slovak Republic and Slovenia do national tripartite arrangements appear to have played any real role in the last three years. Martin and Crestescu-Martin (2004) appear vindicated. Their argument was that the language of 'interest reconciliation' that dominated European political discourse in the early 1990s had evolved easily into the EU language of 'social partnership' from 1996, but that institution building on this 'top-down' discourse was highly partial, fragmentary and largely ineffective. This they argued was particularly because of the employers' lack of organizational coherence. The Hungarian Interest Representation Council, for example, has nine employer organizations, while the Bulgarian National Commission for the Conciliation of Interests has four, which, Martin and Crestescu-Martin (2004, p. 634) report, 'rarely agreed with one another'. The only institutions that are working seriously towards 'national employment relations convergence' appear to be the trade unions, and this is not enough. Thus, with the exception of Slovenia, joint regulation in the other nine CEE new member states, when it occurs, does so predominantly at plant or company levels, and hardly ever at sectoral or national levels.

From the data on collective bargaining coverage, on the role of national-level social dialogue and on claimed union membership density levels, with the single exception of Slovenia, the picture emerges of very wide areas of employment that are virtually devoid of any forms of joint regulation. Why is company collective bargaining limited, sector collective bargaining virtually non-existent and national-level social dialogue so weak? Put differently, why is it that outside the wealthiest in per capita terms of the CEE10 countries (EuroMemorandum, 2008), Slovenia,[6] the EU institutional framework supporting social dialogue as a tool for social change is so rarely used?

TRADE UNION MOVEMENTS IN POLAND, HUNGARY AND BULGARIA

In order to understand better the factors behind the problems CEE trade unions face in retaining and recruiting members as well as in influencing labour market developments, we now consider the experiences of three of the trade union movements: those of Poland, Hungary and Bulgaria. The key post-transition issues for the unions are usefully discussed in terms of their political legacy, their industrial legacy and the challenge of finding employers with whom to engage in dialogue.

Political Legacy

The negative political fallout on the trade unions most closely identified with the pre-transition regimes that had claimed to stand for workers' rights was considerable. The pre-transition official unions had been seen ambivalently both as corrupt tools of management and as powerful ways of accessing solutions to work and non-work problems. These visions of trade unionism distorted workers' understandings of what trade union independence and representative democracy could involve. As a result, while the opportunities available to many trade unions in Central and Eastern Europe to exercise influence on transition were quite limited, workers' expectations of what they could achieve were quite unrealistic. Large numbers of people left trade unions as a natural part of winning political freedom. Many of those who remained in trade unions were disappointed that they no longer had the same influence that they had before 1989. Others considered that even making trade union demands for better treatment in the 1990s might jeopardize the fight for economic survival (Ost, 2000).

The transitions were, however, quite different in different CEE countries, and so too were the roles the unions played in them, and the legacies they derived from. While several features were shared, not surprisingly since these countries had all spent forty years in the Russian sphere of influence, these countries also had their own specific histories and followed different political trajectories towards the post-Communist era. Pollert (1999), for example, argues that the Polish and Hungarian economies had undergone greater economic reform prior to 1989 and had more developed political oppositions than had Czechoslovakia. This, she suggests, was largely because of the greater embeddedness of the Communist Party in Czechoslovakia as a result of its leadership of the wartime resistance.

Perhaps we may also apply the embeddedness argument to Bulgaria, where the Communists also had a long pre-war tradition and dominated the coalition that came to power in 1944, and from 1954 until 1989 had a single dominant leader, Todor Zhikov. In 1990 at the first free elections in Bulgaria the former Communists, now known as the Bulgarian Socialist Party, were elected back to power. Transition, in consequence, was more protracted than in Poland or Hungary.

In Poland, in contrast to Bulgaria, the 1989 defeat of the Communist regime was clearly total. It resulted from nearly ten years of growing mobilization by the Solidarność trade union that had swollen into a mass social movement. In 1989 Solidarność itself won the first partially free elections to be held in a Communist-controlled country, taking 99 out of the 100 Senate seats and 160 out of 161 seats in the Parliament. This enabled the 'union' to nominate the prime minister, and the knock-on consequences were rapidly felt throughout Russia's other satellite states. Within months virtually all of them had also taken the road to transition. The following year, 1990, Lech Walesa, the Solidarność chairman, won an election to become Polish president. Solidarność remained associated closely with Polish political life throughout the 1990s, forming its own political party in 1996, and winning the elections of 1997. Since the end of the 1980s and the early 1990s, NSZZ Solidarność was thus perceived primarily as a political force and only secondly as an independent representative of workers' rights and interests. It has only been recently, and in the light of declining trade union membership, that the trade union's leaders have stated it is necessary to revive the classical purpose of trade unions, to represent workers rather than being dominated by politics and being seen as one of the country's political parties (Contrepois et al., 2009).

In Hungary, by the end of the 1980s reformers already made up a majority of the Communist government, and in 1988 the leader who had helped put down the 1956 Revolution was replaced. Reformers passed new laws permitting trade union pluralism, free expression and free elections. The Communists then also re-badged themselves as the Hungarian Socialist Party and the first free election took place in May 1990, being won by a centre-right coalition. Major structural reforms followed immediately and Hungary was largely opened up to inward investment. After that first democratic election, a political system developed in Hungary approximating to a two-party system, with a left social-liberal or a right-liberal coalition alternating in different elections until 2007, when the Socialist Party was re-elected. This political normalcy seemed to make long-term economic stability appear more credible to foreign capital and FDI. If two distinctly different routes were taken by Poland and Bulgaria, Hungary's transition thus combined elements of both: insider reform and outsider support.

Pollert (1999) argues that these pre-1989 differences continued to mediate the transformation process during the 1990s, affecting the structures of labour representation and industrial relations. In particular the political continuity in Bulgaria may help explain why the pre-1989 official union confederation survived much better in its reformed condition there than in Hungary or Poland, and why 'tripartism' appears stronger there. These new socio-economic systems have been described generally as a form of 'transformative corporatism' (Iankova, 1998). But within this broad label there are still considerable differences. Iankova and Turner (2004, p. 77) view Bulgaria as 'one of the more developed cases of post-communist tripartism, while Poland exemplifies a weaker tripartism that emerged at a later stage of the transformation process'.

Both stronger and weaker forms of CEE 'tripartism' in the late 1990s and early 2000s adapted to and took over the language of European social dialogue. Yet while the negotiating institutional structures created are formally multi-level (national, sectoral and local), in reality, when they take place, negotiations are almost exclusively at national level. They involve the employers, unions and the government and tend to be quite political. But because of the lack of representativeness of the employer and union organizations there is also often an involvement of other civic groups in the tripartite social dialogue process to give it some wider national legitimacy.

Within these broad 'transformative corporatist' settings, the post-transition construction of a 'new' industrial relations system also proceeded differently in different countries. In Poland, a single representative system was enshrined in the constitution drafted by the Solidarność government: employee representation could only be provided by trade unionists.[7] Similarly, in Bulgaria, where the former Communists of the newly founded Socialist Party headed up the first post-transition government, trade unions were constitutionally protected as the unique legal form of workplace employee voice. In Hungary, in contrast, the centre-right transition government not only opened up the gates to privatization and FDI more quickly than did Bulgaria and Poland, but also introduced a dual representation system: workers were given the right to elect works council representatives, but only if the trade unions comprised 50 per cent or higher of the elected representatives would the trade union then secure recognition and the right to collectively bargain.

More recently the legal contexts of employee representation in Bulgaria and Poland have moved away from single channel representation. The 2002 EU Information and Consultation Directive required companies with at least 50 employees and workplaces with at least 20 employees to inform and consult employee representatives about business developments, employment trends and changes in work organization. The Directive essentially harmonized European practice around a dual model of representation that assumed many employee representatives would not be trade union members.

In both Bulgaria and Poland the unions were concerned about what they saw as a potential source of further weakening of their claim to speak for all workers. In Poland its transposition did enable works councils to be established in enterprises from March 2008, but rather than embrace a full dual representation system, the new law guaranteed that where representative trade unions were present these works councils would be controlled by the unions. In Bulgaria the directive became law in July 2006. It enabled the calling of general assemblies to elect representatives, but did not give the trade unions rights to call those meetings where they are not already recognized. The Bulgarian unions were also worried that their influence would be weakened since all individual employees can stand, and any individual can nominate another (Mihaylova, 2009). In Hungary the 2005 change to the Hungarian Labour Code was less dramatic, but it still failed to provide a remedy for the fundamental problem of Hungarian work-place representation caused by the weak Hungarian legislation on works councils, namely that employers are not required to set them up (Fodor and Neumann, 2005). In all three countries the legislation appears so far to have had only a very limited effect.

Essentially, the structure of the trade union movements of the three countries reflects the transition process. In all three the old Communist-controlled unions survived – albeit with new names and much reduced membership. In Bulgaria they even retained their old premises. In each country an alternative (non-Communist-image) trade union confedera-tion centre of varying strength also appeared either before (in Poland) or during the transition period. In Bulgaria and Poland, where the transition to post-Communism occurred under conditions of trade union strength, the new constitutions and labour codes enabled the institutionalization at peak organizational level of just one 'continuity' and one 'alternative'[8] trade union centre. In contrast in Hungary, where there was no strong central trade union influence after 1989–91, and alternating political power between left and right, the constitution and employment relations system discouraged continuity and encouraged the fragmentation of trade union confederations shown in Table 6.2.

Industrial Legacy

A legacy of their pre-transition past is that the trade unions in Central and Eastern Europe are stronger in heavy and extractive industries and in the state sector than in newer manufacturing and the private service sectors. This is for several reasons: there were often major employee concerns that required voicing such as privatization, massive redundancies and take-overs by MNCs; workers in these sectors tended to be organized in quite large units and to be relatively well paid. These factors favoured the main-tenance of collective organization and made it more rational for employ-ers to envisage the collective resolution of change management. In many instances incoming MNCs had to agree with the union before taking over a company that they would not make compulsory redundancies.

The presence of a form of trade union veto was in force when the French electricity company Electricité de France (EDF) bought into Poland and Hungary, for example. For these workers, then, the transition should not

Table 6.2   *'Continuity' and 'alternative' peak trade union organizations in Bulgaria, Hungary and Poland*

Trade union confederations	Bulgaria[a]	Poland[b]	Hungary[c]
'Continuity'	CITUB	OPZZ FZZ	MSZOSZ
'Alternative'	CL Podkrepa	NSZZ Solidarność	SZEF ASZSZ LIGA MOSZ ESZT

Notes:
(a) Bulgaria: CITUB (Confederation of Independent Trade Unions in Bulgaria); CL Podkrepa (Confederation of Labour Podkrepa).
(b) Poland: OPZZ (All Poland Trade Unions Alliance); FZZ (Forum of Trade Unions – a 2002 confederation comprising unions that had formerly split from OZPP); NSZZ Solidarność (Independent and Self-Governing Trade Union Solidarity).
(c) MSZOSZ (National Confederation of Hungarian Trade Unions); SZEF (Trade Union Cooperation Forum); ASZSZ (Alliance of Autonomous Trade Unions); LIGA (Democratic League of Independent Trade Unions); MOSZ (National Federation of Workers' Councils); ESZT (Confederation of Trade Unions of Professionals).

be understood as involving a big discontinuity in trade union representation: in large state-run industries there were already trade union activists in place, and often they had clear formal representative functions ascribed to them. Before transition they were never regarded as really 'independent' and they often played significant HR management roles. But at transition they still had a relatively high status[9] and very often the strong desire to remain in a local position of influence to negotiate with local and company-level management. In most of these workplaces the same people therefore stayed on as trade union representatives through the transition years. In another important example of the effects of continuity, one activist who had gained trade union experience before 1989 renewed her trade union activism after 2003 to help organize the first trade union branch at a Carrefour hypermarket.[10]

This legacy of strong unions also carried over into a handful of privatized service sectors. In Poland, for example, when it took over all or part of the state hotel business, Accor was faced with deeply embedded trade unions. In the major Accor-Orbis chain there are trade union branches in nearly every one of its roughly 80 hotels, although these are made up of many independent union branches and only a few have links to two of the national union confederations. The FZZ trade union groups together three of the different Accor-Orbis hotel branches, while the Orbis-Novotel Hotel Forum local union affiliates to the NSZZ Solidarność region, but not to the sector federation that it does not wish to mandate on its behalf.[11] For several years the company avoided having to send delegates to the Accor EWC by virtue of having an organizational structure in which each of its hotels is an independent company, hence each is below the threshold under which EWC participation becomes mandatory. One manager estimated that in 2006 as many as half of the roughly 3,000 employees were trade union members.[12]

In Hungary, where Accor also took over a big state-owned hotel chain, nearly half of the 1,200 Accor-Pannonia workers were also union members in 2005–2006. This example, however, raises a different form of continuity. The union members there too had followed the leadership of a core of older trade unionists from the pre-transition era and had set up a new union in 1989. Initially the new union had considerable rights: it could veto restructuring decisions for a ten-year period and employees were protected from being sacked for three years. The previous collective agreement had to remain in place and it was also agreed that the next chief executive would be elected democratically. The objectives of the union were to try and ensure protection of their previous working conditions and to achieve better collective agreements and working conditions than elsewhere in the sector. Much of this changed radically when Accor took over in 1993. But the union initiated negotiations and then signed a local collective agreement with Accor-Pannonia providing for a long-term series of wage rises as well as enabling the company to undergo massive restructuring but still by consent with the union.[13]

Within the Accor-Pannonia hotel chain in Hungary there are now lengthy annual negotiations between management and the union covering not only wages and conditions but social provisions as well. They start in April for an agreement that will take effect the following year. The issues discussed in such meetings usually consider an additional 'thirteenth-month' salary payment, extra benefits at Christmas, an annual bonus, individual training and contributions to these trainings, working time patterns, meal allowances, means-tested social assistance, holiday allowances, contributions to sport and cultural activities and to house-building, opportunities for the employees to buy cheap second-hand computers or printers, discounted subscription to the Internet, etc. When conflict occurs, one trade unionist explained that the union still has considerable mobilizing power.

It's enough if the trade union says, 'Guys, we have a sort of problem here'. There are then the secret winks . . . People know what they have to do . . . We won't say it to your face . . . We do what we can do. If this is the solution, this is it – the old method carried over from the Socialist period: passive rejection and sabotage.[14]

The main achievement of the trade union is that overtime has been paid to employees since 2005 (except where they are self-employed workers or members of management, who are not covered by the collective agreement). Although this is stipulated in the Labour Code, this is not the usual practice in the hotel sector. At the same time, the severance payment system is quite generous as well. Even if, for reasons of efficiency, the organization is restructured and some workers dismissed, those laid off can receive significant severance pay – one month's pay for every two years of service.

What is most unusual about this Accor trade union in Hungary is that the members do not pay membership subscriptions. Legally this means they are really only a 'community-based cooperative', but they have all the other characteristics of a union and are organized in hotel-based branches that can bring together between 180 and 200 people in meetings when necessary. The individual hotel union secretaries can ask members for subscriptions to cover local expenditures. The elected union secretary, president and an administrator are given facility time by the company and form the central institution of the union covering all 15 Accor-Pannonia hotels. One union activist explained that, generally, the union and management at Accor-Pannonia Hotels are 'economic organizations [that] agree with each other'. In some ways, then, this represents a real continuity with the pre-transition era.

In the main the service sector was relatively underdeveloped before the transition, and indeed many services are largely new to the CEE countries. Everywhere, the finance sector, including much banking, insurance and real estate, was radically transformed by inward-investing multinationals in the 1990s. Retailing in its present form of supermarkets, hypermarkets and shopping malls did not exist. In most of these sectors the MNCs have tended to make greenfield investments either directly or through joint partnerships or franchises, and to recruit labour within the existing national legal employment relations framework. Yet in doing so the three-year DARES research project (Contrepois et al., 2009) found they have not only deliberately avoided trade unions where possible, but in most cases they have not joined relevant national or sectoral employers' associations or taken any initiative to establish sectoral collective bargaining.

Employer Legacy

A common argument about the difficulties faced in establishing meaningful social dialogue in the CEE10 is that this reflects an employer-side legacy. Employers' organizations were very rare before transition and have not yet had time to establish themselves properly. Thus the EU industrial relations report argues: 'The main problems here are the weak organization of employers, the lack of a mandate to reach multi-employer agreements with unions, and the prevalence of company bargaining, with many (small) firms, areas and sectors left uncovered' (EU, 2009 , p. 33). Yet this concept of 'weak organization of employers' misses the point. The reality is that the transition managers often wielded very considerable power, and that this power imbalance often became further embedded when ownership was privatized – either in the hands of host country entrepreneurs or in the hand of the host country managers employed by MNCs.

As noted earlier, Martin suggests that in the MNC sector: 'Corporate international human resource strategies determine employment relations, with high earnings, relative to national employers, in exchange for high effort and high commitment' (2006, p. 1355). However, in this 'international capitalism' sector, our research into French service sector MNCs found that an associated willingness to recognize and thereby support independent trade unions as a mechanism for ensuring employee voice was largely absent. In an in-depth study of 19 different implantations by eight French MNCs in Hungary, Poland or Bulgaria over a three-year period, we found little support for suggestions that MNCs as a whole are having a benign effect as transmission belts for a European-style social model (Contrepois et al., 2009).

A supportive social dialogue approach did appear to have been adopted in Hungary and Poland when French MNCs were either faced with brownfield acquisitions with strong pre-existing unions and/or were committed to an integrated European HR strategy. Among the eight French MNCs (arguably under some of the greatest pressure among nationally headquartered EU15 MNCs to maintain good HR practices) we identified EDF and Axa as adopting (or in Axa's case just initiating) such strategies.

The other six MNCs all embraced a compartmental approach. Where the latter were faced with existing unions, as at Accor, or saw the successful organization of a union in one of its big Polish stores, as at Carrefour, the MNC was ready to negotiate with unions locally on a site-by-site basis. But where there were no pre-existing unions in their brownfield acquisitions or where they were making greenfield investments then, like the big French banks, Société Générale and BNP-Paribas, or like the other retailers Auchan and Mr Bricolage, they did nothing to encourage a union presence. And, apart from EDF, whose Polish and Hungarian subsidiaries were already signed up to the national electricity employers' organization and sector agreements, none of the other MNCs had joined the host country employers' associations.

Even in the cases of MNCs that either encountered an existing brownfield union presence or experienced union organization in a greenfield site in the host CEE countries, there was little evidence to suggest that they had a commitment to work collaboratively with other employers and still less that they wished to contemplate sector negotiations. This absence of a collective approach (outside of electricity supply) was not about 'employer weakness'; it resulted from the MNCs feeling strong enough to make the choice to 'go it alone'.

Across the service sector of CEE economies, therefore, the individual employers should generally be considered very 'strong' by comparison with the trade unions. It is this that shapes the absence of any serious desire on their part to join employers' associations or to give those associations the right to 'bargain' over wages and conditions. This strategic choice reflects their preference for 'the liberal or uncoordinated model' (EU, 2009, p. 50) of industrial relations.

This should not be a surprise. Collective organizations of private employers in Europe were first created in response to particular external or internal challenges, such as the loss of overseas markets, requiring collective pressure on the government, or concern over the poaching and training of skilled workers, or (most frequently) in the face of the need to combine against the threat of union action (Sisson, 1987). Employer association formation thus occurred when the individual employers believed they would get more benefit from cooperation than in open competition. When these concerns evaporated, as they did in the UK in the 1980s in the wake of the defeat of the miners' strike and the enactment of stringent anti-union laws, the employers simply deserted sectoral collective bargaining and often their sectoral organizations too. Far from 'the main problems' arising from somehow 'weak' employers, the real reason for the partial coverage of collective agreements and the weakness of social dialogue in the CEE economies, with the exception of Slovenia, is the fact that the unions have very little strength anywhere at sector level and only have a toehold in a small number of companies. They lack the power to compel the employers to bargain collectively, and there is no rooted historical tradition of such bargaining to which they can make a public and political appeal.

Where there are exceptions, and the unions have retained high density and strong organizations, as in the electricity supply industries of Bulgaria, Poland and Hungary, a handful of sector agreements has been reached along with a higher number of workplace agreements. However, despite the existence of labour codes permitting them to do so, barely any collective agreements have been legally extended to cover the whole sector by the government: Bulgaria has not extended any agreements; in Poland, where extension must satisfy 'a vital social need', no sector agreements have been extended (Traxler and Behrens, 2002); and in Hungary, although all the sector agreements that have actually been negotiated have been extended, the total is just four (Contrepois et al., 2009). Almost universally workers' wages and working conditions depend largely on local labour market conditions and are conditioned by the benevolence and/or profitability of the firm and their employers' readiness to conform to the labour code and to any national tripartite agreements that might take place.

CONCLUSION

CEE trade unions remain strongest in those sectors and countries where they were most rooted prior to the 1989 transition. Historical continuities still play an important role. In this context the combination of EU 'top-down' directives establishing a 'common law' with the potential leverage some trade unionists might be able to exercise through EWCs may well have provided a safety-net enabling union survival. The 'Europeanization' of employment relations that has taken place has been largely top-down and at the level of national institutions rather than in local organizations. The result, however, has involved unions in regaining a degree of credibility through the consultation processes involved in implementing the social directives, or through the direct encouragement of tripartite negotiations.

Nonetheless, outside a few 'islands' of trade union presence – in the state sector and in the former state sector – the unions are nearly everywhere very weak on the ground. In a few companies there are signs that the unions are beginning to regenerate or create a capacity for the independent articulation of employee voice, but these remain exceptional. The overall context is one where greater job security for some of those who are fortunate enough to secure employment in the 'globalized' sectors of CEE economies is counterbalanced by a huge extension of precarious working in the rest of their economies.

However, nothing appears settled. The combination of the introduction of the European social model with a high rate of FDI makes the employment relations systems of the CEE10 still appear as hybrids. There are islands of 'normal' EU social relations within seas of 'abnormal', imbalanced social relations in which managerial power is total. But if the sea level does not appear to be falling, neither does it appear to be rising.

Recognizably 'Western' European patterns of employment relations with active and viable trade unions are present in many parts of CEE. It is still too soon to determine whether they are expanding, and giving rise to a 'new unionism' – but it does not appear either that they are shrinking. The future of the trade unions of Central and Eastern Europe remains uncertain.

NOTES

1. The research was financed by the Research Department of the French Ministry of Labour (DARES) from 2005 to 2009. See Contrepois et al. (2009).
2. The easier and more lucrative privatizations occurred in the decade from 1995. From 2005 the pace tended to slacken as the benefits of shifting all the way to a fully fledged market economy came under question, and as some evidence appeared of the risks of heavy reliance upon volatile foreign direct investment.
3. The officially recognized pre-transition trade unions in Central and Eastern Europe were often viewed by workers as being too close to management; this created considerable suspicion of anyone who took on an active trade union role; in addition, since before the transition trade union membership was effectively compulsory for anyone who wished to avoid daily bureaucratic problems, many workers decided to leave the unions as soon as they had a real choice.
4. The CEE10 refers to the ten 2004 and 2007 accession countries situated in Central and Eastern Europe and excluding Cyprus and Malta.
5. The data in the table covers private and public sector workers with the exception of Poland. In that country the 14 per cent estimation covers only the private sector; in this case, therefore, given the higher propensity everywhere for union density to be higher in the state sector, it is reasonable to assume that overall union density is around twice that level.
6. For a background to its exceptionalism, see Adam (2008) and Skeldar (2007).
7. The 1974 Labour Code had recognized that collective agreements at plant level could provide more favourable conditions than were stipulated in the sector agreement; in the post-transition 1994 Labour Code collective agreements were made the basic instrument of labour law; however, amendments to the 2002 Labour Code now make it possible (through a joint declaration by the two sides) to suspend a collective agreement for up to three years.
8. NSZZ Solidarność was formed in 1980 while CL Podkrepa was established in 1989.
9. An example comes from one power station where a French EDF expatriate manager was replaced after a conflict broke out following his decision to refuse to allow an elected employee representative on the local board to take up the post of HR manager as before; see Contrepois et al. (2009).
10. See ibid.
11. Non-affiliation to the federal union is for two reasons: first, it means the local hotel union does not have to pay a share of union dues to the national federation; and second, it means that the local union is not bound by what it considers to be the less beneficial levels of wages and conditions that are negotiated nationally. Interview by the authors, Warsaw, 26 April 2006.
12. Interview by the authors, Warsaw, 25 April 2006.
13. Interviews by Melinda Szabo, Budapest, 10 April 2006, 20 June 2006.
14. Ibid.

REFERENCES

Adam, G. (2008), 'Slovenia: industrial relations developments in Europe 2007', *EIROnline*, 23 September.

Contrepois, S., S. Jefferys, A. Kwiatkiewicz, M. Szabo and Z. Vladimirov (2009), *Dans quelle mesure le modèle de relations sociales français est-il transférable? Les multinationales françaises et leur influence sur l'évolution des relations profession-nelles en Bulgarie, en Hongrie et en Pologne*, London: Working Lives Research Institute.

EU (2009), *Industrial Relations in Europe 2008*, Luxembourg: European Commission DG for Employment, Social Affairs and Equal Opportunities.

EuroMemorandum, Group (2008), 'Democratic transformation of European finance, a full employment regime and ecological restructuring: alternatives to finance-driven capitalism', Dortmund: 42, available at http://www.lwbooks.co.uk/ebooks/EUROMEMORANDUM2008_09.pdf.

Eyraud, F. and D. Vaughan-Whitehead (2007), 'Employment and working conditions in the enlarged EU: innovations and new risks', in F. Eyraud and D. Vaughan-Whitehead, *The Evolving World of Work in the Enlarged EU*, Geneva: International Labour Office, pp. 1–52.

Fodor, G.T. and L. Neumann (2005), 'EU information and consultation Directive implemented', *EIROnline*, 31 May.

Gault, F. (2005), 'Les atouts des CE ont conquis les Polonais', *Enterprise & Carrières*, August 30.

Iankova, E.A. (1998), 'The transformative corporatism of Eastern Europe', *Eastern European Politics and Societies*, **12** (2), 222–64.

Iankova, E. and L. Turner (2004), 'Building the new Europe: Western and Eastern roads to social partnership', *Industrial Relations Journal*, **35**, 76–92.

Ladã, M. (2002), 'Industrial relations in the candidate countries', *EIROnline*, 30 July.

Marginson, P. and K. Sisson (1994), 'The structure of transnational capital in Europe: the emerging Euro-company and its implications for industrial relations', in R. Hyman and A. Ferner (eds), *New Frontiers in European Industrial Relations*, Oxford: Blackwell, pp. 15–51.

Martin, R. (2006), 'Segmented employment relations: post-socialist managerial capitalism and employment relations in Central and Eastern Europe', *International Journal of Human Resource Management*, **17** (8), 1353–65.

Martin, R. and A.M. Cristescu-Martin (2004), 'Consolidating segmentation: post-socialist employment relations in Central and Eastern Europe', *Industrial Relations Journal*, **35** (6), 629–46.

Mihaylova, T. (2009), 'The impact of the information and consultation directive on industrial relations – Bulgaria', *EIROnline*, 9 March.

OECD (2009), *OECD Factbook 2009*, Paris: OECD.

Ost, D. (2000), 'Illusory corporatism in eastern Europe: neoliberal tripartism and post-Communist class identities', *Politics and Society*, **28** (4), 503–30.

Pollert, A. (1999), *Transformation at Work in the New Market Economies of Eastern Europe*, London: Sage.

Schulten, T. (1996), 'European works councils: prospects for a new system of European industrial relations', *European Journal of Industrial Relations*, **2** (3), 303–24.

Sisson, K. (1987), *The Management of Collective Bargaining: An International Comparison*, Oxford: Blackwell.

Skarby, E. (2006), *Capacity Building for Social Dialogue in Bulgaria*, Dublin: European Foundation for the Improvement of Living and Working Conditions.

Skledar, S. (2007), 'Industrial relations developments 2006 – Slovenia', *EIROnline*, 13 June.

Streeck, W. (1997), 'Neither European nor works councils: a reply to Paul Knudsen', *Economic and Industrial Democracy*, **18** (2), 325–7.

Traxler, F. and M. Behrens (2002), 'Collective bargaining coverage and extension procedures', *EIROnline*, 18 December.

Vaughan-Whitehead, D. (2003), *EU Enlargement versus Social Europe? The Uncertain Future of the European Social Model*, Cheltenham, UK and Northampton, MA, USA: Edward Elgar.

Webb, S. and B. Webb (1897), *Industrial Democracy*, London: Longman.

7. Seasonal workers in Mediterranean agriculture: flexibility and insecurity in a sector under pressure

Béatrice Mésini

INTRODUCTION

A new 'circular' migration model has been introduced at a European level covering the Mediterranean countries. The European Commission has insisted on the need to intensify labour mobility between the EU and Third World countries and has suggested adjusting labour levels to economic needs by promoting partnerships between countries of origin and host countries. In an already competitive agricultural sector, the Euro-Mediterranean partnership has further increased competitiveness, and is contributing to reshaping highly selective markets through regulating quotas of workers. It is introducing new forms of flexibility, precariousness and social insecurity. The notion of 'circular' mobility, involving migrants working for short periods in the host country and then returning to their countries of origin, highlights a change away from conceptual frameworks seeing international migrations as embedded in post-colonial relations of power and domination (Sayad, 1977) or as representing long historical cycles in expanding world markets (Balibar and Wallerstein, 1988).

In 2000, agriculture in the European Union employed 4.5 million seasonal workers, of whom 500,000 were from non-EU countries. While many worked in appalling conditions, the status quo was maintained through the decade of EU enlargement, which saw both the intensification and specialization of agricultural work and the reorganization of the agricultural lobby at national and international levels. The use of a foreign seasonal workforce, an intrinsic feature of agriculture in southern European countries, has led to a dual reshaping of migratory systems: one has taken place within the EU with the recruitment of an Eastern European workforce, and the second, externally to the EU, with the arrival of Latin American seasonal workers, mainly from Ecuador and Colombia.

Using foreign seasonal workers in France for regulating the agricultural labour market is an old practice. This is shown by the numbers and origins of employees introduced by the French National Immigration Office (OMI) since its creation in 1945.[1] These migrations, which initially took place mainly internally to the EU, compensated for a shortage of workers as French rural workers moved to the towns and cities. The migrations were legally controlled by agreements between France and Italy in 1951 and between France and Spain in 1961, and were followed by agreements with Morocco, Tunisia and Portugal in 1963 and Yugoslavia in 1965.

With the closure of French borders to new migrants in 1974, the OMI has become the only legal channel for introducing foreign workers. Work migration is organized through the Office, which provides workers with temporary contracts, from four to eight months in duration, in exchange for a special OMI levy paid by the employers. The contract, which is signed by the Ministry of Labour, gives the holder the right to enter France and to perform the job mentioned over a period which cannot exceed six consecutive months (out of twelve), but which can 'exceptionally' be lengthened to eight months.

In 1995, under the pretext of controlling rising unemployment, the government forbade entry to new seasonal workers. In the year 2000, under pressure from the Departmental Federation of the Farmers Association (the FDSEA), the Prefecture of the Bouches-du-Rhône again authorized new entries. Thus OMI contracts were generalized in Provence, creating, effectively, a lawless zone in vegetable and fruit farming or viticulture. The Bouches-du-Rhône has become a place for experimenting with labour casualization in the agricultural sector. The result was that the number of OMI contacts doubled in France: from around 7,500 in 2000 to 16,051 in 2004. From that year on, the agreement was only applicable to OMI repeat contracts.

In the Bouches-du-Rhône region, the number of OMI employees exceeds that of permanent workers because of a systematic lengthening of contracts and a current practice for contracts to overlap, some from January to August, others from May to December. A report by two labour inspectors in 2001 in this region found that seasonal workers, 'because of their knowledge and their long experience in many agricultural tasks, satisfactorily fulfil the needs for longer term employment' (Clary and Van Haecke, 2001, p. 14).

This chapter is based on research carried out since 2001 with the Group for the Defence of Agricultural Seasonal Workers (CODETRAS), made up of 15 farm worker trade unions and non-governmental organizations in the Bouches-du-Rhône that provide legal aid to migrant workers.[2] Many 'legal' though discriminatory, as well as clearly illegal, practices have also been identified by the author's analysis of 544 Agricultural Tribunal reports within the area jurisdiction of Arles, and through interviews with lawyers and civil servants involved with the complaints (Mésini 2009).[3]

Legal Channels and Lawless Areas in Mediterranean Agriculture

The tribunal reports show that many legal working conditions and collective agreements were not respected: there was undeclared forced overtime that was either underpaid or not paid at all, underestimated chemical risks, illnesses due to work, accidents at work, etc. The reports show also different kind of ties between employers and employees. For example, OMI contracts are registered by the individual's name and this enables an employer to ask workers to come back, or on the contrary, not to renew their contract in case of disagreement, dispute or litigation. At the end of the first contract, a second one can be subject to tight negotiations between employers and employees and it is common for the OMI tax paid by the employer to be reimbursed immediately by the employees, or directly deducted from their salary. Moreover, this pool of OMI contracts allows questionable dealings: even if there is no guarantee that the first contract will be followed by a second one, it enables the worker to enter France, which in itself is a privilege worth money.[4] Such a contract can be bought for between 5,000 and 10,000 euros in France or in Morocco and such transactions are carried out directly between an employer and an employee or through a member of the family or the head of a team, who may collect all or part of the amount. Another element of this constrained relationship[5] is the docility of many of these seasonal workers. Their contracts are renewed from one year to the next only through 'merit' judged by the employer, and they are kept in a situation of underqualification and lack of recognition of their skills.

The law of 24 July 2006 on immigration and integration introduced new measures for agricultural seasonal workers. A new temporary resident permit was created, which mentions 'seasonal worker'.[6] This permit is for holders of a seasonal work contract, who must commit to keeping their permanent residency outside of France. It is granted for three years (renewable) and it enables its holder to carry out seasonal work for one or more employers over a period which cannot exceed six months out of twelve.

In March 2007, the High Authority for the Fight against Discrimination (HALDE) was asked by CODETRAS to give its opinion on the discriminatory aspect of the 'restrictions imposed by the status of seasonal workers in which foreign workers are kept by the administration' (Case *Ait Baloua*, Decision of the Administrative Tribunal of Marseille, September 12 2006). Written by legal advisors and lawyers, the formal request points to the fact that the majority of seasonal workers are Tunisian or Moroccan, and therefore it is with regard to 'the totality of the non-EU workers' that the issue of discrimination concerning these 'long-term workers' should be examined. In the department of the Bouches-du-Rhône, over one thousand workers are in this category, with contracts stretching over periods of eight months, and being renewed over ten, twenty or sometimes even thirty years by the same employer. The workers have access to only one employer and one geographic area, and are often paid as little as possible. They cannot claim housing benefit or entry and settlement for their family. Despite their contribution to the social care system over very long periods of time, they do not benefit from health insurance when not employed, and do not receive unemployment benefits. Furthermore, as having worked all their working lives on temporary contracts, they are only entitled to half of their retirement pension, which rarely exceeds 100 euros.

On 15 December 2008, HALDE (2008) agreed there was a 'diversion of the aims of seasonal contracts' which gives rise to 'discriminating treatment'. It therefore recommended 'changing the contracts of foreign seasonal workers into permanent contracts' and providing 'compensation for the loss they experienced'. It also recommended that the Ministry of Immigration re-examines their residency status and issues them with permanent resident permits. In early December, about one hundred seasonal workers were given a residency permit and the Marseille regional seat of government committed itself to take care of the situation of three or four hundred others.

Penal Law and the Boomerang Effect

Since 2005, article L. 341-10 of the employment law strictly forbids the reimbursement of travel costs by the OMI-ANAEM[7] to the employer, or the retention of salary for that purpose. In case of an infringement of the law, the employer risks up to two years of imprisonment and a fine of 3,750 euros. Furthermore, receiving money or goods when a foreign worker arrives in France is punishable by up to three years in prison and a fine of 45,000 euros. Further sanctions include being denied employment in the sector in which the offence has occurred, and being excluded from public tenders, while the foreign worker may be barred from entering France for a maximum period of five years. Other restrictions apply to foreign employers. In the case of their infringing the law, it is possible that their entry to France could be prohibited for up to ten years or even permanently, that their goods could be seized and that they could have their civic and civil rights suspended and their premises closed.

The complaints filed with the Agricultural Employment Boards we studied show that since 2002, there have been two major ways of hiding work: concealing work itself or concealing paid work. However, it appears difficult to find proof of this offence, which is therefore rarely punished (Mésini, 2009). Employing a foreigner with no legal right to stay is an offence which can be punished by a fine up to 15,000 euros and up to five years' imprisonment. The fine is multiplied by the number of people illegally employed.[8] If this offence is considered as committed through organized crime, the fine can go up to 100,000 euros and attract a maximum ten-year sentence.

In some cases, the offences committed by employers have a direct consequence for seasonal workers' jobs, who sometimes can no longer obtain an introductory contract. In February 2004, a group of 33 OMI seasonal workers filed a request to the Interior Ministry and to the Agriculture and Labour and Social Affairs Ministries to ask for employment preferences for OMI employees over new candidates to be instituted. These agricultural labourers, all from the Douar Inahnahen in the region of Taza in Morocco, had regularly been coming to work in Entressen in the Bouches-du-Rhône over a period of ten years. From the year 2002, their employer's requests to renew their contracts had been systematically denied. It appears that the reason was that the employer had, in 2001, obtained work visas for new seasonal workers, but had never really employed them on his farm.

Another issue arises when farm inspections by the police and labour inspectors find 'illegal' workers. These are then required to leave the country immediately or are kept in detention before being expelled. This happened in June 2008, when a vegetable farmer from Berre-l'Etang was prosecuted for deceptive goods, concealed labour, assistance in illegal residence and misuse of an agricultural company's assets. This farmer, a member of the main National Federation of Farmers' Associations (FNSEA), and vice-president of the agricultural cooperative of Berre, was buying tomatoes for 0.50 euros in Spain, and selling them as a product of Provence for 1.30 euros in the Marseille wholesale market. One hundred and fifty policemen were on the case and arrested 25 'illegal' workers; 9 out of 12 Moroccan workers said to be in an 'irregular situation' were detained in the detention centre in Marseille.

STATUS FRAGMENTATION AND SEASONAL LABOUR MARKETS

Employing illegal migrant workers in order to reduce costs[9] induces new divisions between workers, increases their competition on the labour market and accentuates the precarization process.

An Increasing Number of Exemptions

Whether it is annual, monthly, regular, occasional or alternating seasonality, the result has been to increase the flexibility of the agricultural worker, which has always been based on varied and rotating tasks, sometimes with geographical changes, according to seasonal rhythms and product sales. As the worker's status has become more and more precarious, the phenomenon of seasonality has also insidiously provoked a weakening of the contractual relation. This is noticeable through a change of terminology. In agriculture, the labourer or skilled worker, whose status is precisely defined in the minutes of the Agricultural Employment Board in 1981, became indistinct from 1991, subsumed under the general term of 'seasonal worker'.

Abuses against foreign seasonal workers are largely facilitated by the fact that OMI contracts are exempted from the Bouches-du-Rhône's Collective Agreement of 12 February 1986. Article 25, dedicated to non-permanent employment, lists five types of contracts 'submitted to the regulations which are specific to them': foreign workers; holders of an introductory contract from the National Office of Immigration; seasonal workers (employees taken on for an increase of work): those employed to replace missing workers; and those employed to fulfil occasional tasks.

There are also other exemptions in agriculture from different protective aspects of labour law. For example, the right to claim legal compensation from the Agricultural Employment Board is excluded from 'initiative work contracts', 'insertion contracts', 'reinsertion contracts', or 'temping contracts'.[10] The law of 24 July 2006[11] prohibits students from working on temporary work permits. The new 'student resident permit' restricts them to working a maximum of 60 per cent of the legally allowable working time (amounting to 964 hours). Lastly, a new category was added to the list of occupations: 'agricultural seasonal helper'. It designates people employed for picking fruit and vegetables, as well as grape harvesting, and it will maintain these employees at the bottom of the occupational scale. The rigid categorization will help deny them upwards occupational mobility.

Increasing yet Insufficient Controls

In terms of the national campaign against 'illegal' employment, 669 agricultural firms out of the 8,689 that were investigated in 2005 were infringing rules. This amounts to 7.7 per cent, compared to 4.8 per cent in the construction sector where investigations are more frequent and thorough (National Commission, 2006). The FNSEA report (2005), concerning 'seasonal workers' living conditions in the South-East of France', underlines the fact that the agricultural farms are not checked very often, and that when checks are made, it always seems to be on the same farms. As a general rule, the farms do not have elected staff representatives. Moreover, there are only two labour inspectors for the whole of the Bouches-du-Rhône agricultural region, which indicates how inefficient these controls are. Inspectors also have very little room for manoeuvre due to a lack of political will and adequate legal framework. One labour inspector[12] working in this region says they have become targets for farmers and he denounces the total absence of interest shown by their senior management when confronted with the generalized exploitation of agricultural workers.

After the dismissal of ten permanent employees from a farm in Berre-l'Etang in 2004, the inspector notified the regional Agricultural Employment Board that 'the employer has dismissed his employees only to import seasonal workers, to sell contracts for juicy profit and to benefit from cheap labour'. Not only did his request for sanctions remain without effect but, he adds, 'the regional Agricultural Employment Board granted the employer the right to introduce new foreign workers, whereas they had the possibility of stopping him'.[13]

One also needs to acknowledge the pressure encountered from the agricultural lobby. On 2 September 2004, two labour inspectors who had gone to inspect a fruit farm in Saussignac (Dordogne) on suspicion of 'hidden work of seasonal workers' were killed by the farmer with a shotgun (Filoche, 2004). In March 2005, at the congress of the farmers' association, the FNSEA, the Minister of Agriculture[14] called for new rules of conduct for labour inspectors to follow during farm visits. These included that they should provide 48-hours' advance notice of the inspection, and precise reasons for their visit.

A circular issued in August 2005 by the Minister of Labour, Gérard Larcher, was sent to all government regional heads. Its aim was to 'reinforce the fight against illegal work'. This circular insisted on the fact that the Commission for the control of immigration which had met on 27 July, had concluded that the results in 'the fight' were insufficient and unsatisfactory. The Commission also underlined the 'undeniable links between illegal immigration and illegal labour'. It came to the decision by 31 October 2005 that every region in the country should carry out at least one thorough check of all workplaces likely to be illegally employing foreign workers.

One labour inspector interviewed considers this text as conflicting with the principles of his job. He reasserts that his job is to enforce the Labour Code, whereas this circular 'asks us to target a particular category of foreigners and to act as substitutes for the police and customs officials'. He adds: 'The government has overstepped the limits of Republican values with regard to the independence of labour inspectors' (de la Casinière, 2005). According to the ILO, which defines their mission, inspectors have to remain 'in charge of the consequences of an inspection and have to be protected against exterior pressures, including political'.

In July 2006, in view of the increase in both detentions and expulsions of 'illegal' workers, the regional Chamber of Agriculture of Marseille held an informal meeting with civil servants from the Agricultural Labour Inspectorate, with members of the CODETRAS campaign group and other associations, and with academics. One of the inspectors at the meeting admitted he was doing 'numerous reports useful only for statistics'[15] and said that he 'had no illusion as far as the utility of his job was concerned: many reports are made without any consequence'. Even when the legal procedure is followed perfectly, the Public Prosecutor's office often classifies the cases as 'uncalled-for visit' or 'insufficient law and order disruption'. The other inspector stressed that he categorically refuses to be used as a 'pass key for State Border Services'.[16]

ETHNIC SEGMENTATION OF THE FOREIGN LABOUR MARKET

On 1 May 2004, when Estonia, Latvia, Lithuania, Hungary, Poland, the Czech Republic, Slovakia and Slovenia joined the EU, France instituted a period of transition of seven years for the free circulation of these workers, who were nevertheless still under the obligation of obtaining a work permit. In May 2006, the government decided to lift certain restrictions concerning access to the work market progressively and carefully, particularly in 'sectors in tension', such as agriculture, where labour shortages were appearing.[17] For jobs that have to be filled, work permits are delivered without previous advertisement at the national agency of work (ANPE).

New Recruitment Channels: Service Providers and International Temping through European Countries

As a result of their accession to the EU on 1 January 2007, service sector companies from Romania and Bulgaria could also operate legally anywhere in the EU. Research in 2005 by the Inter-Ministerial Delegation for the Fight against Illegal Work estimated the top four countries with significant numbers of foreign companies providing services in the French agricultural sector as follows: 151 have their offices in Poland, 44 in Germany, 38 in Spain and 15 in Slovakia.

The increase in the numbers of recruitment networks for migrant workers in the intensive agricultural sector results from different interpretations of rules at national and European levels. Agricultural seasonal workers who are employed for a service provider company based in an EU country are exempted from obtaining a work permit. Thus the European Court of Justice has agreed that non-Community temporary workers who obtain a work permit issued by any European country do not need a new one issued by the country where they are is posted, as long as they are employed 'usually and regularly' by a company providing the services. This rather loose notion of 'usually and regularly' has been restricted by the French administration, which considers that an employee from a non-member state has a 'stable job' in a company if he or she has been working for it for at least one year.

Another source of conflict between EU countries is based on the legal means for providing workers. French regulations do not allow a worker from a non-member state to hold a work permit to fulfil temporary work. Therefore, if the service provider is a temporary work agency, it should not be allowed to send workers from non-member states to France for a mission. In addition, in France, in case the employer fails to pay salaries and social contributions, supplying labour is only authorized for temporary work agencies that have sufficient financial guarantees.

Concerning the delivery of the service itself, temporary work agency subcontractors have to complete a specific and well-defined task (which includes a technical or practical contribution through know-how). This cannot be limited to providing labour alone. Furthermore, the subcontractors must have direct authority over their workers, whom they manage freely; the subcontractors must be paid a fixed price according to the accomplished task, not according to the hours worked by the workers. The law also requires proof that the subcontractor is an individual or a firm employing workers.[18] If the subcontractor employs workers, he will have to give an affidavit certifying that the job will be completed by workers who are employed regularly and that he fulfils his obligations (pay slips, staff register), and a copy of the work permits of non-EU employees. If it is established that the company is not giving a real service but is effectively only providing staff to carry out work, its activity is considered to be a 'lucrative rental' of employees and is punishable by French law under the offence of 'illicit rental of workforce'. Going back to the agricultural sector, the client would then be considered the real employer of the farm workers and would be responsible for them, from both a civil and a criminal law perspective.

Picturing the Segmentation

In the contexts of economic integration of the new states joining the EU and of increased regulation of migration, competition is developing between Eastern European migrants[19] and non-community migrants. The former are sent through European companies and are progressively replacing the earlier generation of migrants, who usually came from the South. On 20 July 2005, around 150 Moroccan farm workers on OMI contracts, of whom 70 were permanent and 35 seasonal, employed on 250 hectares of peaches and nectarines in St-Martin-du-Crau, began a strike over salaries and housing conditions. They obtained immediate satisfaction: a 5 per cent wage increase and the building of a refectory and toilet amenities. According to the General Confederation of Labour (CGT) trade union, the only workers who did not stop work on this site were 30 Polish OMI seasonal workers.

In 2005, for the first time, the OMI recorded more Polish seasonal workers (8,192), than Moroccan (6,941) coming to France. This shows an obvious change in the origin of the migrants. The structure of employment of these seasonal workers according to their nationality shows a specialization in relation to channels and duration of contracts: Poles tend to be employed for grape picking on short-term contracts (two to four months), while Moroccans are mainly employed for harvesting and various other agricultural tasks, with longer contracts of from six to eight months, mostly in the Bouches-du-Rhône. The number of Polish seasonal workers in Bouches-du-Rhône is not yet huge as the channels are still relatively unknown: according to the President of the FDSEA, there were only 98 Polish contracts in 2005 and 114 in 2006. 'There isn't an important increase of Poles. There is a demand, but we do not yet have the networks to introduce them here. Moroccan contracts, by word of mouth or from father to son, we are familiar with. But for the Poles, we don't have the channels yet.'[20]

Infringements of the law are often due to a total ignorance or a partial lack of knowledge of French law among foreigners. Foreign workers experience different levels of knowledge concerning rules and regulations. These depend on the nationality of the worker and the history of immigration from their country: a migration history of more than thirty years for workers from North Africa, ten years for Poles, and no more than four years for Ecuadorians.

In contrast, the new temporary work agencies demonstrate a solid knowledge of both national and European legislation. We have observed new practices with Eastern countries, sometimes through associations or societies that set themselves up in deliberately complex legal forms in order to get away with illegal practices. A statement by a labour inspector describes the case of a Polish company illegally practising 'lucrative rental of workers' through supplying 'landless peasants' as 'independent' workers to a French firm.

> In the packaging unit, the Polish workers were the only ones not to have work contracts and not to clock in, but also the only ones to sweep up the floor after work and to be paid under the minimum wage. In this case the inspectors, who still don't know if this company really exists in Poland, took three months to decipher the legal forms and to write up the report. Without money or translators, they had to translate the documents word by word with a dictionary, while on the other side, the Polish entrepreneur was well informed of the French legislation and had the documents (sometimes fake) written up by a lawyer, in order to avoid sanctions.[21]

The Agricultural Labour Inspectorate of Work, Employment and Agricultural Social Policy (ITEPSA) also investigated a European firm which placed 350 Ecuadorian and Moroccan workers in different French departments (Drôme, Isère, Pyrénées-Orientales, Landes, Gard, Bouches-du-Rhône, Sarthe and Maine-et-Loire), for fruit and grape picking. Legal and political difficulties came to the surface during the investigation, showing flaws in European cooperation as well as in European employment policies. As in the previous example, French inspectors were confronted with the problem of having to wait for very long periods for answers, a major lack of funds for translating documents in both languages and a lack of proper information on temporary work regulations in the other countries.[22]

According to another ITEPSA inspector, the Spanish temporary work company Terra Fecundis is the largest employer in Bouches-du-Rhône, with 480 temporary workers. Two Ecuadorian seasonal workers we met in 2006 in the Crau region, who were employed by this temping firm, explained that they were paid 300 euros a month while working in France. The rest of the salary was withheld in Spain and only given to them on their return at the end of their contract. Paid 7.5 euros an hour, they knew that the Spanish firm received the rest of the amount invoiced to the employer not only on the hours worked but also on holidays and overtime hours. Nevertheless, they preferred this situation to being in Spain, as over there, the usual pay for a day in agriculture is lower (between 45 and 55 euros), and the competition with illegal workers can even sometimes bring the salary down to 3 euros an hour.

In May 2007, in a zone of arboriculture, of fruit and vegetable growing and of olive growing in the Alpilles in Provence, three Ecuadorians were suspended from work by their Moroccan supervisor. Recently taken on (one week earlier), they did not speak French, did not know the name of their employer, and did not know where they were in France. Furthermore, they had no work contract. They told us of the lack of medical care from their Spanish employer. One of the workers had fallen from her ladder the day before, hurting herself. She was sent back to work immediately. Two others also described the sexual harassment they were confronted with from their Moroccan supervisors. They all absolutely challenged the allegation of poor output which was brought forward as a reason to dismiss them, as they considered themselves to be tough and sturdy workers, used to agricultural work. After many telephone calls, the manager finally agreed to send his middle-man to take the woman mentioned above to hospital for an X-ray, and to put them on a different farm. Despite his promises, two hours later, he dropped them off at Avignon train station, with a ticket sending them back to Spain.[23]

All these non-European Community workers prefer to be recruited directly by French farmers, rather than being employed by Spanish temporary work agencies in order to be able to obtain their legal documentations and social rights in France. We have shown here, as Coulon and Flückiger observed (2000), that labour market segmentation is only effective when legal, institutional and economic boundaries exist, preventing a possible change of status for workers.

CONCLUSIONS

As early as 1997 a study commissioned by the European Agricultural Workers Federation trade union showed the existence of 'labour suppliers' who take a commission on their employees' low wages. The report considers this seasonal activity to be 'mercenary'[24] (European Federation, 1997). As a general rule, the middle-man is a permanent employee or an independent worker who supplies work teams. In extreme cases, we find individuals and networks who act as slave traders: in the United Kingdom, around 70 per cent of seasonal workers are supplied by 'gangmasters' who invoice their services to the farm owner and pay their agricultural workers directly.

With intensified competition in the face of pressure from supermarkets, we have seen an evolution from amateurish practices to a well-organized trade. This is now connected into 'illegal' networks of migration from Central and Eastern Europe and Latin America, resulting in the overexploitation and precarization of foreign workers. In Ecuador, the middle-man is called a *coyote*;[25] in Southern Italy it is the *caporale* who is in charge of local recruitment. He escorts the workers to their place of work for 5 euros and decides on the salaries which he invoices to the farmer, without taking any account of the collective agreements.

Ten years after the European Federation study, a report by the Commission of Migrations, Refugees and Demography at the Parliamentary Assembly of the European Council (2006) revealed that in Central and Eastern European countries, cross-border temporary work, both legal and illegal, was on the increase, with the arrival of an even lower-salaried workforce coming from countries still further East. Temporary work agencies were just emerging but the absence of rules, of recruitment procedures and of ways of enforcing the law all led to a fertile situation for criminal activities, undeclared employment and the exploitation of migrant workers. Certain agencies were supplying work contracts which enabled the employer to pay workers much less than they are entitled to in the host country, to demand longer work hours and to by-pass the paying of holidays or extra hours. The Irish Centre for the Rights of Migrants brought to light a case of 15 workers from Latvia and Ukraine compelled to work on a mushroom farm in Ireland. They had given between 1,800 and 2,500 euros to local employment agencies to obtain a work permit. They were working 10 to 17 hours a day without any medical protection.

The European Council has issued several notices to several EU member states requesting them to respect equal treatment between temporary migrant workers as far as salaries, work conditions and social rights are concerned, to regulate the activity of temporary work agencies (through a system of registration and licences), to increase the means of work inspectors, and finally to implement sanctions when the rules are infringed. The 2006 report also regrets that despite the important contribution migrant workers make towards their economic system, none of the industrialized countries that receive migrant workers has yet signed the International Convention of 1990 concerning the protection of migrant workers and their families that came into force in 2003.

Seasonal workers widely employed in Germany, France and Spain in response to the need for unqualified labour now share a precarious legal status that is sometimes purposely maintained. This constitutes a new and important aspect of European immigration policies (Bribosia and Réa, 2002). Using the concept of 'circular' migration appears merely to be a means of helping secure the acceptance of a utilitarian policy that amounts to advocating 'work without (permanent) workers' (Morice, 2004), and acts as an 'injunction for forced mobility' (Morice and Michalon, 2009, p. 16).

NOTES

1. The order of 2 November 1945 set up the National Immigration Office, which became the International Migration Office (OMI) in 1988.
2. http://www.codetras.org.
3. This study is part of a collective project, 'Foreign Labour in Western European Agriculture: Changes in Migration Patterns', funded by the National Research Agency and directed by Swanie Potot, Research Unit Migration and Society-Nice (URMIS-Nice).
4. Interview with Denis Natanelic, CODETRAS, 25 August 2005, Transrural Initiatives, available at http://www.ruralinfos.org, public document.
5. Up to the end of the 1990s, a seasonal worker with an OMI contract wishing to change employer the following year had to negotiate a 'freedom certificate' from his boss.
6. Article L. 313-10 of the Code of entry and residence of foreigners and asylum law (CESEDA).
7. With the passage of a law on 18 January 2005, the National Agency for the Reception of Foreigners and Migrations (ANAEM), which replaced the International Migration Office (OMI), no longer has exclusivity of recruitment in France (article L.341-9l of the Labour Code).
8. Labour Code, article L364-3.
9. A process Terray (1999) described as 'on the spot relocation'.
10. A 1999 ministerial circular stipulates that exemptions can take place where the purpose of the recruitment is to 'ease social integration' through professional activity. In 2004, therefore, the departmental farmers' branch of the FNSEA asked to be able to benefit from 'insertion' contracts as soon as they were created. In this case, the employer receives 450 euros a month from the department (called the 'minimal insertion benefit') and pays only the balance of the wages due, effectively paying directly for just 20 hours a week per worker under the scheme.
11. Circular DPM/DM12/2006/200 from 29 April 2006.
12. Aoudia (2005). 'Death threats, anonymous phone-calls, harassment, they do not leave anything out to intimidate us.'
13. Interview with two labour inspectors from the agricultural sector, Agricultural Labour Inspectorate of Work, Employment and Agricultural Social Policy (ITEPSA,) Departmental Chamber of Agriculture, Marseille, 19 July 2006.
14. Proposing the idea of a charter for the inspection of agricultural sector, already expressed by the FNSEA.
15. Meeting with two work inspectors from the agricultural sector, ITEPSA, Departmental Chamber of Agriculture, Marseille, 19 July 2006.
16. There are three options in case of an inspection on a farm: a double control by police and work inspectors with a rogatory commission, inspectors and police without commission if confronted with a situation in the act (*flagrante delicto*), or a requisition by inspectors.
17. In the agricultural sector, the activities of vegetable or flower growing and arboriculture or grape picking are concerned (both can employ seasonal workers), as well as that of seasonal helpers (amongst whom are the grape pickers) and breeders (pigs, rabbits, poultry).
18. A few documents are needed: registration at the Business Registration Office, affiliation to the Agricultural Social Mutuality (MSA), documents testifying the conformity of the intervention, the certificate for financial guarantee (for temporary work agencies), the certificates of social contributions and the proof of the first employment statement to the work inspector. Circular DPM/DMI/2, 2006-143, 24 March 2006, relative to foreign seasonal workers in the agricultural sector for 2006, *Bulletin Officiel* , 2006-4, entry 64.
19. Franco-Polish accord, 2 May 1992.
20. Claude Rossignol, President of the FDSEA, public meeting on the ANAEM contracts, Atrium, Salon de Provence, 20 April 2007.

21. 'An inspector testifies on the trouble of controlling the agricultural sector: we are always caught in between', *Libération*, 24 May 2005.
22. Service provider in the agricultural sector from foreign countries, Inter-Ministerial Delegation for the Fight against Illegal Work, DILTI, Survey Report, 2005. Available at: http://www.travail-solidarite.gouv.fr/. . ./Bilan_2005_intervention_enterpriseetran-gerers.pdf.
23. Thanks to a swift reaction from the local labour inspector, they were able to claim the wages due to them on their arrival in Spain.
24. This study by the European Office of Research (ORSEU) was carried out in Germany, the United Kingdom, Netherlands, Spain, France, Italy and Brussels.
25. The same name is used for middle-men who buy coffee and agricultural products at a very low price from peasants in Central America (Boris, 2007, p. 37).

REFERENCES

Aoudia, Djaffer Ait (2005), 'Agricultural workers, a new form of slavery?', *Paris Match* **2932**.
Balibar, Etienne and Wallenstein, Immanuel (1988), *Race, nation, classe: les identités ambiguës*, Paris: La Découverte.
Boris, Jean-Pierre (2007), *Fuir l'Equateur: une histoire de clandestins*, L'Isle-d-Espagnac: Hachette Littératures.
Bribosia, E. and A. Réa (2002), *Les nouvelles migrations: un enjeu européen*, Brussels: Editions Complexe.
Chesnais, F. (2004), 'La mondialisation de l'armée de réserve industrielle: la délocalisation interne dans l'agriculture', *Carré Rouge*, **30**, 28–35.
Clary, G. and Y. Van Haecke, (2001), 'Enquête sur l'emploi des saisonniers agricoles étrangers dans les Bouches-du-Rhône', report presented by two general inspectors of agriculture and social affairs, November.
Commission for the Fight against Illegal Work (2006), 'Review of the National Plan to Fight against Illegal employment outlook 2004–2005 and 2006–2007', Paris, 26 January, http://www.travail-solidarite.gouv.fr/. . ./Bilan_du_Plan_National_de_lutte_20060126.pdf.
Commission of Migrations, Refugees and Demography (2006), Resolution 1511 – migration, refugees and population in the 3rd summit of Heads of State and Government of Council of Europe.
Coulon, A. and Y. Flückiger (2000), 'Analyse économique de l'intégration de la population étrangère sur le marché suisse du travail', in P. Centlivres and I. Girod (eds), *Les defis migratoires*, Zurich: Seismo.
De la Casinière, N. (2005), 'Work inspection has to track down illegal immigrants', *Libération*, 13 September.
European Federation (European Federation of Food, Agriculture and Tourism Trade Unions) (1997), *Illegal Work in Agriculture*, ORSEU, European Office of Social Research, Lille, Brussels.
Filoche, Gérard (2004), 'Two work inspectors shot down like dogs', *Démocratie et socialisme*, 3 September, pp. 1–23.
FNSEA (2005), 'Analyse de l'hébergement des travailleurs saisonniers dans le Sud-Est de la France', report from the FNSEA, Paris.
Girod, I. Coll (2000), 'Cohésion sociale et pluralisme culturel', in P. Centlivres and I. Girod (eds), *Les défis migratoires*, Zurich: Seismo, pp. 109–19.

Halde (2008), Resolution No. 2008-283 of the High Authority against Discrimination and for Equality, Paris, 24 December.

Mésini, B. (2009), 'Contentieux prud'homal des étrangers saisonniers dans les Bouches-du-Rhône', *Revue Etudes Rurales: Travailleurs Saisonniers dans L'Agriculture Européenne*, **182**, 121–38.

Morice, A. (2001), 'Choisis, contrôlés, placés: renouveau de l'utilitarisme migratoire', *Vacarme*, **14**, 56–60.

Morice, A (2004), 'Le travail sans le travailleur', *Revue Plein Droit*, **16**, 2–7.

Morice, A. and B. Michalon (2009), 'Les migrants dans l'agriculture: vers une crise de main d'oeuvre?', *Revue Etudes Rurale: Travailleurs Saisonniers dans L'Agriculture Européenne*, **182**, 9–28.

National Commission (National Commission for the Fight Against Illegal Work) (2006), *Bilan du Plan National de lutte contre le travail illégal 2004–2005 et perspectives 2006–2007*, National Commission for the Fight Against Illegal Work, Paris, 26 January.

Sayad, A. (1977), 'Les trois âges de l'immigration algérienne', *Actes de la Recherche en Sciences Sociales*, **15**, 59–81.

Terray, Emmanuel (1999), 'Le travail des étrangers en situation irrégulière ou la délocalisation sur place', in Etienne Balibar, M. Chemillier-Gendreau, J. Costa-Lascoux and E. Terray, *Sans-papiers: l'archaïsme fatal*, Paris: La Découverte, pp. 9–34.

Travailleurs saisonniers dans l'agriculture européenne (2009), *Etudes rurales*, n°182, éd. de l'EHESS, 225 pages.

8. The rise in precarious employment and union responses in Australia

Iain Campbell

INTRODUCTION

Precariousness is a contested concept (Barbier, 2005). In this chapter precarious employment is understood as employment that is deficient in one or more aspects of labour security when compared with the societal standard for a decent job (Vosko et al., 2009). The rise in precarious employment in Australia refers to two distinct but overlapping processes. First, it refers to the resurgence of certain forms of non-standard employment that are characterized by substandard rights and benefits. Second, it refers to the spread of precariousness within sections of what has usually been regarded as the core workforce, supposedly protected by a full-time 'permanent' employment contract.

Not all non-standard forms of employment are precarious. The three forms that attract concern in Australia are: marginal self-employment, fixed-term waged work and casual waged work. Concerns with self-employment are focused on a group of independent contractors who are more properly regarded as 'dependent', that is, subordinate in practice to just one employer. They are often indistinguishable from employees in the way they work within the workplace, though they lack the standard rights and benefits of employees. The current size of this group is small – an estimated 2.6 per cent of the workforce (Table 8.1) – but dependent contracting is common in blue-collar industries such as transport and construction, where it is used by employers to avoid the costs associated with standard employment and union organization (Productivity Commission 2006, pp. 132–8).

Apart from small categories such as apprentices and trainees, the two main types of temporary, that is non-permanent, waged work in Australia are fixed-term and casual employment. *Fixed-term* employees, those with employment contracts that terminate on a specified date or on completion of a set task, are familiar in international comparison and differ from permanent employees mainly in terms of less employment security (Watson et al., 2003, pp. 66–7). The category of fixed-term workers remains small – an estimated 5.3 per cent of the workforce (see Table 8.1) – but they are concentrated in sectors such as education and the public service.

The category of *casual* employment is more unusual in cross-national comparison (Campbell, 2004). Historically, this has been the type of employment specified in labour regulation as the main alternative to permanent employment (O'Donnell, 2004). Because casual employees enjoy little right to protection against unfair dismissal and no right to notice (or severance pay) in case of dismissal, they can be discharged with ease at almost any time. Most dramatically, casual employment is exempted from almost all rights and benefits that are attached to permanent as well as most fixed-term contracts, including even such basic entitlements as paid annual leave, sick leave and public holidays. The central feature of casual work is a simple entitlement to an hourly wage, enhanced in some cases by a so-called 'casual loading' on the hourly rate of pay. As a result, the deficit in rights and benefits separating these jobs from permanent employment is much larger than the deficit separating fixed-term from permanent employment. Casual work is most accurately regarded as a particularly degraded form of temporary employment.

Because casual work is lacking in rights and benefits, it is remarkably plastic in practice and can be used by employers in several ways. It can be full-time, though most of it is part-time (and indeed the majority of all part-time employees in Australia are classified as casual). Similarly, some casual employees can build up long periods of tenure in their job – earning the colloquial title of 'permanent casuals' (Owens, 2001) – but most are in short-term, irregular jobs characterized by high turnover and high levels of employment insecurity (ABS (Australian Bureau of Statistics), 2006). Casual work is more significant in the employment structure than fixed-term employment, and at the latest count just over 2 million 'casual' employees made up 20 per cent of the Australian workforce (ABS, 2009; see Table 8.1). Though there are major concentrations in private sector services, including retail and hospitality, casual employment can now be found throughout the employment structure, including in industries that had previously been dominated by standard employment, such as manufacturing and higher education.

Temporary agency work ('labour hire') is sometimes cited as an additional category of precarious work. Though information is sparse, we know that most agency workers are casual, while another small group are dependent contractors (Coe et al., 2009). Thus most would already have been counted in the previous estimates. The best estimate of the size of the temporary agency workforce is between 2.5 and 3 per cent of total employment (Hall, 2006). It is found in a variety of sectors, but controversy over

Table 8.1   Different types of employment, Australia 2007 (% of workforce)

Weekly hours	Employment relationship				
	Employees			Self-employed workers	
	Permanent	Casual	Fixed-term	Contractors	Non-contractors
Full-time	48.6*	3.6	3.5		
Part-time	12.3	15.2	1.7		
Total	61.0	18.8	5.3	8.9 (2.6)#	5.9

Notes:
*Standard employment.
#Dependent contractors.

Source: van Wanrooy et al. (2007, p. 20), with additional data supplied on request.

its role in lowering wages and conditions is focused on its use in unionized blue-collar areas such as construction and manufacturing.

What is the pace of growth of these forms of employment over the past twenty years? Data are rough, but it is probable that dependent contracting has increased relative to the workforce as a whole (though self-employment as a whole is stable). There is little evidence of any relative increase in fixed-term employment. However, casual work, the largest category of precarious work, has clearly expanded, in particular during the 1980s and early 1990s. In the period of strong employment growth from the mid-1990s to 2008, the expansion of casual employment slowed down, but even in this period it exceeded the growth in the workforce as a whole, with the proportion of casuals rising, according to one estimate, from 16.9 per cent in 1992 to 20 per cent in 2008 (ABS, 2009). Growth is evident for part-time casuals but it has been strongest amongst full-time casuals.

The rise of precarious employment can also be understood in a second sense, as a spread of precariousness within parts of the core or standard workforce. In the past, the category of standard work – identified as in Table 8.1 with full-time, permanent waged work – was largely characterized by an absence of precariousness. Standard work was a good marker for a rich institutional setting, usefully characterized in terms of the 'standard employment relation' (SER) (Bosch, 2006, p. 43), which erected barriers against precariousness and provided decent wages and conditions for many, though not all, employees. In recent years, however, the SER has experienced a fracturing, whereby workers may retain basic aspects such as a 'permanent' employment contract and an elementary wage but lose other aspects. A stark example concerns working time, which was standardized under the traditional model with substantial protections, including compensatory payments and rights to paid leave, but is now extensively 'flexibilized' (Campbell, 2008, pp. 135–41).

In short, standard work can be a further site for the resurgence of precariousness, supplementary to the more obvious process of expansion in precarious forms of work such as casual work. Both processes signal a recommodification of labour power or what can be called a fragmentation of the employment structure (Watson et al., 2003; Campbell, 2008). Though more coherent than the mosaic of employment arrangements found in the United States, the employment structure in Australia is now more disaggregated than in most European countries.

Though the two processes making up the rise in precarious employment are similar in their broad effects, the causal mechanisms are different and the challenges they pose for trade unions also differ. Both processes have roots in economic developments and changing product and labour markets, including the resurgence of mass unemployment. But they differ in their relation to government policy. Erosion of working conditions within the core workforce can be directly linked to government policy, which since the mid-1980s has been heavily influenced by philosophies of neo-liberalism and has pursued a series of initiatives aimed at lowering labour standards and increasing labour market flexibility. In contrast, the rise of dependent contracting and casual employment cannot be so easily traced back to conscious, planned action by neo-liberal administrators. Admittedly, some of the growth in casual work is due to the prohibition of restrictive clauses and the insertion of casual clauses in awards where these had not existed before, as in black coal (Waring, 2003). But more was due to employers taking advantage of existing gaps in the labour regulation system (Stewart, 2002; Pocock et al., 2004, pp. 18–25).

IMPLICATIONS FOR TRADE UNIONS

The challenge of precarious employment for unions must be understood within an historical perspective which recognizes distinct national paths of development (Dufour and Hege, 2005). We allude to one part of that story in the previous section – the introduction of the model of the SER. As in other countries, the trade union movement in Australia led a struggle to establish and generalize this model, conscious that decommodification of labour power is central to its fundamental labour market interests in discouraging competition amongst workers (Offe, 1985). Although the specific form of the SER was marked by its origins and can be rightly criticized as a gendered model that privileged the male breadwinner (Whitehouse, 2004; Vosko, 2005), its establishment represented a major historical achievement for trade unions. As it was consolidated and embedded within a structure of labour regulation, trade unions in turn came to organize around it, that is, to recruit and represent workers who met the criteria of a 'standard worker'. In this way the model became central to the identity, internal structures and strategies of many trade unions.

It is important to note that for much of their history trade unions in Australia have been stronger and less market-oriented than unions in other Anglophone countries. They benefited in their early years from favourable labour markets and prosperous economic conditions. After the Great Depression and strikes of the 1890s, they gained from the class compromises negotiated in the course of federation in 1901, whereby tariff barriers aimed at protecting local manufacturing were linked with expectations of decent wages and conditions (Macintyre, 1989). Trade unions, often craft or occupationally based but with a generous mixture of larger general and industrial unions, were integrated into the rather peculiar Antipodean system of labour regulation, centred on compulsory conciliation and arbitration (Isaac and Macintyre, 2004). Under this system, disputes between employers and trade unions were settled by industrial tribunals and the results were codified in legally binding *awards*, which set down minimum wages and conditions within particular occupations or industries. This became the vehicle by which unions were able to build up and generalize the Australian version of the SER. Trade unions were assisted by the arbitration system – granted rights to recognition, protection from competitors, and occasional help in recruitment through provisions for a *de facto* post-entry closed shop – and in turn they adapted to working within the system, with back-up support through the Labor Party, which from the early twentieth century had won a powerful position in the state and federal legislatures. Many small unions were 'arbitrationist', oriented to legalistic process before the tribunals and with little workplace presence, but others were more readily recognizable as strong unions that relied on mobilizing their members in order to drive collective bargaining, either as a preliminary to securing an award or as a postscript designed to improve on award conditions in specific workplaces (Bramble, 2001).

Since the mid-1970s, the strength of trade unionism has been ground down by the familiar sequence of economic downturns and recoveries, accompanied by extensive economic and labour restructuring and high levels of unemployment. Economic changes have been exacerbated by political changes, in which the class settlement forged at the turn of the twentieth century was dismantled, initially through reductions of tariff barriers, financial deregulation, privatization, corporatization and new competition policies. These political changes in turn reverberated back on the economic structure, helping to foster a more hostile employer class and encourage new management practices that undercut union membership both in traditional areas of strength such as manufacturing, transport and underground mining and in more recently organized areas such as public sector white-collar work. A decisive policy step took place in the early 1990s, when neo-liberal policies were extended to labour markets. This involved slowly displacing the award system with elements of a new system (labelled 'enterprise bargaining') which, as in North America, redefined the scope of unions, confined union activity to a narrow field of single-employer bargaining, expanded the scope of management prerogative in areas where unions were absent or weak, and installed a rather bare 'safety net' of legislated minimum labour standards. The displacement of awards in favour of this new system began under a federal Labor government (1983–96) but it then accelerated and acquired a more distinctive anti-union edge under the succeeding Liberal–National Party Coalition government (1996–2007) (Cooper and Ellem, 2008).

Trade unions are still struggling to respond to the new conditions. The gradual transition to the new regulatory system has had a major impact, though it remains poorly understood and its main features are rarely criticized. Under the system of single-employer bargaining, the interests of trade unions are fractured and they are confronted by increasingly combative employers. Union density plummeted from around 45 per cent of all employees in the mid-1980s to just 19 per cent in August 2008 (ABS, 2008a). This is complemented by an equally catastrophic decline in collective bargaining coverage, which can be estimated to have fallen from around 80 per cent in 1990 to around 40 per cent today (ABS, 2008b; van Wanrooy et al., 2009). Unions have been catapulted from a position where they had a legitimate and central place in the society to a position where they are reviled by policy makers and are struggling to retain influence even in well-unionized workplaces. Declining resources are sapped by increasing demands. Unions have been forced to use their narrowing room for manoeuvre in order to search for paths of 'revitalization' or 'renewal' (Frege and Kelly, 2003; Fairbrother and Yates, 2003). One response, strongly encouraged by the peak union body, the Australian Council of Trade Unions (ACTU) in the late 1980s and early 1990s, was amalgamation (Hose and Rimmer, 2002). More recently, the ACTU, impressed by examples from the USA, has propounded an 'organizing model', seen as a way to revive trade union activism at grassroots level and to boost membership (ACTU, 1999; Cooper, 2003; Crosby, 2005). Several unions have appropriated the rhetoric – and even the practice – of 'organizing' (Peetz et al., 2007), but it is fair to say that most either stumble on with traditional approaches or seek to invent alternative renewal strategies.

The union movement was able in 2006–2007 to mount a vigorous campaign ('Your Rights at Work') against the provisions of the labour regulation system introduced by the federal Coalition government. Although the campaign proved influential in helping defeat the Coalition government in the 2007 election (Muir, 2008), the unions have not benefited as much as they may have hoped from the change to a Labor government. The structure of a US-style system, with a narrow base of single-employer collective bargaining and a minimalist 'safety net' of legislated labour standards, remains largely intact under the Labor government's new framework, and weakened unions now face the added challenge of a major economic downturn (Forsyth and Stewart, 2009).

This brief historical sketch helps to clarify the nature and extent of the challenge that the rise in precarious employment poses for trade unions in Australia. Most immediately, this rise seems to place at risk a major historical achievement of the trade union movement and to restore conditions – albeit in a markedly different context – which trade unionism had fiercely opposed in its formative years. It foreshadows a disintegration of the traditional SER, opening the way for a dangerous recommodification of labour power.

Though it is by no means the only threat to trade unionism, the rise in precarious employment is indeed a significant menace. For example, the rise in precarious forms of work such as dependent contracting and casual work opens up a danger of unfair competition between groups of workers, unleashing downward pressure on wages and conditions and directly threatening to displace standard work and standard workers. The impact readily spills over from individual workplaces to affect broader industries and regions. In spite of expectations that precarious forms of work could work as a 'buffer' for the core workforce in industries such as retail (Carter, 1990, pp. 2–3, 47–8), this rarely proved true in practice. Even when limited in numbers, precarious forms of work threaten the good conditions of the majority section of the workforce. Similarly, where precarious employment has become strong, it can directly undermine the capacity of trade unions to take collective action, to improve wages and conditions, and to recruit and represent workers.

However, the growth of precarious forms of employment should not be considered just as a threat. Workers in precarious employment deserve and need the services of trade unions; they deserve practices of solidarity. As such, the challenge can also be seen as one of extending representation to vulnerable workers; an application of the traditional responsibilities of a trade union movement, understood not just as a service organization but as a social movement. In a certain sense, the growth of precarious employment could even offer an opportunity for the trade unions. The pressure on the SER that is exerted by the rise in precarious employment can be seen as impetus for the trade union movement to modernize this component of its historical goals. Thus, the traditional form of the SER corresponded to a specific workforce, engaged in a particular pattern of participation in paid work, predominantly based on the male breadwinner household. The workforce and patterns of participation in paid work have changed, and as a result the SER also needs to be changed.

TRADE UNION RESPONSES

For much of the twentieth century precarious employment was not considered a pressing issue by Australian unions. Most full-time work was firmly integrated into an institutional setting of decent work, identified with the SER. Indeed the SER appeared to be steadily increasing its sway, as some discriminatory measures aimed at women and indigenous workers were abolished, and as new forms of part-time work in many industries were attached to the model as permanent part-time work. During the decades of economic boom after World War II most employers hesitated to use non-standard forms as a mechanism to impose cheaper forms of labour, and indeed the non-standard forms of most concern to unions seemed small and diminishing. In industries such as entertainment, sport, and visual arts and crafts, unions were obliged to deal with the dominance of intermittent freelance, contract and casual work (Crosby, 1992; Markey, 1996; Dabscheck, 1996), and the rather peculiar circumstances of the waterfront sustained casual labour as the leading form in that industry until the mid-1960s (Sheridan, 1998). But elsewhere, in areas where standard work prevailed, the union attitude to forms such as casual work tended to be one of indifference. The main action, in so far as there was any action, was by means of restrictive labour regulation, oriented to preventing casual clauses from being inserted into the award or, if that were not possible, limiting casual work through devices such as numerical quotas and perhaps operating an informal policy of exclusion from the workplace. Where casual work was permitted under regulatory rules, casual workers were rarely integrated into union membership or, if they were members, as in large retail workplaces, they were rarely represented effectively (Campbell, 1996).

Since the mid-1980s the favourable conditions enjoyed by trade unions have been overturned. Of course, the situation of individual unions is varied, dependent on a range of factors, including the nature and extent of the challenge posed by the rise in precarious employment. Nevertheless, in most cases, traditional union responses have proven to be ineffective and unions have been obliged to adapt and to search for new responses.

As noted above, fracturing within the ranks of the core workforce has been one path for the rise in precarious employment. Most unions, in both public and private sectors, have been obliged to fight employer efforts to remove or differentiate standard conditions, in particular around working-time arrangements such as leave entitlements, controls over schedules and payments for overtime or work in non-social periods. This is a straightforward challenge but one that is by no means easy to meet. In the wake of the erosion of the award system, unions seeking to preserve or improve working-time conditions have been increasingly forced back either onto collective bargaining at single workplaces or onto whatever other campaigning methods have eluded legislative restraints. Vulnerable workforces have suffered the worst results, but the general story for many workers is one of widespread concessions and a trade-off of working-time conditions for wage rises. Even when unions have been successful in holding the line, differential success often exposes union 'hot shops', especially in the private sector, to intensified employer hostility and intensified efforts to de-unionize.

The 1997–98 waterfront dispute pointed to the potential of an approach that engages the community (Wiseman, 1998). Some unions, especially those with limited bargaining power at workplaces, have experimented with new organizing techniques that draw on community support. The Liquor, Hospitality and Miscellaneous Union (LHMU), inspired by the Justice for Janitors campaign in the USA, has campaigned to improve working-time conditions for cleaners working for contract cleaning companies. The campaigns often targeted the building owners or managers rather than the contract cleaning companies, aiming to shift the economic calculations that sponsor increased work effort and reduced hours for cleaners. The union has achieved some success using codes of practice and other forms of 'soft' regulation, initially in government schools in Victoria (Howe and Landau, 2009) and then, more recently, in office buildings in the Central Business District.

The Australian Nurses Federation (ANF) has defied overall trends and achieved a growth in membership over recent decades (Bartram et al., 2007). In 2000, in public hospitals in the state of Victoria, the ANF won a major victory as a result of the introduction, in the context of an arbitrated award, of nurse–patient ratios that require a shutting down of beds if the number of nurses on duty is insufficient (Buchanan and Briggs, 2005; Gordon et al., 2008, pp. 93–178). This regulatory initiative to stave off work intensification is unusual in that it institutionalizes union influence at the crucial level of staffing numbers, and it has proved highly popular with rank-and-file nurses, who have fiercely defended it in subsequent collective bargaining rounds. The success in developing this new regulatory initiative was founded on membership mobilization and support, the relative lack of competitive pressures in public sector hospitals, the ability of the union to 'pattern bargain' across different hospital sites, and the election of a state Labor government. But problems remain and even with favourable conditions the union has not been able to generalize the Victorian model to other states.

The challenge to unions is more complex and blurred when increased precariousness takes the alternative path of an increase in precarious forms of work. Unions have experimented with initiatives both at the level of representation, comprising recruitment strategies, internal union structures, provision of services and representation in bargaining and grievance procedures, and at the level of regulation, targeted at informal regulation at the workplace or formal regulation through collective agreements and government action.

The increase in *individual contractors*, who can be substituted for employees as a way of cheapening labour costs, has long been a source of unease, especially for unions in industries such as road transport (Bray, 1991) and construction (Underhill, 1991; Beaton, 2007). In a slightly different way, concern also applies to home-based workers in the clothing industry ('outworkers'), who were considered as non-employees (subcontractors) until the Clothing and Allied Trades Union (CATU) in 1987, abandoning its previous blanket hostility to outwork, was able to have them recognized as employees, to secure outworker provisions in the federal award, and to recruit some outworkers into the union (Ellem, 1991). In spite of occasional hesitation (see Beaton, 2007), most unions have followed a similar path, seeking to integrate contractors into union membership, perhaps with special membership sections, and then to pursue improved wages and conditions that can reduce exploitation and the risk of unfair competition based on different forms of employment.

Recruitment of contractors can be impeded by the desire for independence that is often linked with self-employment. Recruitment has been easiest in cases, such as amongst technicians in telecommunications or professional engineers in the utilities, where employees were pushed reluctantly into contracting as a result of privatization and outsourcing. Union representation of professional engineers who are non-employees remains largely confined to labour market advice and some specialist services (Macdonald and Campbell, 2008), but unions in other occupations or industries have succeeded in developing more robust approaches.

Regulation of contracting has been difficult, especially as most workplace restrictions are now prohibited (Stewart, 2008), but unions continue to pursue reforms. For example, the initial achievement of the clothing union in securing award provisions was merely the start of a series of struggles to deal with the powerful pressures generating outwork at poor pay and conditions. Modelled on global campaigns against corporations such as Nike and Benetton, recent Australian campaigns have used links with community groups (churches and ethnic women's groups), pressure on retailers (shame campaigns), draft codes of practice, and lobbying of parliamentarians (Weller, 1999; 2007; Delaney, 2007). Similarly, many unions pursue general legislative reforms, seeking to shift the labour law definition of the boundary between employees and non-employees. They have achieved some piecemeal success at state level, through mechanisms that allow independent contractors to be 'deemed' to be employees or that allow 'unfair work contracts' to be set aside, but have not made much progress at federal level, even with the change to a Labor government (Stewart, 2008).

The issue of contractors overlaps with the problem of temporary agencies, since the latter can similarly function as a way for employers to avoid the costs of an employment relationship (Stewart, 2002, pp. 255–6). As in the case of contractors, unions have often pursued restrictive regulation through awards or agreements, and, following on from this approach, some have established their own labour hire companies in the quest to control the flow of agency workers and to equalize conditions at unionized work sites (Waring, 2003, pp. 93–94). But such workplace-based approaches are difficult to sustain (Australian Centre for Industrial Relations Research and Training (ACIRRT), 1999), and many initiatives have been swamped by legislative prohibitions and general labour market changes. Little progress has been achieved so far at other levels, though on occasion unions have been able to conclude collective agreements with larger labour hire companies, and they continue to pursue licensing regulation and other societal controls (Hall, 2006).

Fixed-term employment is concentrated in the public sector and in industries such as education. This form of employment has caused difficulties for unions, in particular in government schools in Victoria, where appointment of new teachers on short fixed-term contracts was encouraged in the course of neo-liberal reforms during the mid-1990s. Although the Australian Education Union (AEU) has since been able to improve conditions for fixed-term teachers, for example by restricting the practice of non-payment of salary in the summer holidays, it has not been able to reduce the high proportion (18 per cent) of fixed-term teachers in the workforce. In a context where employment decisions and finances are devolved to individual principals, the cost advantages and enhanced flexibility that derive from hiring fixed-term employees at the bottom of the salary range have been a powerful barrier to any change. The issue continues to simmer, with evident dissatisfaction amongst teachers in fixed-term positions (AEU, 2007).

Because the deficit in wages and conditions is so large, *casual employment* is often particularly attractive to employers. Where casual employment is freely available to employers it can spread to dominate particular workplaces, occupations or industries. As a result casual employment is widely identified as the major threat to many trade unions, whether casual workers are directly employed or supplied through labour hire companies.

Union responses to the rise in casual employment span the two levels of representation and regulation. Casual workers are hard to recruit into trade unions, partly because of characteristics such as dispersion amongst small establishments, short hours and irregular schedules and high turnover, but also because their lack of rights makes them vulnerable to employer reprisals in the form of reduction of hours or dismissal (Campbell, 1996, pp. 587–8; Walsh, 2002). These factors can foster a passivity that impedes the chances of mobilization inside or outside unions. Nevertheless, some approaches give strong priority to organizing casual workers. One group in Melbourne (UNITE), emerging from the socialist movement, and building on previous experiences in New Zealand, has pursued innovative ways of organizing that are trade unionist in form but fall outside the framework of official bargaining. The union draws on community support but also seeks to sponsor self-organization, using low fees to enrol workers, generally young workers employed as casuals in retail outlets such as fast food, convenience shops and book shops. It has successfully publicized illegal practices such as underpayment and has exposed individual employers to public shame campaigns, but it is unclear whether this model can be sustained in the medium term.

Casual ('sessional') academics in universities have been targeted in one recent campaign. As part of their current collective bargaining round the National Tertiary Education Union (NTEU) has aimed to mobilize casual academics, using low membership fees, conferences and meetings, and encouragement of casual committees (May et al., 2008). The campaign is unfinished, but it seems to be stalling, partly because of the traditional problems of mobilizing casual workers who are vulnerable to employer reprisals but also because of the heterogeneous structure and diverse interests of the casual academic workforce. Although studies show substantial dissatisfaction amongst casual academics, most of whom would prefer ongoing employment, it has proved difficult to aggregate their diverse interests and to build a bridge to the interests of permanent full-time staff.

Trade union campaigns around casual work take different forms. They sometimes appear as 'organizing' campaigns, designed according to a template, ultimately derived from the United States, which seems to prioritize recruitment at the expense of other aspects of union practice (Brown, 2009). Apart from other objections, this risks overlooking the specific Australian context. The point is underlined in a study of the early efforts of the LHMU in organizing homecare workers in Australia since the 1980s. Walsh (2002) stresses the importance of a regulatory dimension to organizing efforts and suggests that the success of the LHMU in this sector was founded on the ability of the union to win a federal award and then to use the award as an instrument to regulate the structure of home-care work. In this way the union could transform the working conditions of the casual homecare workers, who were initially vulnerable because their hours could be cut and they could be dismissed without notice. The conversion of the workers to permanent part-time provided the foundation for the ongoing organizing that is essential in the Australian context, where unions lack the capacity to close off membership through winning elections at workplace level.

Varied approaches to shaping casual work through regulation have been tried. The main option has been a limitations approach, aimed at 'decasualization'. Where they could not achieve a complete ban, unions have pursued mechanisms such as numerical quotas, time limits for employment of casuals, and restraints on methods of use. Union policy slowly turned to an emphasis on time limits in the 1990s, with the aim of confining casual employment to short-term engagements and cutting back the phenomenon of 'permanent casuals'. This in turn often implied a conversion of casual workers to permanent status after a certain time in the job. Although most quantitative limitations were prohibited in awards under the federal legislation introduced by the Coalition government in 1996, unions continued to seek regulations that would require or allow conversion from a casual to a permanent contract after a certain period. In the late 1990s, initially in a case involving clerks in South Australia and then in a case involving one of the most important federal awards, the Metals, Engineering and Associated Industries Award 1998 (the 'Metals Award'), unions were able to win a provision that granted a constrained right to individual casual employees with at least six months' regular and systematic service to 'elect' to become an ongoing employee (Owens, 2001, 2006). Employers could refuse but not 'unreasonably'. Though this regulatory provision is generally seen as a step forward, it is undermined by several problems (Owens, 2006, pp. 346–9). In particular, the reliance on individual choice by the worker can be criticized as providing only a 'weak right' that is unlikely to be effective in a context where casuals remain vulnerable to employer actions and are understandably reluctant to press demands on their employer (Pocock et al., 2004, p. 45; see also pp. 43–44, 49–50). Certainly, the right has in practice only been lightly used by casual workers.

Other regulatory initiatives include efforts to extend protections and improve conditions for casual workers, thereby reducing the deficit that separates casual and permanent employment. Action in this direction, especially for long-term casuals, has been taken at several levels, including in federal and state legislation (Hunter, 2006, pp. 295–300). One obvious path forward would be through the new legislated 'safety net' of minimum conditions, but this net is riddled with exemptions that continue to exclude casual workers (Murray and Owens, 2009, p. 43). Some unions are committed to a further approach, which entails increasing the 'casual loading' on the hourly rate of pay prescribed for casuals. Though often justified as a form of compensation for employees for loss of entitlements, the casual loading has also been attractive for unions as another way of limiting casual employment, in this case by imposing a monetary penalty on the employer who chooses casual employment. The unions have achieved some success in raising the loading, but – apart from other objections (difficulty of enforcement and implicit endorsement of the unfortunate principle of 'cashing out' entitlements) – it is a blunt weapon for limiting casual employment, since it cannot successfully cover the many sources of cost advantage to employers, for example, as a result of only deploying casual labour during peak periods, keeping casual workers on the bottom of classification scales, and not paying penalty rates for work during unsocial hours.

CONCLUSION

This chapter reviews the varied responses of Australian unions to the rise in precarious employment. None has succeeded yet in reversing or even pausing the two processes that have been identified. Nevertheless, it is possible to detect at least a few promising initiatives and a certain amount of experimental energy.

Experimental energy will continue to be needed in the current phase of hesitant recovery from economic downturn. Economic conditions are likely to fuel a continued rise of precarious employment. In particular, as job losses impact disproportionately on full-time permanent workers, and as employers look for less costly and more flexible alternatives, we can expect a resumption of the rapid relative growth of casual workers, both part-time and full-time.

One missing element in the current debate, both at the level of individual unions and at the level of the union movement as a whole, is a strategic perspective that could confidently identify the most promising initiatives, the conditions of success or failure, and the methods for generalizing successful models. Some commentators offer the 'organizing model' as if it were such a strategy for the union movement (Crosby, 2005). The spirit of organizing is welcome, in contrast to some previous traditions of union representation, and it is necessary in a hostile environment where unions have been deprived of much state and employer support (Boxall and Haynes, 1997; Frege and Kelly, 2003, p. 16). But in the Australian context 'organizing' often appears as just a set of techniques designed to improve the flow of recruitment into individual unions. In this sense, it is best seen as a set of tactics that may or may not be applicable to individual unions (Buchanan and Briggs, 2005, pp. 5–6; Probert and Ewer, 2003); at worst it can be criticized as a form of union adaptation to the constraints of enterprise bargaining – a 'recipe for local success within general decline' (Smith and Ewer, 2003, p. 46).

To be fully effective, organizing needs to be anchored in a broader perspective, which extends beyond recruitment in individual unions to an engagement with labour movement politics and with ideas and principles of labour regulation. The need for a broader perspective is especially relevant for unions confronted by the challenge of precarious employment. When the rise in precarious employment appears as a fracturing in the core, it is possible to see the importance of designing controls on intensity, staffing numbers, and caps on overtime. When the rise in precarious employment appears as an increase in forms of employment such as dependent contracting and casual work, it is possible to see the need to determine the appropriate forms of employment in a modern society, the conditions that should attach to these forms, and the balance between flexibility and security. One crucial pivot for new strategic thinking must be the institutional setting of the SER. As Bosch rightly argues (2006), the so-called erosion of the SER under pressures such as those identified above does not imply that it should be jettisoned. The challenge is to preserve the substance, which provides valuable securities for workers, but to redefine the forms, which need to be separated from a male breadwinner model and instead adapted to a more diverse workforce. This will entail re-regulation and the move to a new, more flexible SER, as can be found in some Scandinavian countries (Bosch, 2006).

NOTE

The research for this chapter was supported under the Australian Research Council's Discovery Project funding scheme (DP 0451899). Thanks to Robyn May and Sara Charlesworth for useful comments on an earlier draft.

REFERENCES

ABS (2006), *Forms of Employment Australia*, Cat. no. 6359.0, November.

ABS (2008a), *Employee Earnings, Benefits and Trade Union Membership, Australia*, Cat. no. 6310.0, August.

ABS (2008b), *Employee Earnings and Hours*, Cat. no. 6305.0, August.

ABS (2009), *Australian Labour Market Statistics*, Cat. no. 6105.0, July, data cubes.

ACIRRT (1999), *Regulating Non-Standard Employment in Manufacturing: Summary Report*, Sydney: ACIRRT.

ACTU (1999), *Unions@work*, Melbourne: ACTU.

AEU (2007), 'New teachers survey', available at: http://www.aeuvic.asn.au/professional/files/2007NewTeachers.pdf (accessed 29 April 2009).

Barbier, J-C. (2005), 'La précarité, une catégorie française à l'épreuve de la comparaison internationale', *Revue Française de Sociologie*, **46** (2), 351–71.

Bartram, T., P. Stanton and R. Harbridge (2007), 'Protecting the individual, the profession and the quality of health services: union growth in nursing', in D. Buttigieg, S. Cockfield, R. Cooney, M. Jerrard and A. Rainnie (eds), *Trade Unions in the Community: Values, Issues, Shared Interests and Alliances*, Melbourne: Heidelberg Press, pp. 97–111.

Beaton, L. (2007), 'What do we want? When do we want it? The prolonged battle to organize floor-layers in the construction industry in Melbourne, 1983–2006', in *Diverging Employment Relations Patterns in Australia and New Zealand*, Proceedings of the AIRAANZ Conference, February 2007, CD-ROM.

Bosch, G. (2006), 'Working time and the standard employment relationship', in J-Y. Boulin, M. Lallement, J. Messenger and F. Michon (eds), *Decent Working Time: New Trends, New Issues*, Geneva: ILO, pp. 41–64.

Boxall, P. and P. Haynes (1997), 'Strategy and trade union effectiveness in a neoliberal environment', *British Journal of Industrial Relations*, **35** (4), 567–91.

Bramble, T. (2001), 'Australian union strategies since 1945', *Labour and Industry*, **11** (3), 1–25.

Bray, M. (1991), 'Unions and owner-drivers in New South Wales road transport', in M. Bray and V. Taylor (eds), *The Other Side of Flexibility: Unions and Marginal Workers in Australia*, Sydney: ACIRRT Monograph no. 3, pp. 143–67.

Brown, T. (2009), 'As easy as ABC? Learning to organize private child care workers', *Labor Studies Journal*, **34** (2), 235–51.

Buchanan, J. and C. Briggs (2005), 'Unions and the restructuring of work: contrasting experiences in the old and new heartlands', *Labour and Industry*, **16** (1), 5–22.

Campbell, I. (1996), 'Casual employment, labour regulation and Australian trade unions', *Journal of Industrial Relations*, **38** (4), 571–99.

Campbell, I. (2004), 'Casual work and casualisation: how does Australia compare?', *Labour and Industry*, **15** (2), 85–111.

Campbell, I. (2008), 'Australia: institutional changes and workforce fragmentation', in S. Lee and F. Eyraud (eds), *Globalization, Flexibilization and Working Conditions in Asia and the Pacific*, London: Chandos, pp. 115–52.

Carter, S. (1990), *Casual Employment and Industrial Democracy*, Canberra: Australian Government Publishing Service.

Coe, N., J. Johns and K. Ward (2009), 'Agents of casualization? The temporary staffing industry and labour market restructuring in Australia', *Journal of Economic Geography*, **9**, 55–84.

Cooper, R. (2003), 'Peak council organising at work: ACTU strategy 1994–2000', *Labour and Industry*, **14** (1), 1–15.

Cooper, R. and B. Ellem (2008), 'The neoliberal state, trade unions and collective bargaining in Australia', *British Journal of Industrial Relations*, **46** (3), 532–54.

Crosby, M. (1992), 'Organising a mobile workforce', in M. Crosby and M. Easson (eds), *What Should Unions Do?*, Sydney: Pluto Press, pp. 332–8.

Crosby, M. (2005), *Power at Work: Rebuilding the Australian Trade Union Movement*, Sydney: Federation Press.

Dabscheck, B. (1996), 'Playing the team game: unions in professional team sports', *Journal of Industrial Relations*, **38** (4), 600–628.

Delaney, A. (2007), 'New strategies to organize homeworkers in informal employment: notes from the field', in D. Buttigieg, S. Cockfield, R. Cooney, M. Jerrard and A. Rainnie (eds), *Trade Unions in the Community: Values, Issues, Shared Interests and Alliances*, Melbourne: Heidelberg Press, pp. 173–84.

Dufour, C. and A. Hege (2005), 'Emplois précaires, emploi normal et syndicalisme', *La Chronique Internationale de l'IRES*, 97, 5–22.

Ellem, B. (1991), 'Outwork and unionism in the Australian clothing industry', in M. Bray and V. Taylor (eds), *The Other Side of Flexibility: Unions and Marginal Workers in Australia*, Sydney: ACIRRT Monograph no. 3, pp. 93–114.

Fairbrother, P. and Yates, C. (2003), 'Unions in crisis, unions in renewal?', in P. Fairbrother and C. Yates (eds), *Trade Unions in Renewal: A Comparative Study*, London: Routledge, pp. 1–31.

Forsyth, A. and A. Stewart (eds) (2009), *Fair Work: The New Workplace Laws and the Work Choices Legacy*, Sydney: Federation Press.

Frege, C. and J. Kelly (2003), 'Union revitalization strategies in comparative perspective', *European Journal of Industrial Relations*, **9** (1), 7–24.

Gordon, S., J. Buchanan and T. Bretherton (2008), *Safety in Numbers: Nurse-to-Patient Ratios and the Future of Health Care*, Ithaca, NY: ILR Press.

Hall, R. (2006), 'Temporary agency work and HRM in Australia: "cooperation, specialization and satisfaction for the good of all"?', *Personnel Review*, **35** (2), 158–74.

Hose, K. and M. Rimmer (2002), 'The Australian union merger wave revisited', *Journal of Industrial Relations*, **44** (4), 525–44.

Howe, J. and I. Landau (2009), 'Using public procurement to promote better labour standards in Australia: a case study of responsive regulatory design', *Journal of Industrial Relations* **51** (4), 575–89.

Hunter, R. (2006), 'The legal production of precarious work', in J. Fudge and R. Owens (eds), *Precarious Work, Women and the New Economy: The Challenge to Legal Norms*, Oxford: Hart, pp. 283–304.

Isaac, J. and S. Macintyre (eds) (2004), *The New Province for Law and Order: 100*

Years of Australian Industrial Conciliation and Arbitration, Port Melbourne: Cambridge University Press.

Macdonald, F. and I. Campbell (2008), 'Trade unions and self-employed contracting: new initiatives in representing professional engineers in Australia', unpublished paper for the International Sociological Association Forum, Barcelona, September.

Macintyre, S. (1989), *The Labour Experiment*, Melbourne: McPhee Gribble.

Markey, R. (1996), 'Marginal workers in the big picture: unionization of visual artists', *Journal of Industrial Relations*, **38** (1), 22–41.

May, R., L. Gale and I. Campbell (2008), 'Casually appointed, permanently exploited: how is NTEU responding to the casualisation of academia in the current climate?', in P. Stanton and S. Young (eds), *Workers, Corporations, and Community, Proceedings of the 22nd Conference of AIRAANZ*, vol. 2, Melbourne: AIRAANZ, pp. 255–65.

Muir, K. (2008), *Worth Fighting For: Inside the 'Your Rights at Work' Campaign*, Sydney: University of New South Wales Press.

Murray, J. and R. Owens (2009), 'The safety net: labour standards in the new era', in A. Forsyth and A. Stewart (eds), *Fair Work: The New Workplace Laws and the Work Choices Legacy*, Sydney: Federation Press, pp. 40–74.

O'Donnell, A. (2004), '"Non-standard" workers in Australia: counts and controversies', *Australian Journal of Labour Law*, **17** (1), 89–116.

Offe, C. (1985), *Disorganized Capitalism: Contemporary Transformations of Work and Politics*, Cambridge: Polity.

Owens, R. (2001), 'The "long-term or permanent casual": an oxymoron or "a well enough understood Australianism" in the law', *Australian Bulletin of Labour*, **27** (2), 118–36.

Owens, R. (2006), 'Engendering flexibility in a world of precarious work', in J. Fudge and R. Owens (eds), *Precarious Work, Women and the New Economy: The Challenge to Legal Norms*, Oxford: Hart, pp. 329–52.

Peetz, D., B. Pocock and C. Houghton (2007), 'Organizers' roles transformed? Australian union organizers and changing union strategy', *Journal of Industrial Relations*, **49** (2), 151–66.

Pocock, B., J. Buchanan and I. Campbell (2004), *Securing Quality Employment: Policy Options for Casual and Part-Time Workers in Australia*, Sydney: Chifley Research Centre.

Probert, B. and P. Ewer (2003), 'A near death experience: one union fights for life', in P. Fairbrother and C. Yates (eds), *Trade Unions in Renewal: A Comparative Study*, London: Routledge, pp. 102–16.

Productivity Commission (2006), *The Role of Non-Traditional Work in the Australian Labour Market*, Commission Research Paper, Melbourne: Productivity Commission.

Sheridan, T. (1998), 'Regulating the waterfront industry 1950–1968', *Journal of Industrial Relations*, **40** (3), 441–60.

Smith, M. and P. Ewer (2003) 'Enterprise bargaining and union decline: part of the problem, not the solution', in J. Burgess and D. Macdonald (eds), *Developments in Enterprise Bargaining in Australia*, Croydon: Tertiary Press, pp. 33–49.

Stewart, A. (2002), 'Redefining employment? Meeting the challenge of contract and agency labour', *Australian Journal of Labour Law*, **15** (3), 235–76.

Stewart, A. (2008), 'Work choices and independent contractors: the revolution that never happened', *Economic and Labour Relations Review*, **18** (2), 53–62.

Underhill, E. (1991), 'Unions and contract workers in the New South Wales and Victorian building industries', in M. Bray and V. Taylor (eds), *The Other Side of Flexibility: Unions and Marginal Workers in Australia*, Sydney: ACIRRT Monograph no. 3, pp. 115–42.

van Wanrooy, B., S. Oxenbridge, J. Buchanan and M. Jakubauskas (2007), *Australia@Work: The Benchmark Report*, Sydney: Workplace Research Centre, University of Sydney.

van Wanrooy, B., S. Wright and J. Buchanan (2009), *Who Bargains? A Report Prepared for the NSW Office of Industrial Relations*, Sydney: OIR.

Vosko, L. (2005), *Confronting the Norm: Gender and the International Regulation of Precarious Work*, Ottawa: Law Commission of Canada.

Vosko, L., M. MacDonald and I. Campbell (2009), 'Introduction: gender and the concept of precarious employment', in L. Vosko, M. MacDonald and I. Campbell (eds), *Gender and the Contours of Precarious Employment*, London: Routledge, pp. 1–25.

Walsh, J. (2002), 'Building unionism in non-standard service industries: the case of homecare organising in Australia and the United States', unpublished paper for the International Sociological Association World Congress, Brisbane, July.

Waring, P. (2003), 'The nature and consequences of temporary and contract employment in the Australian black coal mining industry', *Labour and Industry*, **14** (2), 83–96.

Watson, I., J. Buchanan, I. Campbell and C. Briggs (2003), *Fragmented Futures: New Challenges in Working Life*, Sydney: Federation Press.

Weller, S. (1999), 'Clothing outwork: union strategy, labour regulation and labour market restructuring', *Journal of Industrial Relations*, **41** (2), 203–27.

Weller, S. (2007), 'Regulating clothing outwork: a sceptic's view', *Journal of Industrial Relations*, **49** (1), 67–86.

Whitehouse, G. (2004), 'From family wage to parental leave: the changing relationship between arbitration and the family', *Journal of Industrial Relations*, **46** (4), 400–412.

Wiseman, J. (1998), 'Here to stay? The 1997–1998 Australian waterfront dispute and its implications', *Labour and Industry*, **9** (1), 1–16.

9. Hyper-flexibility in the IT sector: myth or reality?

Isabelle Berrebi-Hoffmann, Michel Lallement, Martine Pernod-Lemattre and François Sarfati

INTRODUCTION: THE DEBATE ON FLEXIBILITY

In the developed countries, globalization has generally been associated with more flexibility of work and less stability of employment contract for workers. Since the 1980s, flexibility has been moreover a constant theme with politicians and economists, and has become the criterion of 'excellence'. It is a very variable notion (Boyer, 1986), and can in truth designate the opposite of excellence, such as those totally precarious situations of men and women – in supermarkets for instance – hired on shaky labour contracts to work for very short periods of time and puny salaries. As Sennett (1998) has shown, that sort of flexibility heralds outbreaks of social unrest, for several reasons: because it responds to market exigencies by giving priority to the short term, turns uncertainty into the norm, and transforms the lack of recognition of people's aptitudes into strategies for management. Thus flexibility contributes directly and powerfully to the disintegration of professional communities and the crisis of professional identities.

Other possible models of flexibility in a work environment do, however, exist. Without even mentioning financialization and the economic crisis that ensued, the mutations of contemporary capitalism have also given birth to new forms of activity and new ways of making a career. Boltanski and Chiapello (1999) have pointed to the fact that one of the main figures in the rhetoric typical of today's spirit of capitalism is the highly skilled worker, master of his or her own destiny, mobile, and capable of getting involved in one project after another, at will. At the centre of various networks, this new harbinger of modern times has nothing in common with the 'little people', those working poor for whom flexibility means utter domination. For the 'larger man or woman', 'flexibility and adaptability describe qualities that have nothing to do with docility. The big person in a connectionist world is active and autonomous' (ibid., p. 169).

In the socio-economic literature, the IT sector is frequently associated with both hyper-flexible skilled workers and globalized markets and firms. Software has been considered – and this remains true to this day – a laboratory in which new forms of flexibility and mobility are being experimented with, linked to the organizational model of the start-up, i.e. not being tied to a schedule, working from home, choosing external mobility, training oneself, and endorsing the symbolic figure of worker-shareholder. But, while the exceptional development of the IT sector and its internationalization, profitability, economic performance, and capacity to create jobs and employment are indisputable realities, its merits may be open to question. Is it truly beneficial in terms of new forms of work and careers? Do the new rules of the game – allowing employees to conjugate autonomy, cross-company mobility and individual flexibility – actually apply?

In this chapter, we will reconsider the question of flexibility by investigating the following points, based on a survey carried out in the mid-2000s.[1] First of all, what really goes on in this sector? Is the start-up model really the dominant one? What are the concrete forms of flexibility at play in labour and employment? With regard to that question, do employees really have control over their own working conditions and professional destinies? Lastly, what are the forms of collective action and of flexibility control presently in force? The answers we give largely demystify the vision of a new workforce which is presumed to be flexible by choice.

We will review three of our main results: first, the logics governing flexibility, which can only be grasped at the place where company, national and international marketplaces and networks of professional relations intersect; secondly, flexibility, which here concerns working conditions more than employment per se; thirdly, the impossibility of separating flexibility from the ongoing industrialization of the management of intellectual labour. Finally, we will show that an actual ongoing globalization of markets, which is enabled by the standardization of international intellectual services, does eventually have some negative impact on work conditions through offshoring and increasing international competition

FAR FROM THE START-UP MYTH

Let us begin by surveying the ground covered by our study. Our interest was in studying 'Sociétés de service en ingénierie et informatique' (SSIIs), i.e. consulting firms. SSII activities cover a vast domain, extending from consulting and engineering, through software development, to IT outsourcing. These companies made their appearance in the 1960s, in the form of small production units propelled by engineers knowledgeable in

IT, later joined by consultants previously involved in consulting work. The sector grew rapidly, allowing some small and medium-size businesses to swell by several thousand employees, while discouraging new ones from being created. During the 1990s, the movement was thrown into high gear. In an expanding market, the top SSIIs developed thanks to external growth (by buying other firms) to reinforce their basic skills and diversify their activities. Among the then dominant leaders in the field, particular mention must be made of Cap Gemini, IBM and Electronic Data Systems (EDS). The race towards gigantic entities and internationalization contributed to enlarging the perimeter of activities as well as diversifying the trade. But the frontiers with other sectors are very porous – particularly with the world of consulting and its consultants – making it tricky to give any precise definition of an SSII (Berrebi-Hoffmann, 2002).

On the whole, since its birth, the sector in France has expanded considerably, an average of 8 per cent per year over the ten years prior to the crisis of 2008. According to INSEE (National Institute of Statistics and Economic Studies), it presently employs more than 300,000 individuals and turns over more than 30 billion euros, a figure comparable to that of aeronautics (INSEE, 2009). Despite this rather positive trend, the sector has lived through two serious crises, first in 1993, then at the onset of the new millennium. But since 2003, prosperity has returned, essentially driven by outsourcing activities. It should be added that France is one of the countries where services are cheapest. According to a Syntec review in 2005 (Syntec, 2006) the most profitable markets for French firms in Europe are Great Britain, then Spain, Scandinavia and finally France itself.

A careful look at the situation points to a world far removed from the picture of a fractured territory where the start-up would be the dominant model. The organizational reality is totally different. The IT universe is in fact made up of international corporations of vertically integrated experts, employing a highly skilled intellectual workforce. France boasts groups of world-wide status such as Cap Gemini, Atos Origin for consulting and IT services, Dassault Systems and Business Objects for software publishing. Next to those giants, a multitude of small companies has cropped up. Heterogeneity is thus the rule. To be yet more specific, in the perimeter of Syntec Informatique – the biggest employers' federation in the field – only around 2,000 companies of the 20,000 surveyed have more than ten people working for them.

Even more significantly, the evolution observed over the past few years points to the massive rather than the fragmentary. The weight of the top ten continued to increase through the mid-2000s, with turnover growing from 31 per cent in 1995 to 43 per cent in 2006. According to an AP Management study (2007), the number of SSII takeovers and of independent software vendors (ISVs) takeovers in France came close to making history in 2006, a rise of 54 per cent that represented 126 business fusions-acquisitions (as against 144 transactions, the record in 2000). In 2007, the number went up once again, reaching 140. The SSIIs are still the main unifying force in the sector, with 60 per cent of all fusion-acquisition operations, as against 6 per cent for consulting firms and 34 per cent for ISVs.

The ever-greater concentration of SSIIs can be explained by a combination of factors that depend directly on the customers rather than on the service companies themselves. Over the past few years, the main client companies first wanted to limit the number of their suppliers. With that in mind, they set up an accreditation policy to select subcontractors, a strategy that damages the smaller SSII, unable to respect to the same extent the new norms imposed by the client. The second factor that explains the concentration process in the sector is the industrialization of the means of production of software services and consulting; that, too, depends directly on the clients. The demand is quite simple: rationalize labour to bring down costs and be more competitive, particularly in the emerging markets. The third factor concerns the strong demand for outsourcing, a strategy that allows client companies not only to lower their costs but also to concentrate on their core business.

The small SSIIs which were unable to grow behaved differently. The vast majority chose a niche strategy (whether in the form of technological specialization or by focusing on certain parts of the market), while remaining within the networks of subcontractors dominated by large companies. In the final analysis, it is relatively easy to see how the transformation of the market was able to produce a specific sort of flexibility. This was no thanks to a dominant model of the start-up type, but rather due to organizational segmentation: on one side, the large, multi-activity, multi-specialization, multi-market corporations; on the other, specialized, small or medium-sized companies which have difficulty accessing markets reserved for their client companies – and most importantly procurement contracts.

A NEW PROFILE OF THE 'FLEXIBLE WORKER'?

In France, the software industry employs approximately 300,000 individuals, and 30 per cent of the job opportunities for software engineers and other IT professionals derive from Syntec Informatique member companies alone. What is the profile of the employees in the sector? Do the statistics and survey data corroborate the usual representations that connect performance to complete personal freedom, flexibility to a specific form of employment, technical expertise to continuing education, or exceptional professional investment to good working conditions? To answer that question, let us begin by noting that computer science is still an occupation in great part dominated by men, given that the general trend is not towards greater gender equality. After a period of feminization, there was a backlash in 1990, and today, women represent about a third of the staff in the discipline. The most feminized part is data processing. In IT consulting – the largest branch in the sector – only one quarter of the workers are women. Computer science thus rhymes with masculine . . . though not necessarily with a lack of family life: 73 per cent of the people working in the field live with a partner though over one half are also childless. It is true too that, in the SSII, the qualities habitually associated with the new 'flexi-workers' converge: they are young (one-third are under 30), have superior qualifications (approximately one half possess college degrees – (Bac + 3, i.e. a BA or higher), and occupy high-status jobs (six employees out of ten are managers or in positions equal to a liberal profession) (Fondeur and Sauviat, 2003).

Whilst it might seem that some workers hold all the trump cards of flexibility, in reality the picture is more complex. Contrary to common expectations, the positions filled by IT workers are in their great majority stable: over 90 per cent of employees have open-ended labour contracts. Temporary work is exceptional: barely 1 per cent is hired on that basis. The others (9 per cent) are on fixed-term contracts. The data available unfortunately do not permit us to examine the case of assignment contracts and temporary work contracts, legal formulas which some employers would like to see generalized, since they would allow them to hire an individual for the length of a single mission. The subject was heatedly discussed in the profession, but the symbolic result of the debate – an even stronger identification of the sector with the figure of 'meat markets'[2] – dampened the enthusiasm anyone may have felt for that form of flexibility.

Training is perhaps more implicated in the construction of the new 'multi-task adaptable workers' – for are they not forever on the lookout for more knowledge, eager to learn? In this arena, too, reality has little to do with the myth. Although continuing education is more developed here than in the other economic activities – between 2 and 5 per cent of the total wage bill, depending on the source – it also, more than in other sectors, benefits those workers who are already highly skilled. Above all, as one of the persons sitting on the joint committee that finances and organizes training programmes (FAFIEC) told us, continuing education in software mainly means short training programmes (a few days) and aims merely at keeping up certain skills, not initiating staff into what is new in the domain as long training periods are meant to do. Our own fieldwork (Berrebi-Hoffmann et al., 2010) confirms the fact that training is often a makeshift solution: employees are sent off to train when they do not have a mission to accomplish – though they may be recalled instantly if they have to be posted at a customer site, or if some specific demand lands on the desk of the SSII and somebody has to be trained rapidly to fill it.

Examining data relative to seniority is another way of challenging the image of workers supposedly hyper-flexible of their own free will. It is true that, contrary to what the large number of open-ended employment contracts may lead one to think, people do not spend their entire working life in one SSII: 25 per cent of personnel have been there for less than five years as against an average of 17 per cent in the rest of the French economy. Why is there so much flexibility in the form of mobility? Is it an indication that workers can manage their careers as they wish, free from all social constraint? The answer is no, simply because, more than the employees themselves, it is the companies who control the game. Their main concern is to optimize employees' assignments at a client-company's site (Berrebi-Hoffmann, 2006). The fact they have been delegated forces employees to be flexible, both technically and geographically. Far from being simply an informal requirement, it is explicitly written into their work contract. Since the crisis that followed the Internet bust of 2001–2003, companies have been even more obliged to reconcile two contradictory obligations: on the one hand, they must remain attractive on the IT job market so as to retain a sufficiently large pool of workers to answer growing demand; on the other hand, they must reduce labour costs so as to resist the pressures of international competition. On top of being contradictory, neither of those two obligations is easy to satisfy.

Concerning the first, it can be noted that fewer and fewer young men and women in France today choose to major in the sciences, which makes it problematic to provide the computer labour market with sufficient manpower. Besides, since the SSIIs are not renowned for their working conditions, it is understandable that companies do not always find it as easy to hire as they would like. All the surveys, and ours in particular among them, show the following result: the pressure can be very intense and workers must above all be very liberal with their time, always ready to get up and go. Added to the fact that career prospects are rather thin, it is easy to understand that once their youthful enthusiasm has faded, employees would prefer a less invasive job that leaves more time for private life, and chiefly for their roles of mother and father (Lallement, 2003).

As mentioned above, there are cost pressures inducing firms to resort to offshoring – European firms signing services agreements with countries where IT engineers cost less, e.g. India or China, is no longer a figment of our imagination (Geyer, 2007).[3] Syntec Informatique considers that off-shoring is both a consequence of and a stimulus to globalization. In 2007, Syntec's president explained that

> the trend towards offshoring is lasting, but bears on more specific aspects, such as software development and Third Party Application Management. We're not yet at the end of the Indian mirage, in the sense that we'll continue to go there. But it'll be for development of software applications, in which local engineers are competent. Besides, today the professionalism of that line of work has been recognized'.[4]

What is the real situation? Though the data available in France is scarce, it shows that 29 per cent of the companies employing ten or more workers resort to subcontracting service providers for tasks requiring knowledge and know-how in matters of IT and communications technology (Jlass and Niel, 2008). The first projections showed there was no reason to be unduly worried. It was forecast in 2008 that by the end of 2010, for all sectors of activity in France taken together, approximately 40,000 jobs would be lost due to offshoring (Houdré and Lelièvre, 2008). However, a more recent survey (Berrebi-Hoffmann et al., 2010) shows that the impact of offshore should nevertheless be taken seriously. Not only are some businesses already including the rate of offshoring in their quality indicators, but in reality a multiplicity of forms exists that actors often do not even identify as such: offshoring through buying-acquisition, offshoring by creating branches or local offices with local staffs, offshoring by networking with allied companies; these have just as dire a consequence for the employment and working conditions of French workers as do straightforward offshoring operations.

THE SECTOR AND ITS ACTORS

The reality of flexibility in the computer industry cannot be grasped if one ignores the fact that reforms and transactions have taken place not only within the companies but also at the sectoral level. In particular, there is a significant collective labour agreement (Syntec) that covers over 550,000 employees and concerns 46,000 companies, in which flexibility takes the form of negotiated rules and regulations. Who are the main actors involved?

On the employers' side, for historical reasons, the interests of the smallest companies (with fewer than ten employees) are defended by a small organization that does not carry much weight in the social scheme of things. Companies of over ten employees (SSII and software publishers) are represented, as we have seen, by Syntec Informatique, which in turn belongs to the Syntec Federation, a conglomerate of various IT occupations. Syntec Informatique represents the interests of the SSII, software publishers and maintenance companies. A major actor in the realm of professional relations in IT, it boasts 300 members among the SSII and over 200 in software publishing, i.e. over 160,000 workers. According to the employers' federation, the total comes to more than 85 per cent in terms of turnover and personnel taking, all the sectors it covers together. Its influence can be measured by the scope of its activities: Syntec Informatique takes responsibility for things usually dealt with by employers' organizations, such as defending and promoting collective professional advantages, dealing with social, political, economic, technical and deontological questions. Syntec also provides its members with certain services: aside from legal advice (especially in matters of employment), it produces data that allow companies to see where they stand and eventually improve their position, and it organizes workshops allowing members to get acquainted and function through networks. Parallel to these missions, Syntec has sought for several years to enhance its image and rid itself of the negative one it sometimes has of 'body market'. To accomplish this, besides reinforcing its communications policy and working more closely with the trade unions, the employers' organization has also developed influential networks. A strong point in that direction was the election of L. Parisot as the head of MEDEF (Mouvement des Entreprises de France): before becoming president of the largest employers' confederation in France, she headed up a Syntec company.

On the employees' side, the number of those belonging to a trade union is small and minutes of several meetings report a shortage of candidates during branch elections. All the large confederations (CGT, CFDT, FO, CFTC and CGC) nevertheless have a foot in the door through their unions. They are not alone, though, since one atypical actor is playing a role that can hardly be called trifling: created by a young, unemployed software developer, the MUNCI (Mouvement pour une Union Nationale des Consultants en Informatique, or Movement for a National Union of IT Consultants) was officially launched on 9 July 2003. In 2005, it claimed 800 members and declared sympathizers (30 per cent job seekers, 50 per cent employees and 20 per cent freelance). According to the MUNCI person with whom we spoke,[5] the real figure is closer to 200, and was thought to have dropped to 50 in 2006. Moreover, 'there were 30 people at the General Assembly last year, this year only six of us attended; also, nobody agrees on what we have to do or how we have to do it' (MUNCI activist). The declared aim of this Tom Thumb is to fight against the sector's tendency to promote blatant flexibility and to oppose the compromise agreements negotiated by the traditional trade unions. MUNCI also offers a whole range of services (legal aid, individual career coaching, a website reserved for members, reductions in certain bookshops and rebates for subscriptions to the specialized IT press, a newsletter, etc.).

Should one see in that sort of small organization the promise of a new style of professional relations setting in? In any case, the MUNCI activist whom we met has a number of significant acts to her credit: she has taken six people to the labour courts for harassment, unfair dismissal, discrimination against a union member and not adapting the workplace to persons with disabilities. Aside from that, MUNCI is regularly invited to various events (meetings in Parliament, meetings with Syntec). A journal as influential in the sector as *01 Informatique*[6] publishes some of the forums posted by MUNCI on the internet. When, in March 2007, Syntec suggested that the French Presidential candidates should make the regulations on work and labour more flexible, it was MUNCI that *Le Monde de l'Informatique* interviewed to offset the Syntec proposals. But, as the Syntec delegate remarked, 'MUNCI is an uncontrolled actor whose positions are not always very clear.' Because of that and because MUNCI is not as big or as legitimate a union as the CGT, the CFDT, etc. it is seen as difficult, under these conditions, to negotiate with it.

NEGOTIATING FLEXIBILITY

Though they reveal the transformations affecting French professional relations generally, the new actors who appear on the scene and upset the established rules have not had, if truth be told, any devastating effects on negotiations. Syntec can even be considered an actor that gives priority to collective bargaining. For the Syntec president of the Northern Region of France, the balance for professional contacts in the branches is even positive.

> We work enormously at the level of the sector and the union but also Syntec, we have an enormous number of agreements on certain problems in the sector. It's a bit more difficult today with the CPE [Contrat Première Embauche, First Employment Contract], positions are hardening, but on the whole in the sector we've always known how to find a compromise on major issues . . . The real problem that ruined relations with our partners for two years, was the crisis of 2001-2003, a lot of people were fired . . . [In spite of everything], we have a real policy inasmuch as contracts are concerned, even the CGT signs, besides you don't often hear talk about this sector.

Though we cannot go into the entire contract system here, we can mention a few major issues concerning flexibility in recent negotiations. We will present three of them below: working hours, contracts and training.

The first stake, working time, stirred up a large amount of conflict – which was new for the sector – when the 35-hour working week (Aubry laws) was being negotiated (Lallement, 2003). After six months of talks, a Syntec agreement was signed on 22 June 1999 by the employers' sector organizations and two trade unions (CFDT and FO). It was partially extended on 21 December 1999, totally on 10 November 2000. Aside from the fact it allows working time to be organized more flexibly, the most important result was that the negotiation linked flexibility to individual status. The Syntec agreement established a three-way typology that distinguished managers with 'full autonomy' from 'assignment managers' and 'other managers'. While for the first, the norm merely consists in not exceeding 219 workdays per year (reduced to 217 after Aubry 2), the second are caught in a double-bind, their number of days being limited to 217 a year and their number of hours to 35 per week. For the third group, the rule is 1,600 hours a year. That typology is peculiar to the sector and integrates at the same time the parameters connected to working conditions – assignment managers are typically employees who, in an SSII, are sent out to customer sites – and a hierarchy within the typology – fully autonomous managers are the best paid. As to working hours, although they have been officially regulated in the sector and in the companies, we know that in practice, in periods of economic tension, they are subject to all sorts of abuse.

The question of employment flexibility, our second subject, is top of employers' agendas. As we saw previously, the sector is not very hungry for particular forms of employment; the constant temptation is rather to make employment more flexible. In an interview published in the professional press on 10 July 2003, J. Mounet (executive officer of Syntec) declared, for example:

> we need work to be more flexible, when allocating days of reduced working time (*RTT*), for instance, or work on Sundays. Those are domains where a little more flexibility would be a good thing, both for the client-companies, the companies in the sector and collaborators . . .; short time employment is another question that has to be broached, so that we can be more competitive.

Among the instruments of flexibility that the federation tried to implement (see Syntec, 2003) are: individualizing short-time work; reducing the two-month deadline for posting vacation dates; setting up an assignment contract (corresponding to Mr de Virville's project contract[7]); and last but not least, the invention of a procedure to lay people off 'for lack of conformity to the state of the market'. But before the document was finalized, information leaked out from the employers' federation,[8] provoking an immediate outcry from the unions. Following the lead of the CFDT and the CGT, a petition made the rounds of the sector, and gathered 23,000 signatures in two months. The employers' vague attempts at reform were nipped in the bud, and only recently, during the presidential elections, did their organization come back to the subject.

Where, then, are those pockets of negotiated flexibility? In fact, as we have already mentioned, they can be found in the 'inter-contracts' – the periods between two assignments. Before 1999, inter-contracts were paid the same as working time. At the start of the negotiations, the employers proposed including the time between assignments in the bulk of hours and days of reduced working time. One can see why the unions protested so vigorously – it was even a major cause for conflict. At sector level, the way of solving the problem was by throwing it back to the companies, making them responsible for deciding how inter-contracts should be managed. A classic solution consists in sending the employees to train, thus outsourcing flexibility costs (our third object). Professional training is a major stake that has allowed a multitude of innovations to be introduced: an agreement was signed in February 1999 to integrate young people by setting up school-and-work programmes; a branch agreement to open an equal-representation observatory to supervise all IT, engineering, consulting and market research jobs was signed in March 2000; a definition of nine occupations requiring new skills boosted by the development of the Internet was hatched in July 2001; the signature of an agreement on the individual right to continuing education was signed in December 2004, followed by a professional certification in IT skills in 2005. Above all, the sector's equal-representation committee (in which there are as many members representative of the unions as of employer's organizations) in charge of fundraising for occupational training administers a considerable budget (more than 200 million euros in 2007). Our attempts at investigating that committee encountered a good deal of resistance. However, though we are not immediately able to put our hands on all the empirical elements that would show in detail how the largest businesses resort to professional training in order to externalize their flexibility costs (see above), we can interpret as a form of explicit denial what a former president of the OPCA (organisme paritaire collecteur agréé[9]) told us when asked if large companies did not profit from the system more than small ones:

> We're careful about that because there are people who really know how it functions, because you've . . . you've got the unions on one side and the employers on the other, there are employers who know perfectly well how things work; we're very careful that they – the big companies – don't delve into the FAFIEC budget before anyone else, we're very careful about that.

CONCLUSION

Frequently likened to a model of professional activity that has managed to reconcile what employees today demand (autonomy, being multi-tasked, diplomas, voluntary mobility) with the requirements of a modern economy (being reactive, in touch with the clientele, active in networks), the engineering and IT consulting sector is in reality far from the image generally associated with it and which still prevails. Its structure has little to do with the idea of a space filled with myriads of start-ups, each more groundbreaking than the next. The leading companies are the large multi-national consulting firms which more than ever steer the profession on the road to rationalization – of products, systems and norms. If they coexist with a multitude of small companies, it is all the better to lean on them if needed and use them as a bulwark against economic hazards.

Besides, everything does not take place in the firm or get negotiated there exclusively; flexibility is also a matter of industrial relations. As we have seen, a multitude of stakes has structured the conflicts and negotiations of these past years, in the name of flexibility: recomposing the manager category, financing training programmes, inventing new forms of repre-sentation to defend the interests of personnel. Flexibility has disrupted not only the substantive rules relative to work and employment, but also other rules, whether substantive – when they concern occupational hierarchies – or procedural – negotiations on working time, for example.

In the end, the typical profile of the IT engineer and consultant in France cumulates characteristics that prevent us from putting him or her in the same bag as the hyper-flexible worker. The great majority of jobs in the sector are based on open-ended labour contracts, which does not in itself rule out flexibility. Based on assignment at customer site, the job implies much moving about. Spatial mobility is compounded by temporal flexibility. In a sector where the contents and forms of labour are regulated by the client company and team of peers, working hours are long, and meted out in a highly unpredictable manner. Inter-contracts are also a lever for flexibility, frequently used by companies to handle difficult demands as needed. In short, the elastic quality of professional time and working conditions – which at a time of offshoring, many employees feel are getting harsher (Berrebi-Hoffmann et al., 2010) – as well as relatively uncertain and muddy career perspectives (Lallement and Sarfati, 2009), oblige us to paint a landscape which decidedly has little in common with the fascinating image drawn by the advocates of out-and-out flexibility. Even if the stability of the contract is still the rule in French IT services, the trend is towards a work intensification and harsher conditions for workers who have to build a client relationship in a more competitive environment.

Globalization through offshoring in the sector has led to shorter service contracts and an increasing pressure on productivity because of competition from Indian and Chinese firms.

NOTES

Our thanks to Gabrielle Varro for the translation.
1. The research was carried out within the framework of 'Dynamo', a European networking project piloted by the Arbeit und Qualifikation de Gelsenkirchen Institute. For further details, see the report in Berrebi-Hoffmann et al. (2006). When writing up the report, we also used data from the survey carried out by Berrebi-Hoffmann et al. (2010).
2. 'Meat markets', like 'body markets', is a pejorative expression used by some workers to explain that their employers can sell their services to any client whenever they want.
3. At present, the most sought-after countries for outsourcing software activities are India (80 per cent of offshoring world-wide), the Philippines and China. The United States and the United Kingdom are among the first importers of offshore activities. For France, the McKinsey Global Institute (2005) calculated that approximately 2 to 6 per cent of software jobs were offshore.
4. http://www.zdnet.fr/actualites/informatique (accessed 2009).
5. At the time of our interview, she was part of the MUNCI steering committee but also belonged to a 'classic' trade union and, as such, represented her company's personnel.
6. In 2008, *01 Informatique* averaged a circulation of 57,567 per issue (source: Association pour le Contrôle de la Diffusion des Médias), available at:http//www.ojd.com/.
7. A report on employment law reform, commissioned by the French government, was issued in January 2004. The most controversial proposal in the 'Virville report' is the creation of a new 'assignment contract' or 'project contract', enabling employees to be recruited for the duration of a particular project.
8. It appears that the preliminary document may have been sent to the CGT by members of Syntec themselves.
9. An OPCA is a public organization in charge of collecting a national tax in order to build a national training fund for workers. The fund is financed by companies of the sector according to their turnover.

REFERENCES

AP Management (2007), 'Concentration du secteur logiciel et services: comment le marché se consolide?', available at: http://www.apmanagement.fr/Francais/etude_concentration.pdf (accessed 2007).

Berrebi-Hoffmann, I. (2002), 'Les multinationales du conseil', *Sociologies Pratiques*, **6**, 47–69.

Berrebi-Hoffmann, I. (2006), 'Les consultants et informaticiens: un modèle d'encadrement de professionnels à l'échelle industrielle?', *Revue Française de Gestion*, **32** (168–9), 157–76.

Berrebi-Hoffmann, I., M. Lallement, M. Pernod-Lemattre and F. Sarfati (2006), 'The IT sector in France: an overview', 'Dynamo', IT workshop, Paris, December.

Berrebi-Hoffmann, I., M. Lallement and O. Piriou (2010), 'La division internationale du travail dans les services informatiques: off shore et politiques de ressources humaines dans les grands groupes de service et d'ingénierie informatique (SSII)', Paris: Document de Travail de l'Agence pour l'Emploi des Cadres.

Boltanski, L. and E. Chiapello (1999), *Le nouvel esprit du capitalisme*, Paris: Gallimard.

Boyer R. (1986), *La flexibilité du travail en Europe*, Paris: La Découverte.

Fondeur, Y. and C. Sauviat (2003), 'Les services informatiques aux entreprises : un "marché de compétences"', *Formation Emploi*, **82**, 107–22.

Geyer, D. (2007), 'L'externalisation offshore de système d'information', *Revue Française de Gestion*, **8** (177), 129–39.

Houdré, T. and M. Lelièvre (2008), 'Le off shore, un phénomène de mode?', *Problèmes Economiques*, **2949**, (4 June), 44–7.

INSEE (2009), 'Travail, emploi', available at: http://www.insee.fr/fr/themes/theme. asp?theme=3.

Jlassi, M. and X. Niel (2008), 'La sous-traitance des tâches liées aux nouvelles technologies', *INSEE Premières* (April), **1183**.

Lallement, M. (2003), *Temps, travail et modes de vie*, Paris: Presses Universitares de France.

Lallement, M. and F. Sarfati (2009), 'La carrière contre le travail? Savoirs, activités et trajectoires de jeunes experts de la finance et de l'informatique', *Cahiers Internationaux de Sociologie*, **126**, 115–30.

McKinsey Global Institute (2005), Emerging Global Labor Markets.

Mounet, J. (2003), 'Une plus grande flexibilité du travail est nécessaire à notre secteur', 10 July, available at: http://www.journaldunet.com/solutions/ itws/030711_it_mounet.shtml.

Sennett, R. (1998), *The Corrosion of Character: The Personal Consequences of Work in the New Capitalism*, New York: W.W. Norton.

Syntec (2003), *Document de position* (17 December), Paris: Syntec.

Syntec (2006), *Situation actuelle et développement de l'off shore dans les services informatiques en France (SSII)*, Collection ThémaTIC (January), **4**.

10. The increasing use of 'market' concepts in negotiations, and contextualizing factors

Jens Thoemmes

INTRODUCTION

This chapter is based on a series of research projects on the negotiation of working time relating to company-level agreements in France (and in other European countries) from the early 1990s. Collective bargaining between employers and trade unions has profoundly changed the working conditions of companies. We propose to trace this change from what we have achieved over fifteen years of research in this field. Our aim is to deepen the theory of negotiation with particular respect to the role collective bargaining on working time plays in organizational structuring. Collective bargaining in French companies is framed by legislation. We therefore address the whole process of regulation of working time, which combines the activities of trade unions, employers and the state.

Our theoretical framework draws first on the theory of social regulation (Reynaud, 1979), and then on the theory of organizational work, developed by Gilbert de Terssac. De Terssac (2003a) argues that work also involves organizing; the organizational component cannot be separated from the productive. The usual distinction between the work of management viewed as organizational work, and the execution of work as productive work without an organizational dimension, is meaningless. On this theory, collective bargaining can be considered as work that takes place in the productive sphere, which itself is characterized by a relationship of subordination. In this sense the work of negotiators produces social change, and modifies working conditions. Our chapter aims to focus on this change.

The negotiation process developed over a period of 150 years, initiated originally by the labour and union movement. The impetus for changes to working conditions was linked to the protection and health of workers at their workplace. However, the years from 1982 to 2002 have seen a new direction, where market concepts are increasingly employed in negotiations. A particular emphasis on changes involving variable norms of work duration, as well as incentives to maintain or create employment, show new forms of co-ordination of labour and product markets. The use of market concepts is generally widespread in the developed economies. Historically as well as in the current period, globalization results from the application of market concepts; but the collective bargaining experience in France still concerns a fairly regulated state of labour. We will show that there is no necessary contradiction between the use of market concepts and a regulated state of labour, and that trends towards the introduction of market concepts go beyond narrow conceptions of precarious forms of labour, like part-time work or temporary work, to penetrate the core of the workforce.

From some perspectives, working conditions may worsen as a result of the use of new market concepts. We will see that the focus of employers and unions is not on precarity in the classical way (part-time, temporary work), but on stability of employment and on collective agreements. Nevertheless, public policy and different pieces of legislation aim at commodifying working time and working conditions. But the introduction of new market methods is a negotiated terrain. Companies and unions do not blindly follow legislative intentions: there is a complex give-and-take process that changes the outcomes of collective agreements.

REGULATION OF WORKING TIME AND THE MARKET

Trends Towards the Reduction of Working Time Over the Last Century

While issues of employment and flexibility tend to focus on the importance of labour markets and product markets, a brief review of the legislation of working time in France shows, by contrast, that the slow emergence of working-time regulations was based on other concerns.

For a century and a half, working time has been constructed as a collective norm, a measure of stability around what might be called a standard by an anchoring of rules in labour law, and the creation of special inspectors charged with overseeing the implementation of these regulations in business. This standard of working time emerged in three great periods: the first (1830–41) established state intervention in the relationship between employer and employees, and the second (1841–1904) dedicated inspectors as the actor responsible for enforcing the law and punishing abuses by employers. The third (1904–82) established the time standard for all with a stable week, fixed daily hours, two consecutive days off and five weeks of leave.

A law in 1906 established a weekly rest day on Sunday. The labour law stipulates, however, that 'some exceptions (concerning weekly rest days) may occur in some cases, with a weekly rest day on another day than Sunday' (article L. 221-2, quoted by Grossin, 1992, p. 249). The 8-hour day established by law (23 April 1919) had been a trade union issue from 1888. But its implementation was gradual and sectoral. This law was passed after World War I, following the conflict that led the government of Clemenceau to avoid a test of strength with the trade unions. Strikes with factory occupations in May–June 1936 led to two further laws 'establishing the first 40-hour week without loss of pay', and introducing paid holidays (Fridenson, 1993, pp. 25–6).

The four main components of the working time standard temporal order are (Thoemmes, 2000):

- a standard or social norm (covering weekly and daily rest times and holiday entitlements);
- state intervention as a normative power;
- creation of collective recipients by the common rule;
- highly developed sanctions.

The search for competitive flexibility from the 1980s saw a revision of this conception of time and was characterized by the abandonment of the traditional scheme of collective bargaining around the limitation of working hours which was at the centre of discussions for a century and a half. The length of daily and weekly working hours in itself, which were the subject of the very constitution of the labour movement, was abandoned by unions, employers and public policies in favour of the logic of production and its extension through various methods of temporal flexibility.

This chapter aims to explore this new way of dealing with working time. What is the content of this new direction? By what process has this direction become widespread? Does this new tendency mark the end of protections for individuals at work? Or is it a new way of negotiating under the auspices of markets that actually retains an established way of seeing working time?

Shifting the View from Health to Markets

Employers and unions, backed by the state, have clearly changed the way of conceiving working time. That does not mean a shift in power to employers, but certainly a change in union policies: 'less health and more employment' could be the summary. How does this view fit with the shift to markets? Our contribution will address the period 1982–2002. Collective bargaining has indeed changed the nature of the process. The rationality of the process based on the health of the worker has been replaced by a rationality linked to markets. In just 20 years of collective bargaining, the variability of working hours, the desire to be 'close' to product markets, and employment stability replaced the trend towards reducing working hours and improving employee welfare. The first two of these issues are employer aspirations, while the third is on the labour movement agenda. This evolution is also reflected in the legislation. This is what we have termed the arrival of 'market times' (Thoemmes, 2006a). However, the change in rationality of the process and the outcomes for organizations have been neither predictable nor inevitable: they are the result of the work of the negotiators, which can be considered as organizational work.

Theories of industrial relations (primarily Anglo-Saxon) already addressed the issue of markets in the context of collective bargaining. The work of Dunlop (1958) and Kochan et al. (1986) shows the importance of the environment in general and the influence of the market in particular for the content of collective bargaining. In their book *The Transformation of American Industrial Relations*, Kochan et al. (1986) discuss changes in the industrial relations system in the United States explicitly referring to Dunlop's (1958) *Industrial Relations Systems*: key players such as employees, management and the government produce rules, while incorporating the surrounding context, including economic, technical and other legal and social forces. Thus the introduction of concepts such as 'markets' and 'environment' in addition to the analysis of the traditional forces of collective bargaining is central to the understanding of the system of industrial relations in the United States.

With respect to Europe, we would also like to stress the presence of another element in the relationship between industrial relations and markets, namely the construction of Europe as an entity: the creation of a common market which could influence the industrial relations system of European countries. Does Europeanization, the political construction of a market, ultimately produce a harmonization of social systems? And what are the relationships that emerge within the industrial relations systems, which remain national? Regarding relations between the state of industrial relations and the market in Europe, the arguments in *Industrial Relations in the New Europe*, edited by Ferner and Hyman (1992), remain valid. Their analysis is based on 17 nations and their industrial relations, following the Maastricht Treaty agreements on the single currency and the social charter. The context of Europeanization cannot conceal the extreme variety of situations from one state to another. In the introduction (ibid.), the authors emphasize the progressive integration of European economies in a global economy dominated by multinational enterprises. By refusing to view the development of industrial relations as a simple passage from a Fordist to a post-Fordist (the theory of economic regulation), the authors focus on the link between the economic context and regulatory institutions. Regarding the decentralization of industrial relations, Ferner and Hyman put forward, *inter alia*, the promotion of decentralization through political choice with a legitimacy linked to market forces, as was the case in England. While the conclusion focuses on a weakening of unions in most European countries, Ferner and Hyman emphasize that the effects of recession and growing instability did not originate through labour market competition, but rather through the uncertainties generated by product market competition.

In sum, market-related concepts, working time and working conditions can be understood in a wider perspective as a globalization issue linked to political choice and new forms of legitimacy. This issue is particularly pertinent for developed countries, especially the United States and the European Union.

The Use of the Concept of Organizational Work

We would argue that industrial relations must also incorporate the theory of social regulation (Reynaud, 1979; de Terssac, 2003b). With respect to social regulation and the market, we would like to deepen the concept of 'organizational work' put forward by de Terssac (2003b). For us, collective bargaining is itself a genuine form of 'organizational work' undertaken by employers, unions and the state. Market times are the results of a long-term process in which collective bargaining is considered as work producing a result. Indeed, in the words of de Terssac (2003b: 123), the learning process represented by organizational work goes through different phases of experimentation, generalization and differentiation before reaching a more or less stable state. Outcomes or results are achieved through the confrontation of different projects and collective actors.

The main reason for using this form of theorization is to consider 'organizing' activities as a job itself, as an activity that serves productive activities, and should therefore be analysed as work (de Terssac, 2003b). Collective bargaining is part of organizational work in the sense that it structures the world of work and defines its conditions. From this perspective we can trace the slow introduction of a new form of French collective bargaining, one that did not arrive unprepared or without any actors.

What is the interest of using this concept of organizational work? The analysis by de Terssac and Lalande (2002) is based on the reorganization of an existing company, the management of SNCF (rail) freight. The reorganization passes through three stages of learning. A first phase called 'experimental' covers the invention of new working rules, while a second phase of 'generalization' applies it to all equipment and facilities. Finally a third phase of 'differentiation' adapts this pattern to specific projects. For them, according to Reynaud's preface, 'organizational learning is not a long river, it is characterized neither by the continuity of the progression of ideas, nor by harmonious collaborations nor by an equilibrium of power' (Reynaud, 2002, p. 11).

In a concluding chapter entitled 'Sociology of the organizational work of maintenance', de Terssac et Lalande specify the scope of the three phases: 'the experimental phase is characterized by learning by trial and error: to invent effective solutions and to test them compared to the objectives; the focus is placed here on experience, practice and observation which builds knowledge of maintenance' (2002, p. 187). After this first phase, which aims to seek solutions to problems, the second phase of generalization induces learning by application to indicate that the goal is well known (aligning the production sites on the same pattern and showing the outcome: the objective is to generalize the patterns established in the previous phase (ibid., p. 188). We will show by analogy that the 35-hour law implemented a generalization of a new pattern of organization, coupled with the collective bargaining of businesses. Finally comes the adjustment phase, where a learning process takes a third way. 'However, there is no questioning of the founding principles: one is in a logic of improved operations at the margin' (ibid., 189). We will build on the concept of organizational work occurring in three phases to analyse the dynamics of collective bargaining in connection with the legal framework.

Of course we recognize the limits of this approach in relation to national policies covering all businesses. While in an individual company a modernization project can be clearly identified by actors heading in the direction of modernization, or by those who oppose the project, with governments that change and with a wide variety of situations to be resolved it seems more difficult to identify clearly a national-level policy. Instead of using the term 'modernization' here, we use the term 'social change'. There is indeed a difference between a company and larger territory. The single company gives rise to a form of regulation with clearly demarcated borders, and linkages between projects and production rules. National public policies, however, produce standard-setting covering a range of extremely heterogeneous situations, without an explicit sense of organizational development over time. The great planner does not exist. Social change over a long period in our case is established without being consciously put in place. In sum, this application of organizational theory and the concept of work to collective bargaining – which is a work of negotiation (Dugué, 2005) – is of course an *ex post* construction that we use to explore our empirical findings.

THE ORGANIZATIONAL WORK OF COLLECTIVE BARGAINING IN FIVE STEPS: INTRODUCING THE CONCEPT OF MARKETS (1982–2002)

The concept of organizational work at a regional or national level raises questions. Indeed, the complexity of this approach is linked to the multiplicity of actors and levels of regulation: the national level and the level of business, the level of legal initiatives and collective agreements. This association between company and public policy is mediated in many cases by regionalized branch agreements, which redefine the balance between law and company agreements (Jobert and Saglio, 2004). In this chapter we report primarily on the interaction between law and company bargaining. The analysis of collective bargaining over a period of 20 years in a French region[1] shows the organizational work that was needed to establish a new rule which we call 'market times' (Thoemmes, 2006a). This rule was not the automatic result of a process. It has suffered setbacks, especially when collective bargaining did not follow the proposals of lawmakers.

Genesis (1982–93)

Working-time laws changed considerably from 1982. The initiative clearly came from the government, combining working-time reduction and flexibility issues. The influence of employers and unions on the different laws remains unclear. While working-time reduction and employment creation have always been union objectives, the give-and-take process related to flexibility was clearly also in the employers' interest. Three legal rules affected the period in question. The order of 16 January 1982 reduced legal weekly working hours from 40 to 39, introduced a fifth week of paid leave, and invented the principle of 'modulation' (varying duration of work over a defined period) to 42 hours per week. The Delabarre law of 26 February 1986 then defined the reduction of working hours as a trade-off for the 'modulation' of working hours. Finally, the Seguin law of 11 June 1987 allowed 'modulation' agreements in which the reduction of working hours was only optional.

This first phase of collective bargaining deals with the genesis of the collective variability of working hours, here specifically the method called 'modulation annualization', a varying duration of work over a defined period, especially a 12-month period (Bunel, 2004). This concept is understood by us as including several methods introduced over time which institute a 'corridor' allowing for the variation of weekly working hours (between 32 hours and 44 hours, for example), and where hours that exceed the average (35 hours, for example) are not regarded as overtime. Of course, overtime already allowed negotiators or entrepreneurs to vary working hours, and partial unemployment benefits already allowed for the compensation of employees for loss of employment activity. But the peculiarity of this phase from 1982 to 1993 relates to an early normalization of changing working time (including variability for all) by means of collective agreements. The first types of 'modulation' (1982, 1986 and 1987) indeed included this variability in different forms and conditions within the 'normal and usual' working hours. The variable standard thus first emerged in these laws. The genesis of the particular types was formalized by law and by 'exploratory' use by negotiators. But in fact they were rarely used by businesses; few such agreements came through: in our sample there were only eight such agreements per year.

Experimentation (1993–96)

Two laws characterized the next period focusing on the above-mentioned give-and-take process and on the possibility of individual time saving. Once again the government drove the changes. The first was the 'five-year law' of 20 December 1993. It established an extension of the period over which hours of work could vary, and put in place an experimental subsidized incentive to reduce working hours (an annual reduction of 15 per cent in working hours, compulsory reduction of salaries, and recruitment of at least 10 per cent). This was followed by the law of Time Saving Accounts (TSA) of 25 July 1994, which allowed the accumulation of worked hours and days giving rights to extra paid leave. The extra paid leave had to be taken before the expiration of a five-year period. The individual TSA was permitted only within the terms of a collective agreement. The TSA could also be used by the employer to vary within certain limits the effects of a reduction of working hours over a period of several years. The variable standard (modulation) of working hours was linked by the legislature to compensatory methods (reduction of working hours) and to complementary methods (TSA).

The second phase thus begins in 1993, with the experience of a new give-and-take process between working-hour cuts and modulation annualization. This could be seen as a consequence of the little impact that the latter method had had during the previous phase. It is not that a give-and-take process would not have been possible before, but the innovation of article 39 of the 1993 Act explicitly laid down a new opportunity to experiment with modulation, combined with the reduction of working hours and employment, funded with financial compensation by the state (Morin et al., 1998). This innovation introduced by the 'five-year law' underlines our analysis of the phase from 1994 to 1996 as 'experimentation' or 'testing' of a new give-and-take process through collective bargaining. However, this did not succeed – the 'testing' failed. On the one hand, it was drowned in a set of pre-existing flexible time mechanisms: the negotiation seemed 'broken'. Indeed, we identified 28 different topics on working time in the agreements. On the other hand, only a few companies proceeded to this kind of give-and-take: the annual rate of use of 'modulation' decreased in our regional sample to only six agreements per year. However, the failure of this experiment laid the foundations for another period, initiated by the de Robien law, from 1996 to 1998, which succeeded in 'repositioning' collective bargaining in the give-and-take process already suggested by the previous laws.

Refocusing (1996–98)

This period covers a single piece of legislation which was very important in influencing the process of ongoing negotiations. This law reflected the organizational learning process that had taken place through company-level negotiation but also through the back-and-forth relationship with Parliament. The de Robien law of 11 June 1996 provided state funding where companies created or maintained employment within at least 10 per cent of the original situation while voluntarily agreeing to reduce average working hours by at least 10 per cent. While initiated by the government, this law responded to demands from local actors, both employers and unions, in a period of economic uncertainty. The goal was primarily to avoid layoffs and to support employment.

From the perspective of company bargaining this third phase, after genesis and experimentation based on article 39 of the 'five-year law', again attempted to establish an exchange: 'reduction' against 'variability' in the framing of a single law (de Robien). Indeed this law focused more strongly on 'jobs' than the previous laws. This time, collective bargaining finally and effectively decided between various mechanisms of temporal flexibility and proceeded to their association with the reduction of working hours.

What changed and why do we consider that this law is a turning point in collective bargaining? On the one hand, certain articles were modified: there was an extension of the period of subsidies, the inclusion of job creation, the reduction of working hours, and no corresponding obligation to reduce wages. On the other hand, it was a single piece of law with no other intention than focusing on the question of working time. This law profited from a media or publicity effect which, according to some of our interlocutors, played in favour of the acceptance of the method. It promoted a kind of collective 'local time sharing' to prevent unemployment and which tried to end a certain industrial relations logjam indicated by the low number of company agreements.

Now, although collective bargaining still had 'no obligation to reach an outcome', it effectively moved into a concession bargaining give-and-take process. The reduction of working hours was traded against modulation annualization and established a new standard. In this 'refocusing of collective bargaining' phase the variable standard of working time definitely entered collective bargaining. New agreements (one in two) were increasingly negotiated at the regional level over a two-year period: 49 out of 96 new agreements. This time the law was able to induce the desired response in companies, but without becoming a systematic or a widespread form of agreement. However, the total number of agreements remained at a relatively low level (48 new agreements per year).

Let us summarize this evolution: genesis, testing and refocusing can be used to describe the phases of negotiations induced by the law. These phases led qualitatively and quantitatively to the production of a new type of agreement. The pivotal position of the de Robien law can be seen to have highlighted the exchange of working time cuts with the maintenance of employment to enable the greater use of flexible time arrangements. One could say that in a particular context the law created the conditions for a more favourable response by companies: based on clear commitments in terms of jobs, on an extension of the duration of the subsidies (up to seven years) and without obligation to reduce wages. But wage moderation was also experienced in this phase. Some agreements limited wage increases in future years. Under these conditions, the unions seemed to accept some flexibility related to the variability of working hours in order to maintain or create jobs. The 'variable standard' effectively entered collective bargaining.

The genesis, experimentation and refocusing are subsets of the experimental phase of organizational work within the analysis of de Terssac and Lalande (2002). If we have chosen to qualify these three sub-phases as distinct phases, it is because the orientations of legislators and negotiators show clear differences between them: the genesis phase is followed by the formal creation of an experimentation phase that leads to a choice between different methods; refocusing then introduces a variable standard of working hours that corresponds to the actual social practices taking place, proposed by the legislature and accepted by the company negotiators.

Generalization (1998–2002)

The laws on the 35-hour week in France then generalized this new blue-print for collective bargaining, while the reduction of working hours was extended to all businesses. Moreover, the terms of the trade-offs (annualization, jobs, subsidies, future wage moderation in some cases) clearly derived from the previous phase.

There were two parts to the generalization law. The Aubry law (1) of 13 June 1998 established legal working time as 35 hours per week from January 2000 for companies with more than 20 employees and from January 2002 for the rest. The subsidies given to companies were related to the volumes of employment created. The Aubry law (2) of 19 January 2000 set a ceiling of a maximum of 1,600 hours per year, without any obligations for employment volume. From a collective bargaining perspective this fourth phase can be viewed as the generalization of the new action plan for collective bargaining. The 35-hour law of 1998 moved the situation from 'voluntary' to 'mandatory' negotiation. The pressure exerted by the spectre of legally enforced reductions in working time promoted company-level bargaining. It also disseminated widely the new general standard in business. The agreements followed in the path of previous de Robien agreements: significant reductions of working hours, state subsidies and variable norms of duration. In our sample of 1,232 new regional agreements (Aubry law 1 and 2), two out of three companies, more than 800 companies, agreed modulation annualization mechanisms. Only 37.9 per cent (under Aubry 1) and 30.7 per cent (under Aubry 2) of agreements did not introduce this type of mechanism.

Differentiation (1998–2008)

The fifth phase of differentiation begins at the same time as the generalization in 1998. With Aubry 1 and 2, this phase went beyond the time extensions given to very small businesses to implement the law. The laws also created three different categories of managers (those time-measured in hours worked, those measured by days worked and those whose working time was not measured at all) (Aubry 2), and allowed exceptional treatment for certain industries. The assumption was that the generalization needed adaptation to different contexts in order to become effective. From an organizational point of view, this phase of differentiation should not be seen as inconsistent with generalization, since in our view, the global objective is not only to generalize the reduction of working hours, but also to promote 'market times' including in this specific form, its variability, employment and state subsidies.

Does this interpretation of a change in pattern of action apply to newer developments regarding overtime, for example? We believe that we are still in the stage of differentiation of the legal rule and are neither in a phase of abandonment of the 35 hours, nor in the case of a return to a process of rationality putting 'health' and well-being at the centre of discussions which had opened up the reduction of working hours 150 years ago. Without being able to push our analysis beyond our regional sample of the 2,000 agreements of the period 1982–2002, we believe that recent developments none the less reinforce our analysis on two points.

First, laws and decrees on overtime in recent years have opened the possibility of increasing the quota of overtime and of further fiscal subsidies regarding overtime (no more income tax on overtime). Recent laws could result in an extension of real working hours (laws 2005–296, 2007–1223). However, this type of extension of working hours does not change the legal duration of work (remaining at 35 hours a week) and is perfectly in line with the variability of working hours. The legal duration has not changed but its potential variability is expanding with the increasing use of traditional means (such as overtime).

Secondly, collective bargaining has produced some emblematic agreements in the region demonstrating the new logic of 'market times'. Thus recently an important subcontractor to the auto industry reached an agreement on a working week of 38 hours without derogating from the 35-hour law. The additional quantity of work performed by each employee was actually placed on a time-savings account and called 'time capital'. This account was maintained for several years (2008, 2009), until the company, for the purpose of reorganization, gave the time back without any individual choice for the employee (2009, 2010), thereby absorbing the voluntary accumulated leave (company agreement, July 2007). This was an example of 'market times' based on a time-savings account on a multi-year time horizon. A new standard driven by the needs of production has entered into a collective agreement.

The entire cycle of organizational work we described is coming to an end. The phase of differentiation will perhaps initiate a new cycle. The 35-hour rule could be abolished, but what would happen to the give-and-take process which promoted flexibility? The variability of working hours and the issue of labour and product markets could survive the abandonment of the reduction of working hours. Certainly, we could see a return to a focus on diminishing the legal duration of work 'in itself' (before 1982), or we could experience its extension. The first option seems unrealistic given the initiatives in favour of overtime and given the recent political pressure against further working-time reductions. Nevertheless, the current crisis could provoke a new debate on further working-time cuts. But this would be compensated for by new market-related mechanisms as shown by the Aubry law. The second option, the unconditional extension of legal working time, would change the terms of trade between unions and employers, and its legitimacy would also be viewed differently. It would be hard to explain why the unions would accept giving up the advantages of working-time reductions in favour of accumulating flexible market-related mechanisms alone.

DISCUSSION

An analysis of collective bargaining over 20 years shows that the negotiators have not complied with a planned political initiative that would have produced a new rationality for negotiation. Rather, this result was achieved by trial and error and a give-and-take process including changes in the legal framework. Negotiators are framed by legal action, but retain their freedom to change and to interpret it. This is precisely the purpose of the phases that we have identified.

We discussed successively five phases of the negotiation of company agreements: genesis, experimentation, refocusing, generalization and differentiation of the rule. The rule has been produced by law and by collective bargaining. Its meaning can be seen as the arrival of market times, and as another way to negotiate labour conditions. The first element of the rule is related to the introduction of mechanisms to implement and control the variability of working hours (variable standard or norm). The second element concerns the issue of employment, including its stabilization. This new articulation of labour and product markets is gained by reducing the duration of work and has been heavily subsidized from 1998 to the present day. Negotiators could very well have had recourse to a shift to part-time work, night work and weekend work as traditional forms of precarious labour. This is not the option that the negotiations that we have discussed put as central.

Although the new scheme of action is also a generalization of temporal flexibility, it is by no means an obvious shift to 'standard forms of insecurity or precarious work'. Employment stability, with the control of variability of working time, circumscribes the new pattern of collective bargaining: the rationality of the negotiation process has shifted from health to markets. This perspective suggests analysing collective bargaining as the scope of an exchange between groups which have to take into account changing environmental conditions. This view of negotiation as a combination of the effects of markets and the production of arrangements seems fundamental (Kochan et al., 1986). Working time has been the tool of choice for spreading 'market times', under specific conditions, to a large number of French companies. The five phases of organizational work which led to this new scheme are certainly only one way to describe an evolution in the long run. From an analytical perspective we are dealing indeed with an accumulation of specific practices, an aggregation of partial results, framed by laws, and produced by variable groups, political parties, unions, employers and governments. One cannot easily compare a region or a nation to a productive enterprise in which 'modernization' may pursue an objective involving all parts of the company (de Terssac and Lalande, 2002). Yet the advantage of using the concept of organizational work is, in our view, its heuristic value, based on longitudinal analysis, the line of laws and negotiations, the analysis of their parentage and the learning process even through the boundaries that usually separate groups. Companies have interpreted the legal framework reflecting at the same time the concerns of local negotiators. We are certainly experiencing a shift of the production of standards to the company and to the local businesses. Negotiated public action (Groux, 2001) has more a sense of encouragement of negotiation, rather than a rigid and unifying law. The instruments are not only the laws on working time (Lascoumes and Le Galès, 2004), but also the various agreements that have been formulated through an effective 'work of negotiation' (Dugué, 2005). Indeed, collective bargaining did not always follow particular incentives and legal recommendations. This view suggests a focal area for collective action. Negotiators have felt that the 'market' is an area of compromise and conflict, not just an 'external pressure' (Haipeter and Lehndorff, 2004). The market is not an external reality, but a stage upon which social groups operate (Chessel and Cochoy, 2004).

CONCLUSION

In sum, if working time over 20 years of collective bargaining was emancipated, a longitudinal study of more than 2,000 enterprise agreements shows a change of substance. We observed a trend for collective bargaining to replace an emphasis on action related to the health and well-being of the worker with one related to priorities determined by markets. The rationality of the action has changed. This does not mean that all protection for people at work has been abandoned, but does mean that a change of perspective and preferences has nevertheless been made. This change of perspective does not favour precarious work in the traditional way: part-time, temporary work, temporary unemployment or other forms of precarious contracts. This change concerns a far bigger number of employees.

The point is that the majority of 'non-precarious' employees are submitted to the new regime. In other words the core of the workforce is experiencing market times, because the change was made through law and collective bargaining. Finally, market times bring us back to globalization. As we showed recently (Thoemmes, 2008), the German automaker Volkswagen, while having a completely different system of industrial relations, seems to be taking a similar route. German companies are adopting more and more market times without being as systematic as in the French case. Other societies may experience market times in different ways. We think, nevertheless, that collective bargaining is necessary to establish new rules. This is especially the case over measures in favour of employment and offering protection against unemployment, which cannot be negotiated or explained with a theoretical conception that markets are 'out of control'. On the contrary, regulation was necessary to establish the scheme of action in the French case. One might call this 'negotiated globalization'.

NOTE

1. This chapter reports on a series of studies on company bargaining in a region of Southern France over two decades. In all, we had access to an exhaustive sample of 2,000 agreements covering the period 1982–2002. Partial results were published in the form of either reports, articles or book chapters. The objective of this chapter is not to go into the detailed analysis made during these studies, but rather to submit for discussion a sociological assessment covering the whole period.

REFERENCES

Bunel, M. (2004), 'Modulation/annualisation dans le cadre des 35 heures: entreprises et salaries sous contrainte', *Travail et Emploi*, **98**, 51–65.
Chessel, M.-E. and F. Cochoy (2004), 'Autour de la consommation engagée: enjeux historiques et politiques', *Sciences de la Société*, **62**, 2–4.
De Terssac, G. (2003a), 'Travail d'organisation et travail de régulation', in G. de Terssac (ed.), *La théorie et de la régulation sociale de Jean-Daniel Reynaud: débat et prolongements*, Paris: La Découverte, pp. 121–34.
De Terssac, G. (ed.) (2003b), *La théorie et de la régulation sociale de Jean-Daniel Reynaud: débat et prolongements,* , Paris: La Découverte.
De Terssac, G. and K. Lalande (2002), *Du train à vapeur au TGV: sociologie du travail d'organisation*, Paris: Presses Universitaires de France.
Dugué, B. (2005), *Le travail de négociation*, Toulouse: Octarès.
Dunlop, J. (1958), *Industrial Relations Systems*, Carbondale: Southern Illinois University Press.
Ferner, A. and R. Hyman (eds) (1992), *Industrial Relations in the New Europe*, Oxford: Blackwell.
Fridenson, P. (1993), 'Le temps de travail, enjeu de luttes sociales', in J. Y.

Boulin, G. Cette and D. Taddei (eds), *Le temps de travail*, Paris: Syros pp. 19–28.

Grossin, W. (1992), *La création de l'Inspection du travail*, Paris: L'Harmattan.

Groux, G. (ed.) (2001), 'L'action publique négociée: Approches à partir des 35 heures – France–Europe', coll., *Logiques politiques*, Paris: L'Harmattan.

Haipeter,T. and S. Lehndorff (2004), *Atmende Betriebe, atemlose Beschäftigite?*, Berlin: Edition Sigma.

Jobert, A. and J. Saglio (2004), 'Ré-institutionnaliser la négociation collective en France', *Travail et Emploi*, **100**, 113–27.

Kochan, T., H. Katz and R. McKersie (1986), *The Transformation of American Industrial Relations*, New York: Basic Books.

Lascoumes P. and P. Le Galès (2004), 'Introduction: l'action publique saisie par ses instruments', in P. Lascoumes and P. Le Galès (eds), *Gouverner par les instruments*, Paris: Presses de la Fondation Nationale des Sciences Politiques, pp. 11–44.

Morin, M.L., G. de Terssac and J. Thoemmes (1998), 'La négociation du temps de travail: l'emploi en jeu', *Sociologie du Travail*, **2**, 191–207.

Reynaud, J-D. (1979), 'Conflit et régulation sociale: esquisse d'une régulation conjointe,' *Revue Française de Sociologie*, **20**, 367–76.

Reynaud, J-D. (2002), 'Préface', in G. de Terssac and K. Lalande, *Du train à vapeur au TGV: sociologie du travail d'organisation*, Paris: Presses Universitaires de France, pp. 5–16.

Thoemmes, J. (2000), *Vers la fin du temps de travail?*, Paris: Presses Universitaires de France.

Thoemmes, J. (2006), 'Les 35 heures en rafales', in J. Thoemmes and G. de Terssac (eds), *Les méthodologies d'analyse du temps de travail*, Toulouse: Octarès, pp. 45–60.

Thoemmes, J. (2008), 'L'évolution d'une règle d'organisation sur 10 ans: l'accord collectif chez un constructeur d'automobiles en Allemagne', *Sociologie du Travail*, **50** (2), 219–36.

11. Trade union responses to privatization and restructuring of production in Argentina in the 1990s: similarities and differences in two state-owned companies

Juliana Frassa, Leticia Muñiz Terra and Alejandro Naclerio

INTRODUCTION

Neo-liberal policies in the 1990s brought about significant transformations in the economic models of several countries. In the context of globalization, the world economy underwent a profound transformation which resulted in the erosion of former production models and the emergence of what were later called 'productive restructuring processes'. Such dynamics fostered the emergence of new production and work forms with new features according to each country's existing economic structure and regulatory framework.

In Argentina, globalization trends were experienced jointly with the implementation of a neo-liberal economic model which resulted in, among other things, market deregulation, more open trade and a profound productive restructuring and privatization process. The productive restructuring process implied the transformation of the different socio-technical aspects of companies (the technology, the organization of the work process, the management of the workforce, the work relationships and the corporate culture) as well as the relationship of the companies with clients, suppliers and subcontractors. This process caused a precarious condition for a large part of the employed workforce, which started working in unstable jobs, for a determined period of time, without employee benefits (health insurance and retirement plans).

This chapter will examine and compare the track records of two state-owned companies with divergent ways of dealing with the same privatization context and state adjustment: the shipyard Astillero Río Santiago (ARS) and the oil company Yacimientos Petrolíferos Fiscales (YPF). The analysis will focus on company dynamics and environment at the time of Argentina's economic structural transformation, and on the actors' behaviour.

First, we discuss the theoretical foundations which guide this analysis. Secondly, the main characteristic features of both companies will be described as well as the structural transformations of the Argentinian economy during the 1990s. Thirdly, the responses of the organizational actors of ARS and YPF developed to confront this new context will be analysed in order to present some conclusions regarding the multiplicity of factors involved in the examination of a company and its context.

THE COMPANY, THE CONTEXT AND THE ACTORS' STRATEGIES

When it comes to the definitions of a company and its environment, the premises stated by the French 'sociology of organizations' line of thought (Reynaud, 1989; Bernoux, 1985; Crozier and Friedberg, 1990) will be followed. A company is seen as a productive organization made up of diverse groups of actors which interact, creating and following rules, values and particular symbolic meanings. This point of view states that each organization is a social construct made up of semi-autonomous actors, with specific resources and skills that, even with divergent orientations, cooperate to meet a common goal. Thus, the behaviour of organizations can only be explained from the existent interactions of the actors participating in them. The organization is considered 'the result of a series of games in which different organizational actors take part and where the formal and informal rules . . . limit a range of possible rational strategies' (Crozier and Friedberg, 1990, p. 114).

Apart from that, the oganization is 'a universe of conflict' and its functioning 'the result of struggles between the contingent, multiple and divergent rationalities of relatively-free actors using the available sources of power' (Crozier and Friedberg, 1990, p. 77). Far from adopting a deterministic point of view, we emphasize the contingent and indeterminate characteristic every collective action has because the actors are those who, within the constraints imposed by the system, always have a range of freedom that they strategically employ in interactions with each other. In short, our premise is that the organization is a contingent construct, a space of social rules production, in permanent reconstruction, accepted and legitimized by relatively free actors (Bernoux, 1985) who interact within a schema of limited rationality, but always keep a range of liberty to use the available sources of power (Crozier and Friedberg, 1990).

Each organization is placed in a larger power system which makes up its environment or the context in which it participates and from which it adopts characteristic features which will be integrated into its own action system. The environment, however, also constitutes the main source of uncertainty for the organization. Formed by several fragmented fields, it exerts fluctuating and usually divergent pressures which may constitute sources of change for the organization (Coller and Garvia, 2004).

Organizational change can be understood and analysed from two distinctive points of view, depending on the social theory adopted (Bernoux, 2002). On the one hand, one perspective holds that socio-economic structures play a determining role and impose change on organizations. This view, which usually follows an economic logic, states that factors such as technology, competition conditions or the degree of stability and complexity of the environment are unavoidable coercions which ultimately explain every organizational change. The Theory of Contingency, in organizational analysis, was the first to maintain that the organizational structure design is always 'contingent' on the environmental conditions (Lawrence and Lorsch, 1967; Burns and Stalker, 1966).

On the other hand, another point of view maintains that change is only possible inasmuch as it is accepted and put into practice by organizational actors. This line of thought accepts the significance of external coercion but does not consider it to be a determining factor, and it believes that change will ultimately depend on the way in which actors perceive, accept and manage it. The authors sharing this perspective (Linhart, 1997; Bernoux, 1985) stress the capacity of individuals and groups to modify their relationships and, by doing that, to transform the organization's development; that is, organizational changes would not be produced only by external coercions but also endogenously. Thus, the strategy adopted by each company in the face of external changes varies, within a group of options limited by the existing socio-technical development, due to several factors. The particular type of resistance and/or adaptation of each company to the contextual situation will depend, among other things, on the power-relationships set in the organization, the existing organizational culture, the existing political framework and the skills and knowledge accumulated by the company (Linhart, 1997).

From this second perspective, we believe that organizational change 'can be understood only as a collective creation process through which the members of a certain group learn together, that is, invent and determine new forms of playing the social game of cooperation and conflict and acquire the appropriate cognitive, relationship and organizational skills' (Crozier and Friedberg, 1990, p. 29).

OUR CASE STUDIES: A BRIEF HISTORY OF TWO PUBLIC COMPANIES

The companies which are the subject of this chapter (ARS and YPF) may be understood as paradigmatic examples of the will of the state, beginning in the 1930s, to take on the direction of national economic development. Both companies present inescapable productive and organizational differences[1] but it is possible to observe certain similarities in their conception as instruments promoting economic sovereignty. This characteristic feature is shown in their organizational cultures, built around their state-owned, national and industrial profile.

Astillero Río Santiago: 'National Will, Building for the Sea'[2]

Astillero Río Santiago (ARS), created in 1953 under the Navy's ruling, was conceived as part of the strategic industrialization plan set in motion by Perón's second term to strengthen heavy industry and promote the creation of a nationwide industrial framework. The shipyard, specializing in manufacturing and repairing various capital goods (navy constructions as well as mechanical), was created to meet the needs of the domestic merchant navy and the Argentine Navy.

With a regulatory protectionist framework promoting the construction of ships in the country, the development of the naval industry was characterized by strong state intervention. Argentina's government had an important participation in supply, being the owner of large shipyards, and also in demand for ships for the Navy and its main transport and production companies, constituting an important public, productive and commercial framework. In this area, the government played four significant roles: producer and consumer of ships, market regulator and provider of financing.

As the years went by, ARS underwent an expansion process in terms of production and employment as well as installation capacity. In the industrialization model of substitution of imports, the company developed a wide range of production connected to the Navy[3] which implied the creation of important productive links, incorporation of new technologies and development of know-how and specific skills (ARS, 2004). As an integrated company, ARS built almost all the ship components, having an important technical and administrative infrastructure and highly qualified workers.

In short, until the mid-1980s ARS could be characterized as a diversified production company with a high value, extensive auxiliary industry, strong dependence on the state, and high levels of employment. Due to its military origin, the internal organization was characterized by a very bureaucratic, pyramidal and hierarchical structure, and a state-oriented organizational discourse, stressing the consolidation of economic and commercial sovereignty through building ships locally.

Yacimientos Petrolíferos Fiscales: 'The Great National Company'

Yacimientos Petrolíferos Fiscales (YPF) was created by the national government in 1922, after the discovery of crude oil in the south of Argentina. Years later this company expanded its productive activity country-wide and became the most important natural resource research company in the country.

As in other oil-producer countries in the world, a vertically integrated company was developed, that is, 'an active company in all production stages: exploration, development, transport, storage, refinement, distribution and retail sales' (Organización International del Trabajo, 1998, p. 5). The final products obtained and commercialized were very diverse; different oils,[4] with their by-products. and a large number of raw materials for the oil industry were produced (Repsol YPF, 2004). YPF was also one of largest Argentinian public employers. Before its restructuring in 1989[5] it had 37,000 workers, 33 per cent of whom were technicians and professionals (Instituto Argentino del Petróleo y el Gas, 1989). The fast development of YPF met the domestic need for oil, the increasing exploitation of this natural resource and the consequent reduction of dependence on foreign supply. The state vision for oil-related activity stressed the strategic control of natural resources as the grounds for economic sovereignty.

As a public company, YPF's objectives were closely linked to the economic policies of the government in office. Its long history was tightly linked to the different national economic models, both in state-oriented versions (Juan Domingo Perón, Arturo Illia) and in others oriented towards being open to private investments (Arturo Frondizi).

The significance of this oil company was not, however, limited to its dynamic productive activity but also helped socio-economic and labour growth in the regions where it was located, promoting the development of a social model which embodied the guarantees and opportunities the Argentinian government offered to workers (Svampa and Pereyra, 2003). YPF launched an urban and regional development strategy by sponsoring the local areas where it was located, going beyond its productive function to became part of the ordinary life of the inhabitants of the region, oil workers and their families.

Transformation of the Economic Context in Argentina During the 1990s: Privatizations, Productive Restructuring and Trade Union Strategies Towards Change

At the beginning of the 1980s the change of political orientation in the USA and Great Britain intensified the neo-liberal offensive. The policies applied in these countries had a direct influence on the international context, resulting in a truly global deregulation and privatization dynamic that, at the same time, was promoted and consolidated by several international organisms. Based on the neo-classical concepts of market self-regulation and promotion of competition, the neo-liberal line of thought presented state-owned company assets as an obstacle to economic growth.

Regionally, the industrialization strategy through substitution of imports implemented in several countries was not feasible in the long term, because of the internal limitations and contradictions as well as the changing pattern of international accumulation, and this situation was an advantage for the arrival of liberal 'winds of change' with a tendency to make the role of the state in the economy the devil and emphasize the virtues of the market's 'invisible hand' (Fishlow, 1990). Thus, between the 1970s and 2000s, governments have returned to their regulatory policies benefiting, with the opening up of economies, the free play of supply and demand.

In Argentina, at least three key elements present in the economic strategy initiated in the 1970s and consolidated in the 1980s and 1990s can be identified: fewer state-owned assets, and the privatization of public companies which provided goods and services;[6] deregulation or reconfiguration of the regulatory framework[7] of the general economy and of special areas; and more open trade with foreign markets (Azpiazu, 1995; Neffa, 1998). Those elements had a significant impact on industry and dramatically modified its level and composition.[8] The structural reforms implemented in this period were sustained in the agreement between the government and private actors (domestic and foreign) which played a determining role in the implementation of public policy (Schvarzer, 1995; Basualdo, 2000).

The FDI flow associated with the privatization process and the merger and acquisition of large national corporations were fostered by the state, which guaranteed high benefits through cost flexibility. The buyers were multinational corporations looking for expansion in internal and external markets, while the sellers were national groups looking for the monetary appreciation of their assets. In other words, since 1995, the core of the productive national system has been undermined by the increasing involvement of foreign capital in the economy along with policies of open markets.

Apart from that, the national government started to foster a series of measures which allowed the implementation of what was then known as the process of industrial and productive restructuring. While the concept of industrial restructuring refers to the process of global reconversion of industrial markets searching for higher competitiveness, the idea of productive restructuring is much more specific. It refers to the changes occurring in, at least, some of the socio-technical aspects of companies: technology, work process organization, labour relationships, labour management and work culture (De La Garza Toledo, 2003).

In Argentina, the industrial restructuring implied a break with the protectionist industrial and internal market policies of previous decades, and helped the implementation of some aspects of productive restructuring in big companies.

When faced with the transformations resulting from the new macroeconomic policy, trade unions tried different strategies (Orlansky, 1997). As stated by Murillo (1997), whose focus is on the innovative capacity of unions when facing market reforms, some trade unions resisted the reforms and others negotiated specific proposals in exchange for accepting the general process. These latter could be divided between those who adapted to the process and got new advantages for the union (organizational survival) and those who kept their traditional guidelines for action in the face of the state (subordination). The reactions of trade unions derived from the distribution of their resources (political, industrial and organizational) as well as from their own legacy and the new political and economic conditions which affected the strategic options. The strategies the unions adopted implied a reformulation of historical patterns of submission to the state and a profound change in the relationship between them and the Peronist governments in office in the previous four decades.

FACING CHANGE: THE STRATEGIES OF ACTORS IN THE EVOLUTION OF THE BUSINESS

The new macroeconomic policy and the profound transformation of the role of the state in the economy strongly affected and conditioned the companies hereby analysed. Both ARS and YPF experienced the withdrawal of the state as employer, market regulator, and goods and service provider. Each company, however, responded to the change of environment in a different way, following divergent tracks. The particular strategies launched by the actors participating in each organization are as follows.

ARS: Labour Resistance and State Grant

The high exchange rate, the sudden opening of the market and the closing and/or privatization of the largest state-owned companies[9] were the new features of the context ARS had to deal with. In the sector, new policies of liberalization were introduced which established the deregulation of maritime transport, elimination of cargo reserve requirements for national ships, elimination of tax benefits, dissolution of the Fund for the Merchant Navy (the main source of financing) and implementation of strategic privatizing practices in state-owned shipyards (Frassa, 2006). Thus, in 1991 the ARS was declared subject to privatization, under the Economic Emergency and State Reform Acts.[10]

The decreasing demand for ships and the changes introduced in the regulatory framework produced the almost complete paralysis of ARS. Moreover, aiming at 'healing' the company before it became private, the government implemented a rationalization plan to cut down on employees. Between 1990 and 1993, through voluntary retirements, the ARS reduced 60 per cent of its staff (from 2,460 employees to 1,036).

During those years, there were severe conflicts within the company, in which workers, together with their union leaders, argued for the reactivation and permanence of ARS as a state-owned company (Pérez Pradal, 2003). As a result of the particular articulation of strategies, the ARS was finally able to avoid privatization and was transferred in 1993 to the government of the province of Buenos Aires. The company's 'rescue' by the provincial government did not save it, though, from the policies of adjustment applied. In 1995, the installation of a free trade zone on a lot owned by the shipyard was approved, leaving only 23 of its 229 hectares to the shipyard. This measure resulted in the loss of several facilities and of equipment, that is, a reduction of its installed capacity. Moreover, the provincial budget adjustment caused the company's equipment to become obsolete due to lack of replacement, a personnel freeze and lack of financial resources to embark on new projects.

It is noteworthy that the company could avoid privatization and keep its productive operation with its traditional organizational structure but that this adjustment process was not accompanied by a business strategy of modernization and restructuring (Dombois and Pries, 1993), which were the options adopted by the most important ship-manufacturing countries as a result of the strong recession and deregulation suffered by the sector from the 1980s (Cerezo, 2004; García Calavia, 2001).

Summing up, due to the implementation of neo-liberal policies which transformed the macroeconomic context, the ARS experienced a lower level and degree of diversification of production, loss of auxiliary industry and domestic market competition, reduction of qualified personnel and less productive capacity, and a deterioration and/or loss of certain organizational routines.

The actors' strategies towards change

The actors developed strategies influencing the company's future within a scope of action set by the transformation of the environment, with certain restrictions and opportunities. We maintain that avoidance of privatization and the productive subsistence of ARS can be explained by the specific articulation of the actors' strategies and the environmental conditions.

Between 1990 and 1993 ARS workers belonging to the trade union Asociación Trabajadores del Estado (ATE)[11] started more and more politicized open labour disputes[12] in response to the attempts at privatization and company adjustment. To make its resistance stronger, the union committed the local community to the claim and made alliances with other workers in the area. The conflict's visibility was another key element for the acts of opposition and resistance. Since the company was public, the 'pluralization' and 'publicity' of the labour dispute were fundamental for the strategy's success. The history of struggles in the 1970s and the democratic and pluralist characteristics of the ARS structure (a board of designees, an interim board and a general assembly) contributed to the resistance (Montes, 1999; Pérez Pradal, 2003). This structure fostered democratic decision-making, control of the union leadership by workers and fast organization of collective action. Moreover, the concentration of workers at the same place and the bond created outside the factory with neighbours in the towns of Berisso and Ensenada might have benefited the united action.

The opposition strategy followed jointly by the union leaders, the workers and the middle management conditioned, mostly, the strategies developed by government officials. In the state sector, however, three actors with different interests and different conduct towards the company must be distinguished. First, the national government, in order to reduce the public deficit, tried to terminate the relationship with every productive asset and implemented a strong and immediate adjustment policy. Due to the difficulty in finding a buyer for the shipyard in the short term[13] and the great level of resistance to privatization developed by ARS workers, the executive decided to 'make a politically-feasible deal' with the provincial government, and transferred the company. This alternative allowed the national government to disregard the social conflict which expanded into the area more and more,[14] and to continue moving forward with its privatization policies in other big companies which represented larger profits. Compared to the size of other state-owned companies participating in the privatization process (the oil company YPF, the national telecommunications company ENTEL, the energy provider SEGBA, the airline Aerolíneas Argentinas, etc.) the ARS was not a priority, and this fact benefited the delay of the attempt at privatization.

Secondly, the Navy, responsible for managing the company since the beginning, launched an ambivalent strategy. While its management depended on the policies set by the executive, it did have a certain room for manoeuvre inside the organization. Even if it followed the central government policies, when faced with workers' resistance, it changed its attitude to let workers keep a certain amount of power over the company. The Navy shared with workers the nationalist ideology which had inspired the company's creation; that is why its goal was to keep the productive operation of the ARS as a bastion of the local naval industry. Although the Navy sought to protect its own interests and resources, which were threatened by the national government's privatization policies, in the end it lost its involvement in the company after the province took over the ARS.

Thirdly, the provincial government's decision to take over the company mainly responded to a political and economic interest: political, because ARS control allowed it to appease the regional struggles which were becoming increasingly more visible, and to add a new source of power for partisan use; economic, because, on top of the funds transferred by the national government, the installation of a free trade zone in that area let the government obtain important commercial profits in a so far non-productive space. The benefits for the provincial government were in exchange for financially sponsoring the shipyard.

As stated above, each government actor launched the rational strategy which best suited its interests, even if they did not always achieve their most important objective. Such strategies, rational in contextual terms,[15] reached a satisfactory if not optimal solution.

ARS workers also developed a defensive strategy to confont the government's privatization policies, taking an active role to keep the company productive and, later on, to reactivate it. This strategy was supported by the organization of production by trade groups, the specific organizational culture and the strong sense of identity associated with the shipyard. With an almost total paralysis of production and without a business strategy for restructuring, the high level of expertise of the workers and the organization by trade groups allowed ARS to keep its operation going using informal labour rules and accumulated productive capacities.[16] Keeping the workers' know-how was vital to being able to reactivate the shipyard later on.

An organizational culture was the ideology the labour resistance was based on. For years the company promoted among the workers a strong nationalist feeling based on the company's public character and on its role in strengthening the development of the local industry. This discourse, together with the material benefits and work stability the shipyard traditionally provided, built in the workers a strong social/work identity closely related to the company. This identity was strengthened by the very confrontation with official power, because it was not only the source of employment that was being defended but also the values and concepts (of sovereignty and national industrial development) that the company stood for. The opposition strategy was against the attempt to privatize ARS as well as against the neo-liberal economic model. Summing up, these material and symbolic supports allowed for the development of a defensive labour strategy that, together with the restrictions imposed by the environment, strongly conditioned the strategies of the government actors.

YPF: Privatization, Adaptation and Business Modernization

The vision of the state that saw oil production as a strategic resource for the nation was abandoned in the 1990s when the Argentinian government, through structural reforms, fostered the privatization of YPF because of considering it a mere economic resource whose sale could bring money in to balance the national budget and help with payment of instalments of the foreign debt.[17]

The process of privatization started specifically in 1990 when the national executive branch signed decree number 2778, under which YPF, a state-owned corporation, became YPF Inc. Therefore, the company could enter the stock market. At the same time, the sale of many historical assets of the company was promoted.[18] Together with the deregulation of the oil sector, the sale of YPF was accompanied by a process of business rationalization. The privatization process continued in October 1992 when, under Act 24145, a part of the available corporate capital was privatized and the public domain of the hydrocarburant wells was transferred to the provinces. Between 1990 and 1993 the productive restructuring of the company took place and entailed the implementation of a new business strategy. Once these transformations were completed, the last stage of the privatization occurred between 1995 and 1999. In March 1995, Act 24474 was passed, under which the sale of the remaining state-owned shares (14 per cent) was allowed. Until 1995, the sale of YPF shares was atomized to avoid their control by a single national or international broker. The situation changed in 1999, when 99 per cent of the shares were sold to the Spanish group Repsol.[19]

One of the most important consequences of the YPF privatization was the crunch in the number of employees. The process of rationalization was pursued through a policy of voluntary retirements and other forms of disassociation such as redundancies and layoffs. Between 1989 (the year in which the company had the largest number of employees) and 1995 (when the retrenchment of personnel finished) the disassociation of 31,356 workers took place, that is, 84.6 per cent of the staff. The rationalization of personnel was the first step in the productive restructuring implemented in the company, because after the streamlining of staff, a reorganization of labour management started (Olivieri, 1991). Since then, the company's strategy has been to outsource qualified personnel for specific tasks. With new management of the workforce, professional and technical knowledge acquired more significance and a large number of workers, mostly skilled people whose know-how had been built on work experience, were made redundant.

The restructuring policy meant implementing outsourcing and incorporating technological innovations. Outsourcing was mostly for maintenance and logistic activities. After the privatization, a series of businesses made up by former YPF employees with specific know-how due to many years of working at the state-owned petrol company was hired. Regarding innovations, new technologies were introduced to the exploration, production, refinement and marketing stages to make changes in the organizational and productive routines and to diversify the final products. In other words, YPF followed the same transformation the world petrol industry was experiencing. From the 1980s, the companies which had been integrated were 'dismantled' to reduce fixed operating costs and rapidly adapt production levels to market demand. Such a strategy implied loss of jobs and employment flexibility (OIT, 1998). After the privatization and restructuring of production, the company managed by Repsol became one of the largest private energy companies in Latin America.

The actors' strategies towards change
The process of privatization and business restructuring was possible due to the strategies adopted by the main intervening actors: national government and worker representatives. It is noteworthy that it was the executive that fostered the sale of YPF. The arguments presented to justify this decision were the chronic budget imbalance which was suffered by all the population, the business inefficiency of management and the need to obtain funds to help with instalments of the foreign debt.[20]

The trade union Sindicato Unidos Petroleros del Estado (hereinafter referred to as SUPE) originated and grew together with the Peronist-oriented governments. SUPE established a close relationship with the Peronist governments in office and promoted less intensive struggle as a strategy to get more benefits for YPF workers. Their strong relationship helped to develop a strategy favouring both sides: the governments supported the union claims and awarded the benefits asked for, and the trade union supported the Peronist policies and became their ally. During the 1990s, this situation underwent a profound change because the 'Peronist' government of Menem fostered the dismantling of the petrol company. This policy was a direct blow to the core of union power because, on the one hand, SUPE lost its important role in the internal market and, on the other, the retrenchment of YPF workers dramatically reduced its number of members and economic resources. The new situation made SUPE, together with other Peronist trade unions belonging to the Confederación General del Trabajo (CGT), start more forceful measures to claim a greater participation in the decision-making process (Margueritis, 2003).

SUPE then decided to accept the general process but negotiated with the government certain conditions to the institutional reforms. SUPE wanted to have more organizational resources to make up for the decline of political and industrial resources and to obtain more autonomy in relation to the state.[21] The SUPE leadership also wanted to distance itself from the demands and pressures from union members, many of whom were against the privatization of the company (Murillo, 1997). SUPE redefined its actions and developed an organization survival strategy by becoming a business trade union (Murillo, 1997). Facing the transformation and a significant loss of power, it decided to accept the privatization and negotiate a series of compromises, such as: ownership of private company shares through the Program of Participated Ownership;[22] grants for the creation and management of a social security system, with the financial resources this entailed; acknowledgement of the monopoly of union representation in spite of the existence of another union in the sector;[23] and establishment of service providers to the company (Orlansky and Makón, 2002).

Now, why did national petrol union leaders decide to adopt this type of strategy instead of a total surrender or an active resistance? One of the main reasons influencing the decision to launch such a strategy had to do with the internal political organization of the trade union: SUPE was a vertical union with a leadership distanced from the workers it was meant to represent. This gap gave room for isolated decisions without too much pressure being exerted by the members, who were dispersed nationwide (Muñiz Terra, 2006). Adopting a policy of collaboration, SUPE refused to resist and dispersed the petrol workers by saying that there was nothing the union could do to deal with such structural reforms. Since its power was completely eroded, it had to adapt to the new times to avoid disappearing.

In the case of YPF, we can consider that the privatization, restructuring and business modernization were, in part, guaranteed by the strategies launched by the actors to adapt to a changing economic environment: both the national government and worker representatives fostered the transformation of the petrol company.

CONCLUSIONS

As shown, the track followed by the companies cannot be explained solely by external logics such as changing market conditions or the macroeconomic policies implemented, which would have imposed universal and homogenized changes on them. On the contrary, if we want to explain the companies' business tracks and assess their differences we must consider the actions taken by the actors within each productive organization versus the restrictions and opportunities presented by the environment. Our analysis shows that the variables explaining the differential track records of the companies under study are the very characteristic features of each company, the international climate of the sector and the strategies developed by the actors versus the privatization policy.

Regarding the characteristic features of each company, YPF was a nationwide company with vital economic significance which produced for both the domestic and foreign markets, fostered the socio-economic development of the regions where it was situated, and was one of the biggest state employers, while ARS was a middle-sized company situated in only one facility with a pronounced domestic market profile. These characteristics explain the different degrees of interest the national government and private groups allocated to the privatization of these companies as well as the availability of resources for each trade union when it came to negotiations with the government. The situation of each sector was also an influencing factor in the evolution of the business tracks because, while the international petrol area presented a continuous expansion due to the sustained increase of demand for by-products, maritime construction globally underwent a severe recession for a decade and was the object of a profound process of rationalization and restructuring. The private interest, therefore, posed different pressures and/or conditions in each case.

Regarding the trade union strategies, first, the hegemonic logics of privatization and adjustment used by the government in the 1990s were dealt with differently. The petrol workers' representatives launched a 'negotiating' strategy of acceptance of privatization in exchange for specific benefits, while the ARS union, in response to the demands of workers, launched a strategy of opposition and resistance to privatization and the new macroeconomic model. SUPE developed a strategy according to its historic model of performance: direct negotiation with the Peronist government in office, looking for labour benefits and/or organizational resources for the union. On top of this, the separation between the leadership and the workers and the lack of a tradition of struggle fostered a strategy based on a mainly adaptative logic. ATE Astillero, on the other hand, developed a sustained strategy of resistance in honour of its tradition of struggle and labour movements, a democratic union structure and a strong organizational culture promoting identification with the company.

The actors from the state also had different positions in relation to each company. In the case of YPF, the national government went ahead with the privatization and restructuring of the company regardless of the price it had to pay for it, while in that of ARS the national government, the Navy and the provincial government, to protect their own interests, launched contradictory strategies which did not achieve their most important objectives but ended up benefiting the permanence of the shipyard in state hands.

Summing up, the intervening actors in each organization, in the pursuit of different objectives, launched, within certain limits, strategies which they considered were rational within the situational framework of environmental transformation, using resources and power sources available to them.

In conclusion, the case studies show how relevant the strategies of the actors are[24] to the business tracks taken by the companies. The actors are the ones who, with a greater or lesser degree of restriction on their actions, perceive, understand and deal with changes in the environment. Accepting that no logic of action imposes itself completely on organizations is the first step in accounting for the true complexity of the social relationships developed within them. Reassessing the actions of individuals within the organization, we believe, is the approach most adequate to explaining the way in which recent global changes (corporate restructuring, production outsourcing, precarious employment conditions, labour market flexibility) affect the world of labour. It is all ultimately about looking at the environmental conditionings and degrees of freedom – through which the actions of individuals permeate – in context. This statement shows the tension existing in every social analysis: how much constraint is there on the social action? Or how much unpredictability and originality of behaviour is not explained by the social system or the macroeconomic determinants? After all, it is about accounting for the central tension expressed differently in each productive space.

Without trying to minimize the structural impacts of applied policies or to disregard the different track records of each sector in the de-industrialization and restructuring schedule of the national manufacturers (Wainer and Schorr, 2006), in the cases studied the strategies of the trade union actors, whether by confrontation and resistance like ARS or negotiations and adaptation like YPF, are explained mostly by the final effects of the policies. In this analysis we highlight the fact that the results of public policies can never be totally predictable because the articulation between the imposition of a macroeconomic policy and the actors' behaviour is always original. The track diversity we analysed is explained by the structural conditions (characteristic features of the companies, national and international conditions in the field) as well as by the actions of the intervening actors, suggesting that the macroeconomic contextual constraints must be considered relatively if the transformation of companies in time is to be explored properly.

NOTES

1. From the physical point of view, production level, income and number of workers, YPF was much more relevant than ARS.
2. Commercial slogan adopted by the company until the 1980s.
3. Among other production lines we can mention: diesel engines, railway elements, locks for docks and nuclear components.
4. Among others we could mention super and normal gas, sulphur, gas oil, petrol carbon, paraffin, lubricant oils, asphalt and fuel oil.
5. It reached its maximum level of employment during this year.
6. This strategy resulted in a sharp reduction of public employment and the beginning of an alleged 'modernizing restructuring' of the public entities.
7. Deregulation did not imply the self-regulation of market mechanisms. As Azpiazu (1995, p. 202) points out, the regulation 'was transferred to certain economic agents that, due to the market's own morphology and their position as oligopolies, had wide scope to regulate the market's functioning'.
8. Generally speaking, the consequences of implementing these policies were asset concentration, consolidation of new monopolies and oligopies, regressive restructuring and loss of dynamism of the industry (Kosacoff, 2000).
9. State-owned companies were the main clients of ARS.
10. Act 23.696 from 1989 declares the state of emergency in the public environment, the takeover of all entities, companies and state-owned partnerships and the privatization of public companies. Act 24.045 of State Reform from 1991, among other things, details the entities to be privatized.
11. ARS workers belong to ATE, which, since its establishment in 1992, is part of the Central de Trabajadores Argentinos (CTA). At regional level, ARS belongs to ATE Ensenada, whose leaders have traditionally been ARS union representatives.
12. These conflicts took different forms: factory seizures, the withdrawal of collaboration, demonstrations in front of government offices, road blockades and public building seizures. The main claims were payment of outstanding salaries, opposition to privatizations and defence of national industry.
13. The deep recession in the international maritime construction sector did not help the production of a buyer for the company.

14. The privatization of the YPF distillery and the restructuring of other factories in the area had a strong impact on Berisso and Ensenada, two industrial towns which started to have high levels of unemployment and underemployment.
15. According to Simon (1969), the satisfaction criteria of the decision-maker are influenced by the characteristic features of context, which is why actor strategies must always be understood within the system of action they correspond to.
16. We are particularly making reference to the maintenance of machinery at times of production paralysis and its adaptability in embarking on new projects in a context of lack of resources.
17. In 1989, before starting the privatizations, a significant deregulation of the oil sector had been fostered to open up the possibilities for some private companies to share in this activity, in the exploration and extraction or refinement stages.
18. This included the sale of petrol fleet and trucks, association with private capital in central areas and ports, sale of navy workshop, incorporation or sale of oilducts and poliducts, etc.
19. Traditionally, Repsol had been a small-sized company with low vertical integration, focused on refining and trading crude oil in the Spanish market. Its exploration activities were mainly in Northern Africa, where 60 per cent of its oil was extracted. At the beginning of the 1990s it adopted the strategy of significant growth in that niche. Argentina was chosen as the hub of expansion in Latin America.
20. It is interesting to note that even if the company's situation was dire, it did not mean that it was not profitable; the company's fall was actually a consequence of the fact that the governments in office, one after the other, had not assigned efficient directors.
21. It is noteworthy that, in Argentina, Peronist trade unions usually adopted a submissive political standpoint while still pressing to obtain benefits when facing Peronist governments.
22. This Program stated that 10 per cent of the company's shares belonged to the workers.
23. We are referring to the Federación Argentina Sindical del Petróleo y el Gas Privados (FASPyGP).
24. This element is usually undermined or forgotten in analyses made from an economic point of view.

REFERENCES

ARS (2004), *Presentación oficial de la empresa: Ensenada 2003*, Buenos Aires.
Azpiazu, Daniel (1995), 'La industria argentina ante la privatización, la desregulación y la apertura asimétrica de la economía', in D. Azpiazu and H. Nochteff, *El desarrollo ausente*, FLACSO, Buenos Aires: Norma, pp. 157–221.
Basualdo, Eduardo (2000), *Concentración y centralización del capital en la Argentina durante la década del noventa*, FLACSO, Buenos Aires: Universidad Nacional de Quilmes.
Bernoux, Philippe (1985), *La sociologie des organizations*, Paris: Editions du Seuil.
Bernoux, Philippe (2002), 'Le changement dans les organizations: entre structures et interactions', *Relations Industrielles/Industrial Relations*, **57** (1), pp. 77–96.
Burns, Tom and George M. Stalker (1966), *The Management of Innovation*, London: Tavistock.
Centro de Estudios para la Producción (CEP) (2005), *La industria naval en la argentina*, Subsecretaría de desarrollo productivo de la Secretaría de Industria de la Nación, available at: http//:www.industria.gov.ar/cep (accessed 10 December 2006).

Cerezo, José L. (2004), 'El sector de construcción naval en España: situación y perspectivas', *Economía Industrial*, **355–6**, 185–96.

Coller, Xavier and Roberto Garvía (2004), *Análisis de organizaciones: Centro de Investigaciones Sociológicas*, Madrid: Siglo XXI.

Crozier, Michel and Erhard Friedberg (1990), *El actor y el sistema: las restricciones de la acción colectiva*, México, DF: Alianza.

De la Garza Toledo, Enrique (2003), 'Las teorías sobre la reestructuración productiva y América Latina', in Enrique De la Garza Toledo (ed.), *Tratado Latinoamericano de Sociología del Trabajo*, México, DF: Fondo de Cultura Económica, pp. 716–34.

Dombois, Rainer and Ludger Pries (eds) (1993), 'Modernización empresarial y cambios en las relaciones industriales en América Latina y Europa', in *Modernización empresarial: tendencias en América Latina y Europa*, Nueva Sociedad, Caracas: Fundación Friedrich Ebert-Colombia, pp. 62–85.

Fishlow, Albert (1990), 'The Latin American state', *Journal of Economic Perspectives*, **4** (3), 61–74.

Frassa, Juliana (2006), 'Políticas públicas de desregulación y sus consecuencias sobre la producción y el empleo: el caso de la política naviera y la industria naval argentina', *Revista Informe IEFE*, **139** (July), 39–52.

García Calavia, Miguel A. (2001), 'La producción de mitos y milagros: la reestructuración del trabajo desde los años ochenta', doctoral thesis, Universitat Autónoma de Barcelona.

Instituto Argentino de Petróleo y el Gas (1989), *Boletín de Informaciones Petroleras*, **17**.

Instituto Argentino de Petróleo y el Gas (1995), *Boletín de Informaciones Petroleras*, **42**.

Kosacoff, Bernardo (2000), *El desempeño industrial argentino más allá de la sustitución de importaciones*, Buenos Aires: CEPAL.

Lawrence, Paul R. and Jay W. Lorsch (1967), *Organization and Environment: Managing Differentiation and Integration*, Cambridge, MA: Harvard University Press.

Linhart, Danièle (1997), *La modernización de las empresas*, Buenos Aires: Edit. Asociación Trabajo y Sociedad.

Margueritis, Ana (2003), 'La privatización de Yacimientos Petrolíferos Fiscales y actividades afines', in Ana Margueritis, *Ajuste y reforma en Argentina (1989–1995): la economía política de las privatizaciones*, Buenos Aires: Nuevo Hacer, pp. 195–234.

Montes, José (1999), *Astillero Río Santiago: su historia y su lucha relatada por sus trabajadores*, Buenos Aires: La Verdad Obrera.

Muñiz Terra, Leticia (2006), 'La erosión del poder sindical en un escenario de privatización: el caso del Sindicato Unido Petrolero del Estado', *Revista Question*, **12**, 1–21.

Murillo, M. Victoria (1997), 'La adaptación del sindicalismo argentino a las reformas de mercado en la primera presidencia de Menem', *Revista Desarrollo Económico*, **37** (147) 22–41.

Neffa, Julio C. (1998), *Modos de regulación, regímenes de acumulación y sus crisis en Argentina (1880–1996): un enfoque desde la Teoría de la Regulación*, Buenos Aires: Trabajo y Sociedad, PIETTE/CONICET, EUDEBA.

Olivieri, Carlos (1991), 'YPF, un modelo de privatización para el mundo', *Boletín de Información Petrolera*, **25**, 24–35.

Organización International del Trabajo (OIT) (1998), *El empleo y las relaciones de trabajo en las refinerías de petróleo*. Informe para el debate. Programa de actividades sectoriales. Ginebra, OIT.

Orlansky, Dora (1997), 'Reforma del estado, reestructuración laboral y reconversión sindical: Argentina 1989–1995', *Revista Estudios Sociológicos del Colegio de México*, **XV** (45), 46–68.

Orlansky, Dora and Andrea Makón (2002), 'De la sindicalización a la informalidad: el caso de Repsol-YPF. Versión preliminar', Workshop 'Programa de estudios internacionales' (PESEI), Buenos Aires, Instituto de Desarrollo Económico y Social.

Pérez Pradal, Cecilia (2003), 'Contra el naufragio: un estudio sobre los conflictos laborales en el caso de Astilleros Río Santiago: 1989–1999', in *CD de Tesinas finales de Sociología*, Vol. 1, La Plata: UNLP.

Repsol YPF (2004), *Revista institucional de la empresa*.

Reynaud, Jean D. (1989), *Les régles de jeu: l'action collective et la regulation sociale*, Paris: Armand Colin.

Sassen, Saskia (2003), *Los espectros de la globalización*, Buenos Aires: Katz Editores.

Schvarzer, Jorge (1995), *La reestructuración de la industria argentina en el período de ajuste estructural*, available at: http://www.clacso.edu.ar (accessed 22 November 2005).

Simon, Herbert (1969), *Sciences des systèmes: sciences de l'artificiel* (French trans. 1991), Paris: Sociedad CEIL-PIETTE/CONICET.

Svampa, Maristella and Sebastián Pereyra (2003), *Entre la ruta y el barrio: la experiencia de las organizaciones piqueteros*, Buenos Aires: Biblos.

Wainer, Andrés and Martín Schorr (2006), 'Trayectorias empresarias diferenciales durante la desindustrialización en la Argentina: los casos de Arcor y Servotron', *Realidad Económica*, **223**, 116–41.

12. Organizing and mobilizing precarious workers in France: the case of cleaners in the railways

Heather Connolly

INTRODUCTION

This chapter explores trade union activity in the cleaning sector in France in the railways. Cleaning has become one of the fastest growing occupations in North America, Australasia and Western Europe (Herod and Aguiar, 2006). In a context of labour market deregulation, there has been an increase in outsourcing and a growth in the number of cleaning companies. In most countries the cleaning sector draws its workforce from the most vulnerable segments of the labour market: women, young people and immigrants (Bernstein, 1986), and working conditions are particularly difficult. For Wills, cleaning work is 'emblematic of "bottom-end" service work in countries like Britain, where the work is poor quality, low-paid, without additional benefits and with little chance to secure workplace organization' (2008, p. 310). The organization and management of employment in this highly competitive sector are based on a quest for maximum flexibility in terms of variation in both employees' working schedule and wages, as well as on external flexibility – by outsourcing. The increasing use of subcontracting is aimed at increasing the competitiveness of companies by compressing production costs to a minimum. Herod and Aguiar (2006), studying cleaners in the global economy, argue that the combined impact of marketization, privatization, deregulation, cuts in welfare provision and an assault on collectivism have eroded the wages, conditions and potential power of cleaners.

The cleaning sector in France is also subject to these trends. The labour force working in this sector is particularly vulnerable and Puech (2004), in her study of subcontracted cleaners in France, argues that workers are often of foreign origin, unskilled, and paid extremely low wages, which does not compensate for a job that is not only difficult but often uninteresting. As in other European countries, there has been an increase in the subcontracting of cleaning services in France in many large public and private sector organizations. In France, cleaners come under a sectoral collective agreement, which has the potential to lessen the precarious conditions of these workers. However, as this chapter demonstrates, French employers have been able to undermine collective agreements by exploiting the precarious status of many cleaning sector workers. This is significant as it points towards the fundamental limitations in the legal and political structures of countries like France to protect its workforce against the worst aspects of global capitalism.

Trade unions faced with a context of growing numbers of cleaning workers with precarious working conditions have responded by intensifying efforts to organize these workers. This chapter builds on a growing number of studies looking at unions' attempts to collectivise cleaners (Herod and Aguiar, 2006; Waldinger et al., 1998; Wills, 2008). Unionization has been particularly low in cleaning, where workers have tended to be 'invisible' to the labour movement, both because of the nature of their work – often conducted out of sight – and because trade unions have not invested in campaigns to unionize them (Herod and Aguiar, 2006). Yet the cleaning sector has become an important arena for union growth since the celebrated victory of the 'Justice for Janitors' campaign led by the Service Employees International Union (SEIU) in the United States during the 1990s.[1] Moreover, the SEIU strategy for organizing is now looked upon as a model for organizing cleaners globally, with its version of 'social unionism', combining community involvement, public demonstrations to shame employers into recognizing the union, and direct action methods, being highly regarded, even inspirational (ibid.).

This discussion draws on ethnographic research in SUD-Rail, a union representing workers in the French railway sector, which forms part of the radical trade union movement *Solidaires, Unitaires et Démocratiques* (SUD). The chapter considers the ways in which activists from a local-level union of SUD-Rail attempted to organize and mobilize subcontracted cleaners. In France, reforms in the railway sector – for example, opening up competition in freight and threatened changes to the employment status and pensions of railway workers – has led to waves of collective action since the mid-1980s. SUD-Rail emerged in the railway sector in 1996 as a radical opposition force against reforms in the public sector. However, the trade union has not limited its activities to defending the core workforce, the *cheminots* (railway workers), but has sought to organize subcontracted cleaners, who have been subject to more precarious working conditions.

The first section of this chapter considers the background to the SUD movement and the rise of SUD-Rail in the context of growing job insecurity in the railway sector. The following sections consider the

strategy and activities of a SUD-Rail local union to do with organizing
and mobilizing cleaners: first, how the union concentrated on building up
union organization amongst these workers, which formed an important
part of the union's strategy for growth and renewal; secondly, drawing
on mobilization theory (see Kelly, 1998), how the activists encouraged
cleaners to undertake collective action. The chapter demonstrates how the
union's strategy towards organizing and mobilizing cleaners had mixed
results.

THE RISE OF SUD-RAIL

This chapter draws on empirical research that was conducted in the
context of a broader study exploring the processes of union renewal in
France (Connolly, 2008). This work builds on an emerging set of research
exploring the nature and activities of the group of SUD trade unions in
France (Damesin and Denis, 2005; Denis, 2003; Sainsaulieu, 1999, 2006).
The first of the SUD trade unions was created in 1988 and since then the
number has grown rapidly to over 50. The majority of SUD unions have
emerged from the second largest trade union confederation in France, the
Confédération Française Démocratique du Travail (CFDT). Groups of
activists within the CFDT, advocating a more 'combative' form of unionism, have at various stages disagreed with the CFDT confederal level's
promotion of concession bargaining and economic and social realism. In
recent years this group of trade unions has managed to make its mark on
a trade union landscape dominated by the five nationally representative
trade union confederations. The growth of these unions at a time of relative union stagnation has stimulated speculation on their activities and on
the possibilities for renewal in the French union movement. The growth
of SUD-Rail to become the second union in the Société Nationale des
Chemins de Fer Français (SNCF) in 2004 and the union's high profile in
the media, thanks to its militant approach, have meant that the union's
significance is increasingly debated in literature on trade unionism, social
movements and social conflict in France.

SUD unions are identified as having three broad characteristics. First,
they seek to revitalize a form of militant unionism, using strategies of confrontation and of non-compromise with management. Secondly, they seek
to develop a form of grassroots unionism, with an emphasis on democracy
and building up membership numbers. Thirdly, the SUD trade unions
have taken on a decentralized federal structure representing workers from
specific occupations or sectors, but they adopt a strategy of forwarding
occupational as well broader societal demands (Damesin and Denis,

2001). The unions have formed mainly in the public sector where occupational identities are strong. Civil servants (*fonctionnaires*) and railway workers (*cheminots*) are associated with certain rights and privileges and SUD has been a key defender of these occupational-specific interests. Yet SUD trade unions refuse to be called company unions and they maintain calls for wider worker solidarity, and seek to represent workers of all status in their sector (Damesin and Denis, 2001).

The growth of SUD trade unions has taken place at a time of reform within the public services sector, with the main discourse uniting the SUD unions being the defence of public services (Damesin, 2001; Sainsaulieu, 1999).[2] From 1986 onwards various governments have engaged in periods of privatization and reform with the aim of adapting public services to the market by approaching the client from a commercial point of view. The French government privatized telecommunications in the late 1990s and the electricity and gas companies in August 2004. Moves have also been made towards privatization in the postal service and the railways, with the opening up of certain services to outside competition. In terms of industrial relations, reforms in public service monopolies have centred on aligning employment conditions, most importantly pension schemes, with those of the private sector.

Privatization and occupational reforms have provoked concerns amongst trade unions in the remaining public service monopolies. With increasing pressures towards privatization in the European railways there has been recurring collective action against reforms. The main criticism from the trade unions has been that privatization means moving away from a public service ethic towards consumerism and a focus on profits. The SUD unions have defended a more traditional notion of the French model of public service. This includes a rejection of the quest for profits, importance placed on keeping all work activity in-house, and the necessity of a special status for workers for carrying out the work in the public sector company (Damesin and Denis, 2005). The success of the SUD unions' approach is evident in the growth of support in workplace elections in their respective sectors. They have taken away support mainly from the CFDT, which has been seen to be supportive of reforms.

However, the SUD unions' defence of public services has been problematic as, not being able to stop the processes towards privatization, for example, in the telecommunications and energy sector and the opening up of freight transport to outside competition in the railways, the unions are increasingly representing the demands of workers in the public and the private sector. This is the case for SUD-PTT, representing workers in postal and telecommunications, and so now representing both private-status telecommunications workers and public service-status postal workers. The transfer of jobs to the private sector presents a problem for the SUD unions in terms of adapting their demands to meet the interest of workers in the private sector whilst also maintaining a representative position in the organization by representing the demands of the core work group (Damesin, 2001). In the railways, the 'core' work groups continue to have the public sector status of *cheminot*, but the unions also represent both contract workers – who are employed directly by the SNCF but with a different status from the *cheminots* – and subcontracted cleaners.

As in other European countries, the railway sector in France represents one of the most important historical strongholds for trade union organization. Trade union density is around 30 per cent, which is significant in relation to the national average of between 5 and 10 per cent. In the SNCF there are nine separate unions representing workers, with five of the union federations being affiliated to one of the nationally representative union confederations: the Confédération Générale du Travail (CGT); the CFDT; the Confédération Française des Travailleurs Chrétiens (CFTC); the Confédération Française de l'Encadrement – Confédération Générale des Cadres (CFE-CGC); and Force Ouvrière (FO). The remaining four, SUD-Rail, Union Nationale Des Syndicats Autonomes (UNSA), Federation Generale Autonome des Agents de Conduite (FGAAC) and Syndicat National des Cadres Supérieurs (SNCS), are considered representative in the SNCF. The FGAAC is occupationally specific and represents drivers, UNSA represents mainly management and administrative employees, and SUD-Rail represents workers from all sectors of activity.

The French government's steps towards changing occupational protections associated with public sector status led to important strike waves in the railways in 1986 and 1995. SUD-Rail was created after the strike waves of 1995. The background to the 1995 strike waves in the railways was the government's attempts to reform the sector's special pension scheme. The railway unions played a significant role in the movement overall and the government withdrew proposals for reforming the railway pension scheme under the pressure of the strike waves. The 1995 movement was characterized by the unions' emphasis on democracy, which was evidenced in the importance of general assemblies in the workplace throughout the strike movement (Chevandier, 2002, p. 340). However, there were grassroots 'co-ordinations' during the movement, some motivated by wider grievances, some representing more specific interests. Trotskyites were important in the movement, with activists from the radical workers' parties playing an important role in the conflict. The CFDT had encouraged self-management (*autogestion*) of the conflicts at the local level, but there were disagreements at the grassroots after the confederation supported government pension reforms. In January 1996, when the strike movement had ended, local unions in the Paris region requested an extraordinary congress, which was refused by the general secretary Nicole Notat. During January and February 1996 between 50 and 80 per cent of activists from local CFDT unions in the Paris region left to form SUD-Rail.

In the beginning SUD-Rail struggled to gain recognition in the SNCF as management and the other union organizations tried to prevent the union from putting forward candidates for workplace elections. In spite of the other unions' actions, SUD-Rail gained around 5 per cent of the vote in the workplace elections of March 1996 (Damesin, 2001). After a successful legal process, the Ministry of Transport declared SUD-Rail representative within the SNCF in December 1997. At the national level the union increased its support in the workplace elections of 1998 (6.5 per cent), 2000 (10.6 per cent), 2002 (12.74) and 2004 (18.15 per cent), and in 2001 the union had a membership of around 5,000, compared to around 3,000 in 1998 (Damesin and Denis, 2005). The CGT still dominates in the sector with around 29,000 members, followed by SUD-Rail with between 5,000 and 6,000 members. CFDT membership declined by almost half in 2003 to 4,000 members.

At the time of the field research conducted with the union in 2004, SUD-Rail was experiencing a period of growth in terms of both membership and workplace election support. This chapter draws on research findings from ethnographic research in a regional union of SUD-Rail. The field research took place over a 12-month period in 2003–2004, with a period of five months full-time participant observation. The SUD-Rail Federation is organized into 24 regional unions, five of which are in Paris and its surrounding areas. The research was carried out in one of the Paris based regions comprising of around 7,000 employees. Membership density for SUD-Rail in the region was estimated at between 7 and 10 percent, which was higher than the sector-level density figure for SUD-Rail, estimated at around 3.5 percent. The CGT and SUD-Rail dominated workplace representative positions in the region with only one other union present on the works council, UNSA, representing mainly management employees.

The regional union was composed of 12 branches and the research involved contact with activists at each of the branches. In total I was in contact with around 70 activists, members and workers; I was in regular contact with around 30 activists. During the first month I was based in a regional union office of SUD-Rail where I was mainly observing meetings and daily union activities. In the second month I shadowed trade union activists in several branches around the region. I also participated in trade union actions, including strike rallies, sit-ins and demonstrations, and continued to attend the regular meetings held at the union office. The following months were spent accompanying activists whilst they carried out their duties. I continued to observe the regular meetings at the union office throughout this period and attended strike rallies and demonstrations within the region and also at the national level.

The rest of this chapter is dedicated to exploring a part of SUD-Rail's activity which has not been discussed in detail within the existing literature and has had less media attention; that is, the role of the union in organizing and mobilizing subcontracted cleaners in the railway sector. This chapter argues that this activity has been an important part of SUD-Rail's strategy for union renewal in a context of fiercely competitive unionism and the threat of constant reforms.

ORGANIZING CLEANERS IN SUD-RAIL

This section draws on the findings relating to the union's activities towards organizing cleaners. The most organized occupational groups for the regional SUD-Rail union were first, the customer services and operations workers, who were mostly in-station employees, and secondly, the subcontracted cleaners. The union estimated that there were around 300 cleaners working in the region. The union had around 159 members in the cleaning companies, which represented a membership density of over 50 per cent. The high level of membership amongst cleaners represented an interesting feature of union organization in the region and reflected the success of the union's strategy of building up union organization in this sector. The union's involvement in organizing these workers showed how the union was not only focused on representing the interests of protected workers, but was also prepared to organize those with a more precarious status. Due to the precarious working conditions and resource constraints of cleaner activists, mobilizing workers in the cleaning companies was an activity mainly undertaken by union activists with *cheminot* status. The main activist in charge of building union organization among cleaners during my research period was Sylvestre (white male, mid-forties).[3]

Four companies were subcontracted to undertake cleaning work in the region. The union had invested resources to gain 'representative status' in the private cleaning companies.[4] They were representative in three out of the four cleaning companies, and at the time of the research they were trying to gain representative status in the fourth company. Cleaners in the railway sector have a specific collective agreement which provides more favourable terms and conditions than the national sector-level agreement. However, SUD-Rail complained that the terms of the agreement were not respected by employers. The majority of cleaners were from ethnic minority backgrounds, and employers took advantage of the fact that many workers could not read or write French to make them sign contracts agreeing to switch to the sector-level collective agreement, with less favourable terms and conditions. In the light of these precarious conditions, SUD-Rail were demanding, in the first instance, that the SNCF withdrew their policy of accepting the lowest-bidding subcontractors and, more generally, the reinstatement of cleaners within the SNCF, having the same terms and conditions as railway workers.

In order to help organize cleaners, SUD-Rail drew on legislation pertaining to trade unions and their activities. SUD unions have adopted a practice of investing in the law and advancing their organization through having an expert knowledge of the Labour Code.[5] This marks out the peculiarity of SUD unions, as they base their identity on a combative form of unionism rather than one favourable towards institutionalized regulation (Denis, 2003): because they are acting outside the framework enjoyed by the legally representative confederations, it has been essential for them to have expert knowledge of labour law. SUD-Rail's legal process for gaining union representative status necessitated an awareness of appropriate union legislation. The development of legal expertise has thus been a matter of survival for the SUD trade unions. In this research, using legal expertise was essential in activities to build union organization in the subcontracted cleaning companies. In French labour law it is considered a criminal offence to interfere with trade union activities and representatives (*delit d'entrave*). The rules governing the establishment and functioning of the institutions of employee representation within the enterprise all carry penal sanctions. Interference with the creation of representative bodies, interference with the free selection of their members, interference with their functioning or with exercise of the right to organize collectively: these offences, covering what is termed elsewhere anti-union behaviour, have been the subject of a considerable body of case law specifying the extent of the rights of employee representatives (EMIRE).

There were three sets of observations where activists used legal tactics to further union organization in cleaning companies. First, the activists nominated union representatives in order to give some protection to cleaner activists who were vulnerable to employer discrimination. This seemed to be a successful tactic for helping to build union organization amongst cleaners. For example, Mai (black female, mid-thirties) was told by the union that if she were nominated as a *délégué syndical*[6] (DS) in her company she would have less trouble with her employer. Talking about Mai, one SUD activist said that she had been 'abused' by her 'boss' and that he had been trying to 'move her around different stations' at very short notice. He said that now she was a union member, and a nominated

DS, she was 'left alone'. This was also the case for a group of workers cleaning drivers' overnight accommodation in the main station in the region. The drivers in this depot were mainly with SUD and this had had an impact on cleaners, who were all either SUD members or supporters. One of the cleaners said:

> We are left alone here because we are with SUD . . . if I have a problem I use the phone and the problem is sorted out . . . we had a problem with the fridge this morning . . . I phoned up the boss and it is going to be replaced by this afternoon . . . we have got no problems being in SUD.

Secondly, SUD-Rail offered a legal advice service to all workers, which helped encourage some cleaners to become union members. The service was held one morning a week and workers could come to the regional union office to obtain legal advice. The service was used mainly by the cleaners, who had more problems with their employment contracts and with employers not respecting terms and conditions of employment. These workers were often unable to read and write in French and they were less likely to be aware of their employment rights and to be able to challenge their employers. Union activists wrote letters for these workers and helped them to put cases together to take to employment tribunals. Several cleaners said that access to the legal advice service was one of their main reasons for joining SUD-Rail. Kamina (black female, mid-forties) said she had been a member of other unions and that they had said they 'could do nothing for her'. However, SUD-Rail activists had offered to help her with complaints against her employer. Kamina had changed employer after being transferred to another subcontracting company. In the process she had not received certain benefits which the new company had agreed to respect in the changeover. The activists wrote letters to her employer setting out her complaint and when the employer ignored these letters, they put her case together to take to a tribunal. With the threat of a tribunal, the employer offered a one-off payment, but the activists refused, took the case to a tribunal and won. That the union was willing to 'fight' for these workers helped create a favourable identity for it.

Thirdly, SUD-Rail activists invested resources in training cleaner activists on employment rights and tactics to enforce these rights. The activists saw this as the union's responsibility as management would not 'respect or even be aware' of cleaners' rights. Meetings and training sessions were held in the union office for cleaners, aimed more generally at encouraging them to become more involved in the union and to take responsibility for the organization of workers in their companies. Another aim was to make cleaner activists aware of tactics that they could employ with employers which drew on existing labour law. Labour inspectors[7] were perceived as an important resource to enforce the Labour Code. Below are some examples of the tactics that the activists encouraged.

> You need to be aware of the laws on trade union activity [the *delit d'entrave* – see above] . . . a labour inspector will not intervene if someone has not been paid their allowance for Sunday working but if the employer has not provided a report from the employee representative [*délégue du personnel*] meeting then he will intervene . . . it is up to representatives to contact the inspector.

> In July and August the boss might say you cannot have a works council meeting because he is on holiday . . . you tell him to nominate someone . . . the meeting has to take place . . . if not you call in the labour inspector.

> An important right to know about is the right to withdraw from work [*droit de retrait*[8]] . . . the boss cannot just do anything . . . if you are in a dangerous work situation you have the right to stop . . . you do not have the right to go home but you can stop and go to the canteen or go and sleep in your car . . . leave your phone on in case the boss calls . . . I work in different stations replacing people who are not there and I worked where there was a broken door so I stopped working and said I would call in the labour inspector unless they fixed it . . . it was health and safety . . . all employees have the right and it is important.

These examples show how SUD-Rail activists used existing labour law as a resource to help protect and organize cleaners and also how they took a militant approach to the workplace. The success of their approach was evident in the number of members amongst this group of workers. It could be argued that the extent to which union activists drew on labour law in organizing cleaners marks out the 'exceptionalism' of French industrial relations. For example, compared to campaigns to organize cleaners in Britain and the US it is evident that labour legislation provides a more important resource for unions in France.

A CAMPAIGN TO MOBILIZE CLEANERS

This section looks in detail at a campaign to mobilize cleaners to take collective action to improve their working conditions. The section draws on mobilization theory to analyse the social processes underlying this campaign and to help understand the relative failure of the union activists to mobilize cleaners en masse. The key question in mobilization theory is how individuals are transformed into collective actors willing and able to construct and sustain collective interests and engage in collective action against their employers (Kelly, 1998). The critical factor for collective interest definition is for workers to develop a sense of injustice or illegitimacy.

In addition, individuals must feel that they are entitled to their demands and that there is some chance the situation can be changed.

Leaders play several key roles in the process of collective interest definition (Kelly, 1997, 1998). First, they use arguments to frame issues so as to promote a sense of injustice amongst workers. This process of persuasion involves the use of 'collective action frames', which can be defined as action-oriented sets of beliefs and meanings that inspire and legitimate social movement activities and campaigns (Snow and Benford, 1988). Collective action framing is the attempt to link the ideologies, goals and activities of the union to the interests, values and beliefs of workers (ibid.). Secondly, leaders encourage group cohesion and identity, which encourages workers to think of their collective interests in opposition to their employer. It is vital that aggrieved individuals blame an agency for their problems and that they have a sense of themselves as a distinct group defined in opposition to an 'outgroup', which has different interests and values (Kelly, 1998, pp. 29–30). Thirdly, leaders incite and justify the need for collective action, and fourthly, they legitimize this action in the face of counter-mobilization by employers.

This section shows how leaders in SUD-Rail tried to promote a sense of injustice amongst cleaners and how they helped justify collective action. Sylvestre was the main instigator of collective action amongst the cleaners and put forward the following proposal to the union executive committee for a sit-in (*envahissement*) during the monthly works council meeting.

> Cleaning section
>   A sit-in during the regional works council is envisaged on 22 June, at 14h 30 without a strike notice. It is a protest against working conditions and changes in working time . . . The works council executive will join the rally and a common statement will be made. A hundred cleaners are expected, supported by railway workers.

Sylvestre also wrote a leaflet to hand out to workers where he highlighted the problems for cleaners in relation to their terms and conditions. He identified the cleaning companies as not respecting 'acquired rights' (*aquis sociaux*) and not paying 'overtime'. In the leaflet Sylvestre encouraged and justified the taking of collective action by saying that occupying the works council would mean the workers would be listened to and their demands could be put forward to managers directly. He also attributed blame for the choice of subcontractor and the standards of working conditions to the *regional management* and not to the respective cleaning company managements. It was the 'SNCF regional director' who was credited as being ultimately responsible for the 'working conditions' of cleaners. This interpretative work by Sylvestre can be seen as an attempt to encourage workers to shift their perceptions of attribution away from the company or manager they worked for in their 'private companies' towards the 'SNCF regional director', and to highlight the regional director's role in choosing the private companies and cleaners' 'bosses'.

Sylvestre organized 'union rounds' (*tournée syndicale*) in the week before the action. Union rounds were the main activity linking the union activists to the workplace and took place once a month, normally in the week before representative meetings. They were held more frequently before strikes or other actions and during certain other periods; for example, in the lead-up to the workplace elections. The union rounds for this action aimed to cover as many workplaces and cleaners as possible. Cleaners were based in two main areas: first, in stations, where they were in charge of cleaning trains and looking after station facilities such as toilets and restrooms for railway workers; secondly, in large depots, where they were assigned to clean train interiors whilst trains were stationed there.

As part of the training to encourage self-organization amongst cleaners Sylvestre organized for Abdul (Arab male, mid-thirties), a cleaner with two years' experience as a member of the union and six months' as an elected employee representative, to accompany him on the rounds. An important incentive was that Abdul was from an ethnic minority background and was able to speak Arabic to those Arabic-speaking workers who could not speak French fluently.

The activists visited several workplaces in the region. In one depot the workers were having lunch when the activists arrived. Sylvestre handed out leaflets to each of the tables and said that they would wait until the workers had finished eating before talking to them. Sylvestre handed out the leaflets and came back over to speak to Abdul:

Sylvestre: You can go round once they have finished and talk to them about why the 22 June is so important . . .
Abdul: I am not used to speaking in front of people . . .
Sylvestre: I will show you . . . [they went over to the group of Pakistani workers] . . . do you know about the 22 June . . . Here is the leaflet . . . it is important for you to be there . . . this is Abdul, he cleans trains at [depot] . . . he is going to be there . . . we need to be out in force so the boss can see that we are serious . . . it is the director of the region that decides what companies run the cleaning . . . it was him who put [the manager of the depot] as boss. . .if you are not happy about that then you should come [the four workers nodded] . . . you will lose an afternoon's pay but it will be worth it to show the boss that we are serious.

Sylvestre used similar arguments for cleaners in other workplaces:

here is a leaflet for the 22 June . . . we are occupying the works council . . . it is important for you to be there . . . there used to be 160 people working at this depot and now there are 130 . . . do you think that is normal . . . the work has not changed . . . you are doing more work . . . you will only lose two and a half hours of work and this will stop people like [manager of depot] being your boss.

In these two observations Sylvestre amplified the necessity of engaging in collective action. In pointing towards particular grievances, he was using arguments aimed at encouraging workers to develop a sense of injustice and to act upon it. There was evidence, however, that the activists were unable to convince some workers of the efficacy of collective action. Sylvestre encouraged Abdul to speak to some workers in Arabic. One set of workers started arguing with Abdul. Sylvestre asked what the problem was:

Abdul: They are saying they supported a strike action with Jean-Paul[9] for three months . . . they say they gained nothing and do not want to talk or hear about unions . . .
Sylvestre: I understand that but this time if we can show we are strong then they will have to listen . . .
[One of the workers replied to Abdul in Arabic]
Abdul: It is disappointing that you are not interested . . .
Sylvestre: You should come anyway . . . here is the leaflet . . . it is still important.

Two female cleaner activists from this workplace arrived and Sylvestre told them to speak to the workers every day and at lunchtime before the action and to make sure that they had a number of them coming to the action. The two activists said they were not hopeful but that at least they would be at the action. Sylvestre and Abdul encouraged participation in the action using these tactics during union rounds over two days. In spite of the number of rounds conducted for this action only around 20 cleaners participated in the occupation, and the majority of these were cleaner activists. There were around 40 activists who took part in the action in total. The other 20 participants were railway worker activists. Sylvestre had expected a higher turnout and was disappointed at the number of cleaners participating. During the action, Sylvestre introduced the cleaners' section and talked about the low pay and conditions in the sector, and the fact that it was because the SNCF was taking the lowest bids for cleaning. The director responded by saying that decisions were outside his control and that 'it is the law in France and Europe to put out contracts for re-bidding . . . we have to be competitive'. Jean-Paul responded 'I understand that but there are laws respecting working conditions . . . these are not upheld.' Once again the director explained that it was outside his control but that he would look into the issue of working conditions and companies that were not respecting collective agreements.

An important feature of SUD-Rail's actions was the union's insistence on the participation and intervention of those concerned in the grievances. During the sit-in, two cleaning activists intervened to talk about their conditions of work. Abdul said he had to work extra hours and that some cleaners worked 12 days without a break. He also said that he had been threatened because he was a trade union activist. The director responded to the intervention saying he would look into the issue. This action was within six weeks of a similar action against freight privatization, and the first action of this kind for the new director of the region. The action could be viewed as an opportunity for putting forward the demands of the cleaners and for highlighting the SNCF policy of taking the lowest-bid company to a new audience. However, according to the activists, another aim of the action was to demonstrate their adversarial position to the new director, and show their confrontational and militant approach.

The failure to mobilize large numbers of cleaners could to an extent be explained by the fact that cleaners would have lost pay by participating in the union action. The finances of the union did not extend to a strike fund for these workers. The local union activists admitted that this was a problem for mobilizing cleaning workers. Another explanation is that the cleaners had been involved in previous campaigns with the union, and had not seen changes in their working conditions. The past experiences of workers alongside the prospect of losing pay in further action undoubtedly lowered the salience of Sylvestre's arguments for taking collective action. This demonstrates the significance, which is drawn out in mobilization theory, of workers needing to believe in the efficacy of collective action in order to take action.

CONCLUSIONS

This case study has shown that the activists in the local-level union of SUD-Rail had some success with organizing and mobilizing precarious workers. Out of all the occupational groups, private sector cleaners were the second most organized group in terms of membership within the region. The activists were successful in attracting cleaners to become members of the union, some of whom were motivated by the legal service it offered. Workers were also encouraged to become members of the union to take advantage of the 'protection' offered by becoming a union representative. The local union activists were involved in activities to organize cleaners, which included meetings and training sessions with groups of cleaning members. The activists encouraged the cleaners to become more involved in their union section and to help build union organization. The cleaners were given information on their legal rights in the workplace and on how to enforce these rights. The SUD-Rail activists also organized mobilizations for cleaners, to improve working conditions specifically, and more broadly to put pressure on management not to accept the lowest-bid offers for cleaning contracts in the SNCF.

The organizing and mobilizing of cleaners in SUD-Rail formed part of a broader strategy to help build the union's organization and identity. In the context of highly competitive unionism, organizing the interests of cleaners allowed SUD-Rail to stand out from its competitors. However, the outcome of the campaign for collective action demonstrates that the union activists struggled to convince many of the cleaners of the efficacy of collective action as a way of improving their working conditions. Whilst the activists had limited success in mobilizing these workers, the local union continued to consider this an important activity in the broader process of building local union organization.

This case study contributes to wider debates on trade union renewal strategies and how unions are responding to vulnerable and precarious employment. Increasing privatization and subcontracting pose significant challenges for trade unions, particularly in sectors such as cleaning, where the most marginalized groups within trade unions and in wider society are employed. The turn towards organizing these workers in many trade unions is important for helping to limit the worst aspects of global capitalism.

NOTES

1. The SEIU has developed an international arm and has been helping unions in Europe and elsewhere with campaigns to organize cleaners. The SEIU were involved in the TELCO (living wage) campaign in the UK and also campaigns in Germany and the Netherlands.
2. SUD unions also exist within the private sector – for example, SUD Michelin was created in 2001 – but the high-profile SUD trade unions exist mostly within the public sector and services. There are SUD trade unions in health and education, but two of the most high profile have been in the post and telecommunications (SUD-PTT) and the railways (SUD-Rail).
3. Sylvestre had worked in the SNCF for 15 years and had been with SUD-Rail for 4 years at the time of the research. He was the works council representative for the cleaning union section at regional level and acted as one of the leaders of this section. He was also one of the four representatives in charge of the legal advice service offered by the union. At the time of research he was requesting training to become an employment tribunal judge. All the names used in this chapter are pseudonyms.
4. In France the five nationally representative unions do not have to go through this procedure as they are legally considered representative in all workplaces.
5. Most (though not all) French legislative and regulatory texts concerning employment as an employee and the relationships which are established in connection with it have been collected together and classified in a document called the Labour Code (EMIRE).
6. Every representative union which has members in an enterprise employing more than

50 employees is entitled, under a law of 1968, to appoint a trade union delegate within the enterprise, chosen from among the unionized employees. Trade union delegates are entitled to move freely about the enterprise and to have paid time off to perform their functions (EMIRE).
7. This is the name given to the established civil servants belonging to the Labour Inspectorate. At enterprise and establishment level, the labour inspector is the official who has direct dealings with enterprise managers, unions, workforce representatives employees (EMIRE).
8. Since 1982, it is a statutorily recognized right of employees, when they have good reason to believe that some condition at work poses a serious and imminent danger to their life or health, to stop work without incurring any penalty or deduction from pay (EMIRE).
9. Jean-Paul was the union activist in charge of organizing cleaners before Sylvestre.

REFERENCES

Bernstein, D. (1986), 'The subcontracting of cleaning work in Israel: a case in the casualisation of labour', *Sociological Review*, **34** (3), 396–422.

Chevandier, C. (2002), *Cheminots en grève ou la construction d'une identité (1848–2001)*, Paris: Maisonneuve & Larose.

Connolly, H. (2008), 'Exploring union renewal in France: an ethnographic study of union activists in SUD-Rail', PhD thesis, University of Warwick.

Damesin, R. (2001), 'SUD-PTT et SUD-Rail face à la transformation des secteurs publics: entre coopération et conflit', *Les Cahiers de Recherche du GIP-MIS*, **77**, 13–57.

Damesin, R. and J-M. Denis (2001), 'Syndicalisme(s) SUD', *Les Cahiers de Recherche du GIP-MIS*, **77**.

Damesin, R. and J-M. Denis (2005), 'SUD trade unions: The new organisations trying to conquer the French trade union scene', *Capital and Class*, **86**, 17–37.

Denis, J-M. (2003), 'Les syndicalistes de SUD-PTT: des entrepreneurs de morale?', *Sociologie du Travail*, **45**, 307–25.

Herod, A. and L. Aguiar (2006), 'Introduction: cleaners and the dirty work of neoliberalism', *Antipode*, **38** (3), 425–34.

Kelly, J. (1997), 'The future of trade unionism: injustice, identity and attribution', *Employee Relations*, **19** (5), 400–414.

Kelly, J. (1998), *Rethinking Industrial Relations: Mobilization, Collectivism and Long Waves*, London: Routledge.

Puech, I. (2004), 'Le temps du remue-ménage: conditions d'emploi et de travail des femmes de chambre', *Socologie du Travail*, **46**, 150–67.

Sainsaulieu, I. (1999), *La contestation pragmatique dans le syndicalisme autonome: la question du modele SUD-PTT*, Paris: L'Harmattan.

Sainsaulieu, I. (2006), 'Syndicalisme critique et défi institutionnel: vers l'individualisation du militantisme?', *Relations Industrielles/Industrial Relations*, **61** (4), 684–707.

Snow, D. and R. Benford (1988), 'Ideology, frame resonance and participant mobilisation', *International Social Movement Research*, **1**, 197–218.

Waldinger, R., C. Erickson, R. Milkman, D. Mitchell, A. Valenzuela, K. Wong and M. Keitlen (1998), 'Helots no more: a case study of the Justice for Janitors campaign in Los Angeles', in K. Bronfenbrenner, S. Friedman, R.W. Hurd, R.A. Oswald and R.L. Seeber (eds), *Organizing to Win*, New York: Cornell University Press, pp. 105–19.

Wills, J. (2008), 'Making class politics possible: organizing contract cleaners in London', *International Journal of Urban and Regional Research*, **32** (2), 305–23.

13. Growing power asymmetries, individualization and the continuing relevance of collective responses

Rachid Bouchareb

INTRODUCTION

The difficulties workers in SMEs have in asserting their rights, in joining trade unions and in breathing life into the formal channels of employee representation are well established. They reflect in a particularly obvious way the inequalities in all waged relationships under private property. Constitutive of the way waged relationships operate is a natural hierarchy, imposed as much by the irregularity of employment or of working time as by the persistence of the asymmetrical power relations that separate an employer from a precarious collective of waged workers (Bouquin, 2006; Bouquin et al., 2007).

In SMEs even the concept of 'social dialogue' that developed over several decades out of a concern for good governance and a degree of democratization of employment relations has almost always proved inoperative. Despite this, the working relationships in SMEs do not appear more 'pacific' than in larger companies. Industrial conflicts occur there as frequently because of the way employers act, even if the conflicts are not expressed in as visible or spectacular a way. Thus, for example, while the use of the strike is quite rare, SME employees make up the biggest group of plaintiffs in industrial tribunals in France (the Prud'hommes), and are getting still more numerous.

How to understand these forms of resistance which, at first glance, appear primarily individual? Does one have to analyse them as interpersonal conflicts, whose speedy resolution is enough to preserve the existing contractual framework? Or, on the contrary, should they be analysed as new forms of mobilization and as indicators of a wider level of conflict in the absence of the traditional mechanisms of collective expression?

At the end of various research projects on SMEs (Contrepois, 2004; Bouchareb, 2005) completed during the last few years, this second assumption appears to us to be the most viable. In order to develop the elements of analysis which enable us to arrive at this conclusion, we will present here three studies carried out in IT services (a software firm) and in the retail and hotel (catering) sectors. These three sectors are interesting in that they include a high proportion of SME employment, often working in flexible forms. If retail and catering are relatively traditional sectors, employing a low-skilled labour force, the software sector is new and in full expansion and has a highly skilled workforce.

In spite of their diversity, we observe a rationalization trend in production which has produced new forms of SMEs and precarious work conditions. This evolution of SMEs has entailed management by 'precarization' and a hardening of work relations. Employees are scattered and individualized in their work but we find a number of attempts at resistance and collective opposition.

SOFTWARE FIRMS: INDIVIDUALIZED WORKERS FACING COLLECTIVE CHALLENGES[1]

This investigation related to several software firms of various sizes ranging from fewer than 10 to more than 50 employees, in the Paris area, and was conducted between 2005 and 2006. About fifteen engineers were studied through long interviews about their experience, job, working conditions, hierarchical relations and relations with other employees. This sector has around 300,000 employees, and software firms are extensive users of subcontracted forms of employment and services.

In a generalized subcontracting system, there are huge numbers of commercial relationships between firms, particularly concerning IT. These IT software firms often play a major part in delivering the main services of their customer's firms. Software subcontracting is thus characterized by a strictly commercial supply of personnel, accompanied by the undermining of the employee's status, which is transformed from being full-time and permanent into a form of temporary work.

The contracts of the software firms are generally completed in missions that last between one and 24 months, with flexible employment that uses very highly skilled graduate labour where the job is only permanent for as long as the contract lasts, thus building in precariousness: 'Even if you get a CDI [unlimited contract], the work is not for life . . . We are only recruited when the company gets a contract at a customer' (software engineer, 30 years old, Paris). Subcontracting is becoming increasingly important; 60–70 per cent of software company activities currently consist of providing services of this nature (Fondeur and Sauviat, 2003).

The subcontracting chain creates a strong individualization of work situations. This is similar to temporary work where the temporary workers are by definition dispersed on different contracts and have the impression of being strangers to their workplace and to the other 'permanent' staff. In addition, the frequent changes of 'customer firms' encourage this individualization and make the link to employment more ambiguous, since the software engineer is perceived more like an 'independent' professional than as a waged worker: 'I have less . . . euh. . . in fact, I do not have working relationships with my company; really, none of the relations that normal employees have, what' (software engineer, 34 years old). Consequently, it is the concept of the firm that loses its meaning with this form of work where availability to the market shapes the nature of employment and work. These software firms are characterized by the extreme frequency of wrongful dismissals, which accelerate when there is a fall in activity. According to a leading official from MUNCI:[2] 'Harassment and forms of bullying are generally the first stages before dismissals "on personal grounds" and also lead to many forced resignations.'

There are many accounts of this repression: ending a mission without observing the proper dismissal procedures, only deciding who will get the work after selections are made both at the IT provider and at the client, prolonging and ending probation periods according to the length of the contract, and so forth. The paradox is that software engineers are only taken on by the software firm when they are sure 'to be engaged' by the client, in reality the true employer.

Weak Presence of Employee Representatives and Individual Conflicts that Rarely Surface

The presence of employee representatives (union shop stewards, personnel delegates, works council representatives) is only found in the large software firms, and even there they do very little. According to several software engineers interviewed, their role is often limited to a formal presence. In the few cases where representatives are present, workers none the less consider they are not very informed or do not consider themselves directly represented. A DARES study (Fondeur and Sauviat, 2003) in both software and 'user' firms found that only 14 per cent of the employees considered the role of the staff representatives as significant, while 48 per cent considered it marginal. But, as we will see later, although some consider the representatives do not fulfil their role properly, for others, it is their weakness in meetings with management that is the principal problem:

'they only take notes, and do not raise significant points with the director' (software engineer, 32 years old).

Faced with this situation and unclear roles, the software companies manage employment relations individually and informally, which leaves room for considerable abuse and bullying, in particular for young graduates discovering the implicit standards of the sector. Consequently, conflicts in software firms appear very opaque for isolated employees who lack any form of collective mediation. A software engineer working in a medium-sized firm reported several conflicts with the management hierarchy: disciplinary warnings from the human resource manager pushing him to leave, intimidation or work pressures (on schedules etc). These were never founded on real mistakes but on reprimands related to the issues usually left to the autonomy of the employee. However, as soon as the company wanted 'to force someone to leave' the employee would be accused of delays or over issues that were never raised in busy periods when temporal availability was being required.

In this situation, the software engineer had access to external advice (networks of friends, the trade unions) to get informed about labour law to be able to carry on his own defence with correspondence challenging management. However, he had never felt well informed about his rights ever since working in the sector. In the absence of a trade union presence or of employee representatives in the company, it is largely personal research that is required in the management of conflicts.

Collective Action Due to More Contact Between Employees

In this fragmented professional world, contacts between employees present at the same place of work – when possible – remain key to the processes through which a precarious group leaves the constraints of individualization and develops a group consciousness. According to a union representative, the work group's importance in certain areas, in outsourcing in particular, cannot be overestimated. If you can see the same person lots of times in the same place, this allows exchanges and information to be passed on, something that does not happen when workers are dispersed between many clients: 'In software firms, you can be really isolated when teams are sent to lots of firms, and even in your own firm, sometimes, you don't know the people who come from your own firm' (engineer software firm, 29 years old).

The low level of mobilization reported here is not related to a lack of interest in collective action, but dispersal and individualization through flexible working simply do not make it possible to invest in the long term in an oppositional attitude. In addition, these employees are involved in producing an intellectual product and generally in an individual way. This situation does not make it easy to develop systematic demands arising out of daily pressures, even if there may be a common, shared feeling that each one of them is experiencing the same degraded conditions of employment.

At the same time the size of the company is important in shaping a collective consciousness. In family-type SMEs the interpersonal and reciprocal relations are stronger and are sources of strong cohesion. Paradoxically, this can permit some room for manoeuvre for opposition to management, and even lead to workers deciding collectively to leave in the event of disagreement about company policy. On the other hand, within the impersonal and hierarchical relations that dominate the largest software and user firms, the dominance of market relations often limits the likelihood that software engineers will challenge company policy.

A Need for Collective Action to Face Individualization

According to the DARES study (Fondeur and Sauviat, 2003, p. 4): 'the collective regulation of working relationships is extremely weak, and, in the event of problems, staff address their line managers rather than go to a trade union'. Our interviews carried out with employees of several software firms, however, show that this argument is nuanced according to the state of the tensions at work. The recourse to trade unions remains present even if it is not systematic. Thus, despite their in-house absence, some workers contact the trade unions when an urgent issue arises, while others will seek information from among contacts of trade unions. They can be guided by an opportunist logic as 'consumers' of services, but their behaviours are better explained by their urgent search for modes of defence in the hope of rebalancing power relations.

This particular form of socialization into opposition seldom leads to co-ordinated or durable actions, but it does not necessarily imply the rejection of the collective. The request for protection, even of activist involvement, is simply latent, in particular when the existing actors or the possible modes of actions are difficult to identify, such as in the expectations of one software engineer: 'If I knew people who are there and who would invite me to participate in a meeting, why not? Because it is an opportunity to get trained and informed. But there, I do not know anybody' (an engineer, 31 years old).

In the face of imposed individualization in software firms, it is not possible to support the thesis that workers whose managerial status masks their very limited autonomy and subordinate relationship within commodified relations between companies have rejected trade unionism. Accessing external trade union activists or their contacts demonstrates the presence both of a sense of awareness that their rights are not being respected, and especially of an awareness of the inequalities inherent within waged work relations.

SMALL SHOPS AND PRECARIOUSNESS OF THE WORKING RELATIONSHIPS

This fieldwork related to two types of shops, independent (small employers) and chain store shops, in the Paris area, and was conducted between 2005 and 2006. We researched in five shops and interviewed 40 workers as well as trade union actors. The retail sector accounts for 1.6 million employees and for 30 per cent of SME employment in France. This sector has had a strong growth in employment (+45 per cent in thirty years) and women occupy 60 per cent of jobs, with the norm being part-time work.

The precariousness of retail workers illustrates the increasing difficulties of employee representation in a highly fragmented sector. Here, we cannot speak about an employment status based on observed legal rules. The situations are very opaque and are often close to manpower leasing arrangements. As a result the employees are divided and have very little collective protection at the place of work.

Everywhere in this sector there appears to be deliberate non-observance of the formal thresholds of employee representation: more than 50 per cent of those establishments that should do so[3] do not effectively set up legal representative institutions, and 49.1 per cent of the workers (over 800,000 workers) face this obstacle to their representation rights (Dufour et al., 2004). Moreover, the non-respect of the legal thresholds is even higher where there are higher proportions of precarious jobs and especially of women workers.

This mass precariousness is observed in the split shifts that have become standard, with part-time work assigned to women and the youngest workers who demonstrate the greatest permanent temporal availability. In this situation, where wages are so low, many employees make few demands and are ready to agree to work public holidays, evenings and weekends, to profit from premiums which remain random and are not always monitored.

Moreover, the trend towards precariousness starts from the moment a person is recruited. The small employer will have already made sure the employees are not trade unionized and that they do not know about the minimum wage level, so as to be able to impose the employer's vision of work,[4] in some ways to detach the post from a sense of belonging to a waged workforce entitled to rights: 'And me, I remember at the beginning when I worked for small employers, it was one of the questions asked: are you a trade unionist?' (shop employee, 32 years old). The social control of labour thus starts very early. The employees will have an impression of tolerated behaviour and of the limits not to be exceeded and the penalties for infringements; they will do what they can to conform to the employers' model, at least for the new starts who are least well prepared to face such a demand for subordination. From there the small employers try to exploit the ignorance of work rights to impose even more flexibility. Consequently, the wage relation is shaped largely by the requirements of the hierarchical system.

Working in a Small Shop

The numbers of workers in small shops are kept as low as possible, which increases the workload and the pressure on employees to achieve sales targets. Repression is systematic. Workers cannot develop a logic of mutual support, which is made particularly difficult by divisive tactics such as favouritism and bullying. The least-well-treated employees describe differences in wages and working hours based on the relational proximity of the owner. They find themselves isolated without any possibility of negotiating different working conditions and more respect. A resignation will then constitute the only form of exit in the absence of visible actions of worker solidarity, or any collective opposition.

The employer is dominant and the repressive regime aims to prevent any hint of autonomy in the working relationships between employees. At the same time, employees do not see their waged condition clearly, since many of the relations between 'collaborator' employees and owners are directed towards interpersonal exchanges shaped by the dimension of proximity, and thereby help attenuate the perception of a waged subordination in which owner and workers are opposed.

The worker's room to act is thus subjected to a total engagement in support of the success of the shop. Individual loyalty remains a major characteristic of working relations in these small organizations; always doing more in an environment where the status as 'worker' is hidden behind that of 'member of the family'. Employees do not have real freedom of speech, and any resistance or challenge (over work schedules, for example) will be viewed badly. As in the shopping chains, the employee will get a label as 'troublemaker', and the traditional strategy will then consist of modifying their working conditions (hours and most unpleasant tasks) until they can be dismissed or have been forced to resign.

Loneliness at work is a major characteristic of the closed world of small shops. Employees have a very limited understanding of the world of work, which is often reduced to interpersonal relations. This loneliness will be even more unbearable in the event of a conflict with the owner, going as far as an employment tribunal. In contrast to shops where staff numbers are higher, repression will be inevitable and will be even more visible if the shop has other employees as well. The owner, or the manager, will demonstrate their power in order to dissuade any others from opposition.

Even more than a precarious status, the employees experience a *relational precariousness* explained by the limited number of employees and often by the absence of an intermediate line manager. As a result, it is particularly difficult to describe what happens at the place of work in ways that would allow other employees to feel a greater solidarity to support each other in the face of the employer and of work that often appears to lack value.

The relational aspect is a determining element in explaining frustrations and suffering at work: a feeling of loneliness, of frequently being alone in the shop with the owner, without the possibility of real interaction. These aspects of the working day are particularly testing: 'it is the boredom, the day does not pass quickly' (former saleswoman, small shop). As the small independent retailer has fewer customers than chain shops where the rhythm of work is more constant, the days feel longer and more difficult to support in proximity to the employer.

This situation pushes the employee all the time to show or pretend to show their usefulness, to show their loyalty and, out of fear of reprimands, to seek to find ways of appearing busy (rearranging the shop and so forth). We are very close to the constrained self-exploitation that was the condition of nineteenth-century retail employees whose servant status was not far removed from slavery (Niermann et al., 1979).

Employers' Opposition to Trade Unions

Unquestionably the shop owner, the 'master of his own house', sees labour relations as being part of the private sphere of the shop, and will oppose any trade union intervention. Such an approach demonstrates the desire both to control behaviours at work and to prevent external interventions that could call into question their legitimacy by unveiling power relations.

According to the type of shop and the number of staff, two responses are possible. The employees submitting to the daily pressure of a small employer or manager could try to turn to a trade union in secret, and out of fear of reprisals ask for an intervention from the outside. In spite of the risks of dismissal, it does happen that employees ask a trade union to intervene directly in an individual conflict. This attitude shows a readiness to resist and inverts the customary subordination that characterizes work discipline in shops. Moreover, daily resistance can show itself through acts of insubordination such as refusing to work overtime or to have their working schedules changed arbitrarily, or even through encouraging other workers to do the least work possible. But in several of the cases observed, systematic repression follows, using the employees' fear of losing their employment, and leading to frustration at not being able to get past the stage of individual resistance. Their previous experience of work relations then acts on their perception of the status of being a worker in a small shop, creating the feeling of being alone in negotiating, and of not being able to exchange freely with other colleagues.

In the case of young employees who are less socialized in the world of work, the meaning of turning to trade unions is interesting and complex. Where such a process starts in a small shop, the individual and collective process involved is worth exploring. There may often be a natural process of socialization that encourages a long-held desire to denounce the workplace relationships: to reject subordination, to seek to interact with colleagues and invest in an open challenge. Often there is a real sense of going beyond the imposed limits and that the only way of doing so meaningfully is through taking back collective rights to expression at work:

> This is what I meant. We stay open one Sunday, and some girls asked for the day off to attend their communions, and then asked if they could make up that day at another time in the week. Well, they were turned down because the shop's turnover is really high on Sundays. And so, on two floors of the shop no one worked for the next few Sundays. So the manager says to me: 'Isn't that awful', and I reply: 'You reap what you sow.' It's like that. Suddenly something happens and the staff have just had enough. (woman member of sales staff, trade union representative, 35 years old)

The desire to resist arbitrary employers is always latent, and can be analysed as being a part of an advanced stage of employment relations and of a reasoning that suggests conflict is inevitable. It is not expressed systematically in visible ways, as through spontaneous trade union membership at the place of work, but through a defensiveness that seeks external advice (from networks and/or trade unions):

> I defend my rights alone, I turn to friends, to my parents. And then if really I have a problem, I contact unions or associations. It is true that at the level of rights, I am a little bit naive; I learn every day [. . .]. The existence of unions is essential. They are there to defend us, inform us and seek for us to have better things. (saleswoman, 23 years old, chain shop)

For the employee, their opposition to arbitrary management has to be considerable to allow them mentally to leave the work relations that dominate in the SME private sector, and choose the long and uncertain route of either individual or collective conflict.

In the face of the absence of trade unions from small shops and of the very low trade union density in the whole retail sector (2 per cent), shop workers are forced to adopt other forms of protest – absenteeism, refusal of overtime working, petitions, meetings – which deviate from the traditional image of the conflict by way of strike (Carlet and Tenret, 2007). But this reality also shows that conflict remains present, and even in the absence of trade unions, it helps define employment relations in the sector. In particular the resistance uncovered is directed against the effects of the forms of subordination that are amplified in this type of firm.

UNDERSTANDING THE TURN TO EMPLOYMENT TRIBUNALS IN THE CATERING TRADE[5]

The analysis of the use of employment tribunals in the catering industry throws additional light on the importance of forms of mobilization that could be described as individual. With 850,000 workers in France, the hotel, restaurants and café sector constitutes the major employer of workers who provide private sector individual services to private individuals. It is characterized by its dynamism – 110,000 jobs were created from 1990 to 2000 – and by the socio-economic importance of SMEs: 92.8 per cent of the approximately 175,000 companies that make up the sector employ fewer than 10 workers, and together employ over half the total sector's total manpower. The workforce as a whole is not very skilled, being very young and with a high turnover, as studies carried out by INSEE testify (INSEE, 2003).

The number who participate in occupational and representative elections in the industry is extremely low. Only 75,000 workers participate in works council elections – not even 10 per cent of all the employees. The sector's collective agreement is highly fragmented: there are nine collective agreements coexisting at the national level, and these are broken down into regional collective agreements. Among these, the collective agreement covering the Hotels, Cafés and Restaurants (no. 3292) is the most significant, and since 3 December 1997 its terms are legally binding on a majority of firms in the sector.

These social and demographic characteristics clearly limit the establishment and development of the trade union movement. In any case it is relatively weak. The strongest trade union in the sector is the Paris area Confédération Française Démocratique du Travail Hôtellerie, Tourisme, Restauration (CFDT HTR), which had only some 4,000 members in 2003. Significantly, a large part of its activity is involved on the one hand in sector collective bargaining and on the other hand in providing legal support for workers taking cases to employment tribunals, and the latter absorbs most of its financial resources.

It was therefore with the aim of understanding the dynamics of conflict in the sector and the forms of action that result from this that we decided to examine employment tribunal cases in the catering sector in one particular jurisdictional area of France. Doing so is not straightforward. Any analysis of these procedures encounters several obstacles of which the most significant is undoubtedly the confidentiality that embraces certain stages of the legal procedures. Only the judgements, which relate to 30–50 per cent of the cases (those which did not lead to conciliation), in the services section of the Tribunal where we carried out the research are the subject of a public hearing and consultable reports.

It was thus on this particular stage that we worked, on the one hand by attending certain hearings and interviewing protagonists when that was possible, and on the other hand by systematically analysing the judgements available for a certain period. In total, 105 cases concerning the catering sector were located for the three years 1999 to 2001. In 85 of them a judgement was given. Eight cases were declared too old to be heard, and six were finished by a friendly agreement between the parties before the judgement. Finally, nine cases were struck off, one was re-examined and two were not the subject of a fully detailed report. Most of these legal complaints involved SMEs. In nearly all the cases (103), the applicant was an employee.

How far can these actions at the Employment Tribunal be understood as part of a broader collective process defending workers' rights? A first indicator making it possible to answer this question relates to the role played by the trade unions. At first sight, this appears relatively weak. In almost a third of the cases the employee represented himself or herself or was assisted by a member of their family (31 cases out of 102). The remainder were more frequently assisted by a lawyer (47 cases) than by a union representative (10 cases). We can, however, immediately nuance this observation by indicating that the lawyers can be provided by the trade unions. The interviews tended, in addition, to show that the workers who defended themselves are those who have contacts with a trade union environment, and that this plays a role in their deciding to take their employer to the Tribunal.

Turning to the contents of the cases, the most frequent reason for the Tribunal claim was a challenge to dismissal for serious misconduct or professional insufficiency (38 cases). Next came cases around the non-respect of employee rights concerning dismissal procedures, overtime pay, wage levels, etc. (19 cases); redundancies, generally related to firm collapses (12 cases); resignations as a result of ambiguous work situations (11 cases); breaches of apprenticeship contracts on the initiative of the apprentice or of the employer (6 cases); and breaches of short-term contracts (2 cases). In nearly all cases these were linked to demands for payment of elements of the wages due (hourly rates not respected, overtime pay, holiday pay and so on), demands which confirmed the existence of a latent conflict.

The study of the arguments exchanged between the parties shows that there are two fundamental issues at stake: on the one hand there is the relation of subordination, and on the other the issue of the continuity of the employment relationship.

Extent of Subordination

One section of the cases was classified as related to 'behavioural problems'. These were stigmatized as such by the employers, but in practice it is very difficult to evaluate precisely the reality and the reasons through the minutes of the judgements. We can demonstrate that a certain number of dismissals for 'serious misconduct' came from serious disputes between the employee in question and the employer. It is then interesting to note that these dismissals were in every case reclassified by the court as 'dismissals without real and serious cause', or even as 'wrongful dismissal', which suggests a certain ambiguity in these situations.

Another section of the cases related to the availability of the workers. Most often they occurred after an absence, whether short or long, justified or unjustified, accidental (sickness) or as a normal part of life (maternity leave). Eleven cases of this type were noted, giving rise to a finding of dismissals without fault in 10 cases and to a breach of a fixed-term contract in another. In all the cases the demand for reclassification of the dismissal put by the workers was accompanied by a demand for overtime payments and even holiday pay.

It can thus be noted that several of the cases gave to the employees the opportunity to claim payment for overtime hours, sometimes significant, that they had carried out; claims that required them to bring tangible evidence, which is not always possible for them in the absence of clocking-in cards and the presence of issues in collecting witness statements from work colleagues.

The Continuity of Employment

The cases that raised the issue of the continuity of employment generally occurred when companies were liquidated – the rate of survival of SMEs is particularly low[6] – or, more marginally, within the framework of a reorganization or an evolution of activities. If some claims focused on an ignorance of the existing measures to support workers (where there was non-payment of wages by the company) or from the non-application of legal provisions, others were based on a certain haziness on the rules regarding transfers or closures. In this last case, few guarantees exist for the employees concerning continuity of employment relation in the context of the changes of owner. Moreover, the application of existing measures is largely left to the decisions of the actors.

Drawing together the key points of this study of Tribunal decisions, it is clear that a key issue is about how far these 'micro-conflicts' relating to subordination and employment continuity can have a wider impact in creating a balance of forces more favourable to SME workers. It is difficult to answer in a categorical way. But we can note that during the three years considered, the Employment Tribunal studied adopted an almost systematic policy of reclassification of the dismissals for 'serious misconduct'. This may be seen as contributing to counter the arbitrary power of these SME employers to discipline their employees.

From this point of view, legal action constituted a somewhat positive experience of conflict resolution for the employees. This is the case not only for the employees who took up the challenge themselves, but also undoubtedly for their colleagues and the members of their networks, who might be more inclined thereafter to follow the same route to assert their rights. Moreover, such experiences also constitute bases from which to consolidate or even sometimes to advance collective rules established through the processes of negotiation.

CONCLUSION

Our research shows that in response to the personalization of conflict by SME employers and the individualization of the employment relations, employees are pushed towards an individualization of the types of defence. But this individualization does not take place without reference to more collective frameworks available in society, as the content of the legal actions demonstrates.

As for collective action in itself, it is clearly much more difficult to organize in the absence of a trade union presence. That does not, however, prevent the emergence of some collective actions (petitions against management, associations of former dismissed employees and so on), suggesting the presence of forms of solidarity between workers and the possibility of opposition in SMEs. But the size of firm remains determining. A close locational relationship of workers to each other in the same place of work is the element most capable of facilitating exchanges necessary to formulate and express demands.

Several social issues appear in the current unequal balance of forces at work, expressed through the importance of disciplinary dismissals in SMEs, including those of so-called 'protected' employee representatives.[7] Ignorance of labour law not only contributes to maintain situations of injustice, but also to some extent holds back the development of the whole body of legal protections that frame the wage relation in France.

Another issue is how trade union co-ordination can be improved across workplaces involving many different SMEs. The role of the sector trade union and collective bargaining remains crucial here. It can weaken the negative effects of the dispersion of employment that results from increasingly flexible forms of production and employment. It remains important to harmonize employment and working conditions upwards in a direction more favourable to all the workers so that those in SMEs are not penalized.

NOTES

1. See Bouchareb and Oyharçabal (2006).
2. MUNCI (http:\\\www.munci.org), an autonomous association of professionals, independents and engineers, had 1,162 members in 2008 (see also Chapter 9 above). Software SMEs have 3,000 union members, that is, 1 per cent of the employees of the branch. This rate is extremely low, in particular by comparison with the general French trade union density for professionals, known as *cadres* (approximately 7 per cent on average for all sectors).
3. The law on collective representation applies to SMEs with more than 11 employees (which should elect staff representatives) and with over 50 employees (which should also elect work council representatives).
4. This vision suggests that small shop employees should not count the hours they work, while managers of chain stores should show complete working-time flexibility.
5. The research into the catering sector described in this section was carried out by Sylvie Contrepois.
6. In this sector the survival rate of companies is only 35 per cent over a five-year time horizon for newly created companies and 40 per cent for companies that are taken over. In the other sectors, these rates are respectively 46 and 57 per cent.
7. In the establishments with 50 to 199 workers which had carried out a request for dismissal of protected employees (staff representatives), 36 per cent of these requests were founded on an economic reason and 64 per cent on a personal reason; for other workers, economic reasons and personal reasons respectively represent 44 per cent and 56 per cent of the dismissals. See Carlier (2009).

REFERENCES

Bouchareb, R. (2005), 'L'emploi et les relations professionnelles dans les PME du commerce de détail', *SMALL: Representation and Voice in Small and Medium Sized European Firms*, vol. 1: *Report of Research*, Paris: IRESCO, pp. 2–31.

Bouchareb, R. and C. Oyharçabal (2006), 'Sous-traitançe informatique et absence de représentation syndicale: des raisons multiples', *Les Mondes du Travail*, **1**, 73–82.

Bouquin, S. (ed.) (2006), 'Relations de travail, syndicalisme et dialogue social dans les PME', *Les Mondes du Travail*, **1** (1), special issue.

Bouquin, S., S. Leonardi and S. Moore (eds) (2007), 'Can Europe's trade unions represent and organise workers in SMEs?', *Transfer*, **13** (1), 13–146.

Carlier, A. (2009), 'Licenciement des salaries protégés et gestion de la main d'œuvre par les entreprises: une analyse des pratiques', *Premières Synthèses*, 06.1, 6pp.

Carlier, A. and E. Tenret (2007), 'Des conflits du travail plus nombreux et plus diversifiés', *Premières Synthèses*, 08.1.

Contrepois, S. (2004), *La représentation des salariés dans les petites et moyennes entreprises: le cas de l'hôtellerie restauration* (results of European contract SMALL), XVIIth Congress of the AISLF, Tours, 5–9 July.

Dufour, C., A. Hedge, A. Malan and P. Zouary (2004), *Post-enquête Réponse. Des institutions et des acteurs dans les entreprises: pour quelles relations sociales?*, report, Noisy-Le-Grand: IRES, 104.

Fondeur, Y. and C. Sauviat (2003), 'Technologies de l'information: normes d'emploi et marché du travail', *Premières Synthèses*, 13.2.

INSEE (2003), 'L'hôtellerie, la restauration et les cafés, un secteur très spécifique en termes d'emploi et de rémunération', *INSEE Première*, 889.

Niermann, C., A. Saur, P. Schöttler and E. Sinner (1979), 'Petit commerce et apprentissage à Brême au début du XXe siècle', *Le Mouvement Social*, **108**, 31–150.

14. Changing lanes or stuck in the slow lane? Employment precariousness and labour market status of MG Rover workers four years after closure

Alex de Ruyter, David Bailey and Michelle Mahdon

INTRODUCTION: GLOBALIZATION, FLEXIBILITY AND PRECARIOUSNESS

A recurrent theme in international policy debates spanning the years 1985–2010 has been the imperatives of globalization and economic restructuring. In advanced industrial economies discussion has centred on the need to reduce trade barriers, reduce costs and improve competitiveness against low-cost NICs and emerging economies such as the 'BRICs' (Brazil, Russia, India and China). Typically, discussions have focused on the need for advanced economies to streamline welfare regimes and encourage greater flexibility in labour and product markets (OECD, 1994). A key manifestation of globalization (in the UK and US particularly, but also other industrialized countries) has been an apparent shift away from manufacturing to services industries; a process which has been typified in the UK by a number of high-profile plant closures (Pike, 2002, 2005; Bailey et al., 2008a, 2008b; Armstrong et al., 2008). In practice, the position is more nuanced than this, with a process of deindustrialization combined with a blurring of the lines between manufacturing and services (Brinkley, 2009).

As such, whilst total employment in industrialized countries such as the UK had grown (certainly until the current economic crisis at the time of writing), many newly created positions required skills that were not found in the industries shedding labour – or else have been in substandard, low-paid, low-skilled, low-job-security occupations (Nolan, 2004). There is evidence to suggest that cycles of recession and structural change have been associated with a more parsimonious use of (now) flexible labour across industries (Peck and Theodore, 2007). Hence, the subsequent labour market experiences of displaced manufacturing workers in particular can provide sobering lessons for the ongoing impact of structural change and labour market adjustment elsewhere. These impacts also provide salutary lessons for trade unions, which have been severely affected by the decline in secure traditional sectors. Trade union density in the UK remains at historically low levels – 27.4 per cent of employees during 2008 (ONS, 2009) – and this masks a growing gap between males and females, with female density higher than male (ibid.).

Under pro-trade and foreign direct investment regimes, MNCs have engaged in the extensive subcontracting and outsourcing of production and employment across developed and developing countries. This has entailed a fragmentation of production whereby MNCs can use the threat of relocation as a means to secure lower costs and higher productivity across individual sub-units in countries as well as enhanced subsidy packages (Bailey and de Ruyter, 2007). Ackroyd and Procter (1998) found that UK manufacturers, for example, had increasingly restructured their operations so as to achieve 'competitiveness' through a reliance on relatively low-skilled flexible labour and the extensive use of subcontracting and outsourcing (ibid., p. 171) – a deliberate pursuit of flexibility in response to financial control imperatives whereby production is evaluated against pre-set financial targets (and non-performing units could be easily dispensed with, given the low levels of training and technology involved). Consequently, this has led to a realignment of production regimes across and within countries (Jones et al., 2005).

In this context, the closure of the MG Rover (MGR) plant at Longbridge (in Birmingham) in April 2005 was one of the most significant in the UK for twenty-five years; with the loss of some 6,300 jobs (Armstrong et al., 2008). However, by April 2008, some 90 per cent had obtained full-time employment or self-employment (Bailey et al., 2008a). As such, in some respects this can be interpreted as a successful example of structural change, with only 10 per cent unemployed or otherwise economically inactive at the same period. However, against this – and of particular interest given ex-prime minister Tony Blair's view that ex-MGR workers would be able to find 'full and fulfilling jobs' – is that the gross average salary of workers had decreased significantly, even three years after closure (ibid.).

It should be noted that 'good jobs' involve more than income but crucially more than income and job security too. Good quality jobs can be seen to comprise: autonomy and task discretion; control; a lack of monotony; an appropriate use of skills; a balance between effort and reward; fairness; support; and the opportunity for development and progression. For example, in a recent analysis of the European Working Conditions Survey (EWCS), Fauth and McVerry (2008) constructed an index of 'good jobs' comprising 18 indicators. Using elements of the EWCS survey, we asked our sample of ex-MG Rover workers about various aspects of their current jobs in order to compile a comparative measure of their job quality. In our survey we asked respondents about 17 of those 18 indicators. In general, the job quality reported by our sample was reported as an average score of 7 out of 17 job quality indicators. However, when compared with national averages collected by the EWCS, the differences were particularly striking when comparing workers from the MG Rover surveys working in 'non-professional occupations'. The ex-MG Rover workers reported lower levels of autonomy, challenge, skill use, progression and opportunity in their post-MG Rover jobs than the UK national average (Bailey et al., 2008a).

This highlights that for many (if not most) ex-workers, significant issues of job quality remain, as well as issues of precariousness in terms of insecurity of income, representation and tenure, with these now exacerbated by the impact of the current financial crisis and consequent economic downturn. Here, the subsequent labour market experiences of ex-MGR workers can provide valuable insights for the many other workers in deindustrializing 'mature' economies currently facing redundancy; and also for policy makers and trade unions. As such, the current economic situation places a renewed emphasis in policy circles on issues of *precariousness* in the labour market and hence security of employment. Hence, it is these aspects of what has been described as 'precariousness of employment' (Burgess and Campbell, 1998) on ex-MGR workers that this chapter seeks to explore; building on the analysis of de Ruyter et al. (2009). It is not the purpose of this chapter to provide a comprehensive account of typologies of precariousness and job insecurity (readers are invited to de Ruyter et al., 2009, and de Ruyter and Burgess, 2003, for a more comprehensive discussion). However, we may note that one key typology of precariousness is that of Standing's (1997) framework of labour security/insecurity (see also de Ruyter and Burgess, 2003), which encapsulates seven aspects of security/insecurity, pertaining to the nature of the labour market, job/task specification, physical nature of work, skill reproduction, representation, income and employment (protection from arbitrary dismissal) security.

In what follows, we focus on precariousness and labour market adjustment as they pertain to tenure, income and union representation, utilizing the findings of a longitudinal survey of ex-MGR workers and qualitative data obtained from interviews with ex-MGR workers and trade union representatives.[1] These findings are then discussed with a view to expounding lessons further for practitioners and policy in these areas.

METHODS AND DATA

The data used in this chapter consists of findings from a three-wave longitudinal survey of ex-Rover workers, building on the findings of Armstrong et al. (2008). Letters were sent to ex-MGR workers inviting them to participate in the research via a telephone interview, lasting approximately for 20 minutes. This was conducted in accordance with the ethical principles of fully informed voluntary participation, anonymity and confidentiality. The third wave of this survey (which is the focus of this chapter) was carried out in April 2008; three years after the closure (see Bailey et al., 2008a, for a complete discussion).

Ex-MGR workers were first interviewed in July 2005 (wave 1, three months after the closure), again in December 2005 (wave 2) and finally in April 2008 (wave 3). In the first wave, 273 interviews were conducted with ex-MGR workers. In the second wave, 232 interviews were conducted, and in the third wave 204 interviews were conducted, with 176 ex-workers across all three waves and 19 new volunteers. The demographic profiles of the samples were representative of the MGR workforce. Similarly to the MGR workforce, the third-wave sample was 93 per cent male, and the majority (over 70 per cent) of workers were aged between 40 and 54 (with an average age of 48 years) and had worked on average for 21 years at MGR. The median yearly salary back in 2005 of the ex-workers interviewed at MGR was £27,624 or a weekly salary of £514, as compared with a median £404 for a full-time worker (£444 for a man) in the West Midlands in 2005. Approximately 80 per cent of the respondents were married, whilst some 93 per cent were home-owners (with 55 per cent still paying a mortgage) in 2008. The composition of our sample was highly representative of the demographics and job type of the MG Rover workforce as a whole, which enabled a high degree of generalization of the findings (Bailey et al., 2008a).

The survey data was supplemented with qualitative interview data (face-to-face and by telephone) obtained from ex-workers (over 20 in total, at the time of writing) and trade union representatives (three, in total). These interviews were conducted between July 2008 and April 2009 and consisted of semi-structured sessions which lasted for approximately 30 minutes, at which issues pertaining to precariousness and income, tenure and union representation could be explored further.

FINDINGS

Prima facie, it could be argued that a majority of the ex-MGR workforce appeared to have undertaken successful labour market adjustments as at April 2008, having noted that approximately 90 per cent of ex-MGR workers were in employment, with nearly three-quarters of the cohort describing themselves as being employed full-time (150 out of 204 workers interviewed), with 12 employed part-time and 23 self-employed (Bailey et al., 2008a).[2] However, another 10 workers described themselves as unemployed and looking for work and 4 as unemployed but not looking for work. Interestingly, approximately half of those employed full-time at wave 3 reported having had more than one job since leaving MG Rover, as had those in full-time education and training.

Against the overall positive picture regarding the number of ex-workers who were back in work of some form, it was evident that the average salaries obtained by ex-workers had declined, even three years after the closure (this in turn conceals significant gains for some workers relative to earnings at MGR; in turn suggesting widening earnings dispersion amongst the cohort). In addition, some 25 per cent of respondents reported that their household was facing financial difficulties. This in itself is indicative of a depressed local labour market situation in the West Midlands (Chapain and Murie, 2008), with the official (ILO) unemployment rate in the Birmingham City Council local authority having remained around 9 per cent for much of the recent period (de Ruyter et al., 2009); the current economic downturn has only added to this. In this context, ex-MGR workers were, in many cases, simply taking those jobs that they could and in turn displacing the already unemployed in the job queue, a sort of 'ripple effect'.

The findings, then, suggest a more complex, mixed picture of the impact of the closure on the overall nature of work entered into, and hence the degree of precariousness entailed by the impact of the closure. Accordingly, in what follows we provide a critical assessment of the degree of precariousness in work arrangements entered into by ex-MGR workers.

Income Levels

As noted above, overall, significant falls in earnings were reported by respondents. Given that more than three years had elapsed since the closure and third wave of the survey, this discrepancy represents a significant decline in annual wages. Our findings also indicate a greater dispersion of earnings, with a third of respondents reporting an increase in salary and two-thirds a decrease in salary, as illustrated in Table 14.1.

*Table 14.1   Median, minimum and maximum annual salaries at MG
Rover and at April 2008 (wave 3)*

Employed respondents at wave 3 (n = 173)	Median (£)	Minimum (£)	Maximum (£)
Last salary at MG Rover	24,000	9,000	70,000
Current salary	20,800	3,588	180,000
Difference in salary	*−3,400*	*−4,680*	*159,800*

Source: De Ruyter et al. (2009) and Bailey et al. (2008a), both from survey.

On the basis of unadjusted wage differences, the survey showed that workers employed at the time of the wave 3 interviews were earning less than whilst they were employed by MGR across most industries, with the exception of those working in construction, where workers were earning about £1,000 more per annum than at MGR (although even here the effects of inflation on this nominal figure would in all likelihood erode these gains relative to their MGR salary, even before considering the impact of the current economic downturn on the construction sector). As one union representative commented:

> Whilst they could earn on average over £24K p.a. at Longbridge they are now typically getting in the range of £16–£19K; to this you then have to add travelling costs. I know people who do three shifts at SupplierCo, only just to earn the minimum £368 weekly rate they were earning at Longbridge. (Union representative 1, October 2008)

For many, this meant having to rely on savings just to enable what they regarded as an ordinary standard of living, as a number of workers commented:

> since I left MGR, we've been living on savings; that won't last me until I die. I won't be able to go on holidays or anything like that. (Worker 1, October 2008)

> My financial situation though, once you factor in the travel costs of going 40 miles each day there and back, has deteriorated I'd say. (Worker 4, November 2008)

These findings were particularly evident for the 5 per cent of respondents who were employed part-time and the 14 per cent of employed respondents who were in temporary or agency work as at April 2008. The financial pressure that an increase in income insecurity has placed on many workers has also been linked to increased family breakdown, stress and alcoholism.

This was commented on by respondents who were only too well aware of the stresses that this placed on family cohesion:

> Your minimum wage would be about £200 a week; for many this meant you had to start again. Many of the guys didn't know how to do that, so they turned to the bottle so you know . . . there's been a bit of family break-up. (Worker 2, October 2008)

> Well I suffer with depression. It's not just from Rover but that has a big part to do with it and I'm on medication at the moment. My wife and I didn't cope very well at first and we suffered a break-up but we've managed to get back together. (Worker 9, April 2009)

Hence, the findings of this chapter suggest that significant issues pertaining to income security remain for many workers, a situation which has become an increasing concern in the current context. The lack of security of tenure felt by many in a depressed economic climate is an issue we explore in the next section.

Tenure

As inferred from the preceding analysis, some 86 per cent of ex-MGR workers who were employed as at April 2008 described themselves as being in permanent employment (virtually all full-time jobs). However, it was apparent that only a quarter of respondents had the same job in April 2008 as in November 2005 (six months after the closure). This suggests that for a significant proportion of the workforce, a lack of automatic entitlement to claim unfair dismissal may be an issue, given that unfair dismissal provisions only pertain to those with more than 12 months' tenure in their current job. Those in position for less than a year are effectively excluded from the coverage of employment protection law as pertaining to unfair dismissal (Waring et al., 2006).

Hence, it is important to examine the number of jobs that ex-workers have had since the closure. It was evident that workers had often had more than one job since working at MG Rover. Approximately half of those employed full-time at wave 3 reported having had more than one job since leaving MG Rover, as had those in full-time education and training. All of the workers in part-time employment and in part-time education and training reported that they had had more than one job since MG Rover. In addition, approximately half of those unemployed and looking for work, and three-quarters of those unemployed and not looking for work, reported having had more than one job since leaving MGR. This would suggest that for many workers, the nature of jobs entered into has been substandard and/or temporary (precarious cycles); and for some at least, a route to exiting the workforce entirely.

Also apparent was that even in jobs described as 'permanent full-time' by respondents, there was no guarantee that the jobs actually had a formal contract attached to them:

> Regarding the job that I had, I was the only person employed 'full time' – though without a formal contract, as I mentioned. I was 'on the books' and regarded it as permanent, even though I didn't have a contract. I didn't get occupational sick pay but I did get holiday leave. (Worker 5, November 2008)

This particular worker was subsequently laid off in June 2008, in the midst of the current economic downturn: 'now here I am, back in the job market; I have an interview tomorrow' (ibid.). As this example indicates, even jobs that at first glance may appear as 'secure' or 'full-time' may actually be highly precarious, 'informal' (or 'permanent casual') jobs, with no real protection from the vagaries of the external labour market. It is therefore evident in the current context that many of these individuals are at high risk of being made redundant again. This was amply illustrated by one ex-worker (a tooling manager at MGR), who in his new (current) role, employed a number of ex-MGR workers:

> When I started with [Tool Co.] they got me to employ more people. I took on 10 ex-MGR workers six months after Rover went bust – but now, of those ten, I only have three left who are permanent full-time. Two others are working on-and-off as casuals, and the other five have all gone.
> I was going to [i.e. supplying] eight or nine companies. Now three of them are out of business and of those that are left, most are on three-day weeks and have lost 40 to 50 per cent of their workforce. It's carnage in the car industry at the moment. (Worker 8, April 2009)

This shift from long-term tenured employment at MGR (where the average tenure for the sample was 21 years) to the current context is demonstrative of increased precariousness of tenure (that is, a rise in *employment insecurity*; de Ruyter et al., 2009). In this context, self-employment could also be regarded as displaying a high degree of employment insecurity: of the 23 workers (11 per cent of the cohort) describing themselves as 'self-employed' at wave 3, it was notable that the majority of these individuals had just one client – that is, that they were in effect dependent contractors. For these individuals, despite the fact that they tended to be more highly skilled 'consultants', it could still be argued that they had experienced a decrease in employment security, as they were reliant on one 'customer' for their livelihood; hence they could be considered as 'surrogate employees', but without the protection generally available to employees.

For ex-workers trapped in unemployment or casual employment arrangements in particular, there were clear negative implications for psychological well-being and a solid sense of self-worth, reinforcing earlier studies that demonstrate the negative effects that this can have:

> If my current situation goes on much longer I'll be unemployable. Even I will start to believe at some point that it's pointless to do anything else other than casual work, and that . . . upsets me. I have a great deal to offer. (Worker 1, October 2008)

Overall, this discussion suggests that considerable issues pertaining to security of tenure remain central to concerns expressed by ex-MGR workers, a situation exacerbated by the current recessionary context. In the next section, we link concerns around tenure and redundancy to the related issue of voice and representation in the workplace.

Representation

As noted in the introduction, structural change and plant closures have been key factors behind the fall in trade union density in the UK; and hence a fall in *representation security* (that is, secure voice mechanisms in the workplace). The findings of wave 3 strongly indicate that representation security had declined for ex-MGR workers, with only 37.5 per cent of respondents indicating they were currently members of a trade union. Whilst this is higher than the reported national average of 27.4 per cent during 2008 (ONS, 2009), it represents a severe fall from the virtually 100 per cent union membership at MGR. Indeed, the previously reported strong camaraderie and good working conditions experienced at MGR held strong positive memories that were hard for new jobs to compete with (Armstrong, 2006). As a union representative who had been at MGR put it:

> I'm slightly detached from it now working in Coventry; but you know, I have no intention of moving from here, due to the real [local] community that I feel part of. I moved here from Wales 30 years ago and then my brother was also able to get a job here. (Union representative 1, October 2008)

However, also evident is that the decline in union membership possibly indicates a decline in collective identity felt by many ex-workers. Evidence from the worker interviews revealed feelings of disillusionment and even resentment at the union movement in a perceived failing to be more proactive in averting the closure, with a consequent feeling of 'being alone' and 'having to look out for one's self as no one else will':

the union ain't strong like they used to be; they're just for themselves. They [the union] wrote to me askin' 'do you want to maintain your membership' and I said 'why?'. I would never again trust a government in this country. (Worker 2, October 2008)

This development in itself could be cause for concern – particularly given that in the current context many workers may struggle to cope in an atomistic flexible labour market where an economic downturn could result in many of those currently in employment being made redundant again, but without the recourse of having a trade union to 'police' their employment rights.[3] Union representatives in turn were aware of these types of concerns. It was acknowledged that an overriding emphasis on maximizing redundancy payouts (albeit not in the MGR case) had perhaps occurred at the expense of pursuing alternative measures of preventing plant closure, such as reduced hours:

Historically, when redundancies have occurred, our focus has been on enhancing the amount of severance pay. In that sense though, we [the union movement] have almost become architects of our own downfall; where those privileged few in manufacturing get a good payout. (Union representative 3, October 2008)

It was also pointed out that workers themselves in such situations were often only all too eager to go for a redundancy payout, and that (multinational) companies in turn were aware of this and sought to use it to their advantage:

every time we have been through a serious vote on strike action to protest against plant closures rather than taking redundancy payments, our members go for redundancy payments. Ford are a classic at this; heated debates at the negotiating table with our reps – that's fine – but then they tell us that 'the cheque book is open and we are confident that your members will take it'. Ford still find generous redundancy payouts [in the UK] cheaper than plant closures elsewhere. (ibid.)

However, in the current context of widespread redundancies in the UK economy, other ex-MGR workers reported a different view of unions, namely that they increasingly recognized the renewed value of having a collective voice – particularly those respondents who had subsequently obtained work in a non-union environment and had questioned the fairness or veracity of the management decision-making process, particularly in matters pertaining to major workplace change or redundancy:

in rejoining a union, I think that having a collective voice does help – at the last place it was all individual and you just don't know the accuracy of what the company is telling you half the time do you? Having that voice could make a difference in things like discussing redundancies. (Worker 17, April 2009)

I rejoined UNITE in November 08 because I could see what was coming. The company was getting rid of people for what I thought were very dodgy reasons . . . how management work without a union being present has completely changed my view of the unions. (Worker 11, April 2009)

In the absence of traditional forms of collective representation at the workplace, workers resorted to bodies such as the Citizens Advice Bureau (CAB) network, ACAS (Advisory Conciliation and Arbitration Service), the Inland Revenue and the providers of legal aid to obtain advice on any employment or redundancy-related concerns they might have had. However, the capacity of these overstretched bodies to provide substantial support to workers was extremely limited, given the volume of enquiries they had to process:

Well I rang them [the CAB], but they are always very busy . . . they have a lot of problems with the number of people nowadays who are in debt and are having trouble making payments, back in 2005 and more so now I reckon. It took awhile to get though on every occasion I rang them – more than 30 minutes each time! (Worker 13, April 2009)

The Inland Revenue, for example, which investigates violations of the national minimum wage and is responsible for its enforcement, only employs around 100 compliance officers to investigate complaints and undertake actions nationwide (Croucher and White, 2007). Similarly, as alluded to above, CAB are also heavily utilized with some 26,000 staff (15,800 on a volunteer basis) in 448 bureaux across England, Wales and Northern Ireland having dealt with some 1.9 million people (for 5.5 million issues) during 2007–2008 (CAB, 2008). Employment concerns were significant, with 500,000 employment-related issues arising during 2003–2004 alone; typically relating to terms and conditions, redundancy and unfair dismissal (NACAB, 2004, cited in Abbott, 2006, pp. 443, 439). However, intervention was limited to responding to individual complaints and thus provided a contrast to the ability of unions to have sustained workplace presence. As such, CABs did not extend their influence within an organization by mobilizing workers around a single common issue (ibid., p. 443).

These findings suggest that, in the absence of trade union revival and renewal, further measures need to be put in place to improve worker voice and representation, that go beyond reliance on an overburdened voluntary sector; a theme that is taken up further in the following section.

DISCUSSION: IMPLICATIONS FOR POLICY AND PRACTICE

Our findings suggest that significant issues remain for workers with respect to income, tenure and representation, which in turn are indicative of broader trends and problems in the UK labour market. With the median wage in the UK at some £23,000 p.a. and only 10 per cent of workers earning more than £40,000 p.a.[4] it is evident that low income (combined in many cases with insecurity of income) has become the norm for many. In addition to low(er)-wage jobs, some 30 per cent of workers interviewed reported a lower occupational status than at MG Rover, suggesting a shift for many into low(er)-skilled jobs (particularly in the services).

Hence, a key issue for government – particularly pressing in the current context – is whether 'bad' jobs can indeed be turned into 'good' jobs (Armstrong et al., 2008). As part of this, and recognizing that a 'bad job' is not just a low-paid job, a more focused and sophisticated effort needs to be made to improve the wages of the working poor that goes beyond a reliance on the minimum wage. In the UK, the wages of the very low paid have been supplemented with tax credits, with those on minimum wages able to receive the maximum entitlements (Armstrong et al., 2008). This is commendable and has greatly assisted those at the bottom. However, there is a need to go further, in also considering low-paid jobs above the level of the national minimum wage. The concerns around giving the lower paid a genuine living wage and making work pay are issues that have been commented on by ex-workers themselves, reiterating an awareness that income inequality in itself imposes social costs on society:

> It's no good saying to me that 'we'll put 10,000 retail park jobs into Longbridge' when you had 20,000 real jobs at Rover. We've just not given the kids any real opportunities; who wants to work for £5.73 an hour? People would be better off on benefits. They moan about benefit spongers, but they've created the problem . . . yes one could say 'cut the dole' but if you've got two or three kids, then if you've got nothing, you've got nothing to lose . . . Let me tell you, half the problems of the world stem from there being the haves and the have-nots. Poverty is the biggest problem in the world; it causes crime, obesity, sickness, war and terrorism. (Worker 8, April 2009)

These concerns are also integrally linked to broader concerns of reinvigorating industrial policy and promoting high-tech jobs (De Ruyter et al., 2009; Bailey and MacNeill, 2008). However, the promotion of a living wage and providing quality, fulfilling jobs are also in turn related to issues of representation. What is especially evident from the interviews with union representatives is that the current regional development agenda, whilst emphasizing skills acquisition and 'competitiveness', has lacked any clear employment relations component, despite research that suggests that 'efficiency wages' and the promotion of positive labour relations are an essential ingredient of fostering innovation and dynamic efficiency (Kleinknecht, 1998). As one union representative commented:

> AWM [the Regional Development Organization] don't get involved in labour market issues . . . they don't think of productivity issues as being part of employment relations. The idea that positive employee relations could be conducive to productivity enhancements and hence competitiveness is completely alien to them. They just don't see the importance. (Union representative 3, October 2008)

Finally, a climate of positive labour relations is also integral to measures to shield workers from the undue impacts of plant closure and redundancy in future. In part this requires more effective consultation rights in order to engage and involve the workforce at as early a stage as possible, and where possible slowing down the closure 'process' or finding alternative routes to preserve jobs and skills. The manifest decline in representation security also points to the need to ensure that workers caught in subsequent cycles of closure and redundancy have ready access to advice and advocacy that goes beyond a reliance on an overburdened voluntary and not-for-profit sector – and of course, further regulatory measures to stop companies reverting to mass redundancies as a 'soft' or 'easy' option.

CONCLUSION

This chapter has presented a discursive analysis of the nature of labour security pertaining to issues of tenure, income and representation for MGR workers four years after closure. The findings suggested that at one level, the short-term assistance epitomized by the government's task-force approach (Bailey et al., 2008a; Armstrong et al., 2008) facilitated relatively successful labour market adjustment for the ex-MGR workforce by April 2008, with approximately 90 per cent of ex-MGR workers having obtained some form of employment. At a time when over 6,000 workers lost their jobs, the agencies involved in assisting the workers should be praised for their efforts in helping so many workers in such a short space of time. By April 2008, only 5 per cent were still unemployed and looking for work. The findings also revealed a shift away from manufacturing towards jobs in the services sectors.

However, the research also unveiled sharp declines in income security, with a majority of respondents reporting a significant decline in earnings from when they worked at MGR and also a greater turnover of jobs, with – by implication – less access to employment protection rights. Furthermore, a quarter of respondents reported that they were experiencing financial difficulties. Concerns over tenure and income security are even more important now in the current recessionary context (as revealed by the supplementary interviews); successful adjustment in 2008 is no guarantee that a worker could not have been made redundant *again* by 2009 (and/or that workers had not experienced three years of security but instead had been changing jobs). The implications of this analysis are that low pay and insecurity of tenure are now the norm for many in the workforce and that more needs to be done to provide quality jobs and 'make work pay' (Armstrong et al., 2008). The decline in representation security also highlights the need to ensure that workers have adequate recourse to advice and advocacy (traditionally provided by the union movement), and raises issues about union renewal and encouragement. It suggests too that measures are needed to avoid a repeat of sudden and catastrophic plant closures. All of these in turn combine to form significant challenges for policy makers in the UK and internationally in defending high-quality manufacturing jobs. Simply transferring policy from one environment to another rarely works, but we would suggest that examples of 'good practice' need to be identified in different countries in terms of how to safeguard jobs during a severe downturn, as well as in terms of how to deal with plant closure situations.

NOTES

1. Our data suggests that other aspects of job quality were also lower in 2008 on average for ex-MG Rover workers than before.
2. Ninety-eight per cent of the sample had worked full-time at MG Rover (Bailey et al., 2008a).
3. From a very different perspective, the involvement of unions at Jaguar Land Rover has been seen as critical in workers and management agreeing a 'pain-sharing' deal through the current downturn.
4. See http://www.guardian.co.uk/commentisfree/2008/nov/25/pre-budget-report-economy1 (accessed 26 November 2008).

REFERENCES

Abbott, B. (2006), 'Determining the significance of the citizens' advice bureau as an industrial relations actor', *Employee Relations*, **28** (5), 435–48.
Ackroyd, S. and S. Procter (1998), 'British manufacturing organisation and

workplace industrial relations: some attributes of the new flexible firm', *British Journal of Industrial Relations*, **36** (2), 163–83.

Armstrong, K. (2006), *Life After MG Rover: The Impact of the Closure on the Workers, their Families and the Community*, report commissioned for BBC Radio 4, London: The Work Foundation.

Armstrong, K., D. Bailey, A. de Ruyter, M. Mahdon and H. Thomas (2008), 'The impact of plant closures on workers: a comparison of MG Rover in the UK and Mitsubishi in Australia', *Policy Studies*, **29** (3), 343–55.

Bailey, D. and A. de Ruyter (2007), 'Globalisation, economic freedom and strategic decision-making: a role for industrial policy?', *Policy Studies*, **28** (4) 383–98.

Bailey, D. and S. MacNeill (2008), 'The Rover task force: a case study in proactive and reactive policy intervention?', *Regional Science Policy and Practice*, **1** (1), 1–16.

Bailey, D., C. Chapain, M. Mahdon and R. Fauth (2008a), *Life after Longbridge: Three Years on. Pathways to Re-employment in a Restructuring Economy*, London: The Work Foundation.

Bailey, D, S. Kobayashi and S. MacNeill (2008b), 'Rover and out? Globalisation, the West Midlands auto cluster, and the end of MG Rover', *Policy Studies*, **29** (3) 267–79.

Brinkley, I. (2009), *Manufacturing and the Knowledge Economy*, London: The Work Foundation.

Burgess, J. and I. Campbell (1998), 'The nature and dimensions of precarious employment in Australia', *Labour and Industry*, **8** (3), 5–22.

CAB (2008), *Citizens Advice: Annual Report and Accounts 2007/08*, London: Citizens Advice Bureau.

Chapain, C. and A. Murie (2008), 'The impact of factory closure on local communities and economies: the case of the MG Rover Longbridge closure in Birmingham', *Policy Studies*, **29** (3), 305–17.

Croucher, R. and G. White (2007), 'Enforcing a national minimum wage', *Policy Studies*, **28** (2), 145–61.

de Ruyter, A. and J. Burgess (2003), 'Growing labour insecurity in Australia and the UK in the midst of jobs growth: beware the Anglo-Saxon model!', *European Journal of Industrial Relations*, **9** (2), 223–43.

de Ruyter, A., D. Bailey G. Bentley and C. Chapain (2009), 'Precariousness of employment and regional disparities: an analysis of the labour market status of MG Rover workers 3 years after closure', paper presented at the Regional Studies Association Annual Conference, Leuven, April.

Fauth, R. and A. McVerry (2008), *Can 'Good Work' Keep Employees Healthy? Evidence from across the EU*, London: The Work Foundation.

Jones, R., H. Kierzkowski and C. Lurong (2005), 'What does evidence tell us about fragmentation and outsourcing?', *International Review of Economics and Finance*, **14** (3), 305–16.

Kleinknecht, A. (1998), 'Is labour market flexibility harmful to innovation?', *Cambridge Journal of Economics*, **22**, 387–96.

Nolan, P. (2004), 'Editorial: shaping the future: the political economy of work and employment', *Industrial Relations Journal*, **35** (5), 378–87.

OECD (1994), *The OECD Jobs Strategy*, Paris: OECD.

ONS (Office of National Statistics) (2009), *Trade Union Membership 2008*, London: Department of Business Enterprise and Regulatory Reform.

Peck, J. and N. Theodore (2007), 'Flexible recession: the temporary staffing industry and mediated work in the United States', *Cambridge Journal of Economics*, **31**, 171–92.

Pike, A. (2002), *Task Force and the Organisation of Economic Development: The Case of the North East Region of England*, Discussion Paper 02/3, Centre for Urban and Regional Development Studies, University of Newcastle upon Tyne.

Pike, A. (2005), 'Building a geographical political economy of closure: the case of R&DCo in North East England', *Antipode*, **37** (1), 93–115.

Standing, G. (1997), 'Globalisation, flexibility and insecurity', *European Journal of Industrial Relations*, **3** (1), 7–37.

Waring, P., A. de Ruyter and J. Burgess (2006), 'The Australian Fair Pay Commission: rationale, operation, antecedents and implications', *Economic and Labour Relations Review*, **16** (2), 127–46.

15. 'Politics of production', a new challenge for unionism: workers facing citizens in the French civil nuclear energy

Patrick Chaskiel

INTRODUCTION

If the globalization of economic activity is obvious in many ways, it does not mean that all productive activity is now run on a world-wide scale. Many industries are still at least partly managed in the national arena. The chemical sector of production, for example, has not experienced the same type of upheaval as other industries – assembly (automobile) or process (steel industry) – in the sense that the relocation is not massive and, therefore, job losses do not mainly result from relocating production to areas with lower wage costs. For economic reasons electricity also has to be produced as near to the 'consumers' as possible. In some cases, transfer attempts have not succeeded because of problems in exporting the technological 'knack' or skills.[1] In other cases (such as that of chemical fertilizers), production is relatively regionalized, even if it affects cross-border zones. The costs bound up with the transport of hazardous materials increase with distance since the risks (for example, of explosions or toxic leaks) are the object of more and more restrictive regulation.

Nevertheless, while French chemical, petrochemical and energy companies have not relocated jobs to Asia,[2] they have cut labour costs. This has been achieved first through automation, and then through subcontracting and creating precarious jobs: an oil refinery plant may thus have as many subcontracting workers as 'direct' ones. This is a classic, well-known scenario.

In fact, cost reduction is not the only threat to workers in high-risk industries. A new challenge has emerged as dangerous activities are increasingly being questioned by environmentalists who form a part of new social movements (Luhmann, 1993; Offe, 1984; Touraine et al., 1980).

Environmental movements have developed on an international scale making it much more difficult to set up new sites in Europe and particularly in France.[3] The companies involved in high-risk industrial production have therefore been forced to adopt the strategy of preserving existing production sites. To this extent, it is the very globalization of ecological protests shaped by non-governmental organizations (such as Greenpeace, Friends of the Earth, WWF and national voluntary associations which tend to be very similar in most industrial countries) that are restricting the breathing space of high-risk industrial firms.

Such questioning can be effective, as shown by the social conflict that arose from the AZF factory disaster, when a chemical fertilizer stock exploded, killing 30 people in and around the plant, in September 2001 in Toulouse. This disaster created a confrontation lasting several months between the inter-union committee of the employees of the chemical site and a constellation of voluntary associations, public sector trade unions and political anti-authority groups. This coalition was opposed to the continuation of activities and even to the existence of the chemical site where the factory was located. Thus, taking into account the dangers argued by the protesters and despite the fact that the work involved was said to be profitable by the company, a *secret* government decision closed down the workshops at the chemical site which were making a highly toxic gas (Chaskiel, 2007; Suraud, 2007). In other cases, after campaigns by voluntary groups and under the pressure of the local authorities, companies have closed factories – calling the closures 'reconversions' – on the grounds of diminished profitability in the face of pressure to bring them up to the environmental standards.[4]

These tensions and conflicts result from an increased tendency towards the 'politicization of production' (Offe, 1984, p. 176) that arose in the 1960s and 1970s with the emergence of the environmental movement, in particular that aimed against the development of the civil nuclear energy (Touraine et al., 1980). This raises questions for trade unionism in a different way from the historic focus on employment relations: from now on, employment protection must also be achieved through a legitimization of the activities concerned in order to face criticisms addressed to these very same activities as being dangerous. This legitimization turns out to be more complex than a 'simple' justification concerning the volume and skill level of jobs (direct or indirect). With the rise of the environmental movements, factories are no longer or not solely considered as spaces of wealth production, but also as pollutants and sources of risk. These difficulties cannot then be handled within the traditional framework of the conflict/negotiation process and institutions of employment relations. To the extent that ecological movements have a general and universal claim, which abstracts from the monetary or politico-strategic requirements of the 'system',[5] no collective bargaining is possible between civil society and decision makers. Moreover, tensions run through unionism, which is confronted with general claims (the refusal to run the risk of major disaster) that the unions do not control.

Paradoxically, these tensions are rarely researched, and the objective of this chapter is to fill the gap in information regarding an issue considered, with the growing impetus of the environmental theme, as a *new challenge* for trade unionism. We here advance the thesis that, far from having widened its field of demands, trade unionism has focused for the main part on the traditional protection of the worker-consumer, and has left to other groups the role of citizen on environmental issues. In other words, rather than participating in political protests against polluting and high-risk production and arguing for a reconfiguration of products and the means of production, trade unions as a whole have given priority to an approach within the existing framework of employment relations, where little dynamic articulation between workers and citizens is observable.

French civil nuclear power production is an example of the politicization of production and its effects, not only because it reveals a 'French' exception,[6] but also because it may be an indicator of the difficulties experienced by trade unionism in approaching questions of public opinion, where the flow of discussions is not regulated by money or power dimensions. The issue of French civil nuclear energy enables us to show how trade unions have changed from an appropriation of both the worker and citizen roles to a unique reassertion of the workers' role, abandoning, for the most part, the problem of politicization of production.

This chapter draws on research conducted in 2006–2008 into unionism and industrial risks,[7] in particular through a study of a nuclear power station located in the southwest of France (Golfech).[8] The research involved around 30 interviews (with union activists from CFDT, CFE-CGC, CGT and FO, elected representatives, members of voluntary organizations, managers, administrative staff), the analysis of various documents (including leaflets, minutes of workplace Committee for Hygiene, Safety and Working Conditions (CHSCT) and joint production committee meetings, press clippings, and minutes of public meetings) and many informal discussions.

FROM THE LABOUR/UNION DIVISION TO THE WORKER/CITIZEN DIVISION

If France is the country which has proportionately the most nuclear plants of the world, it owed this to a government plan in the 1970s[9] to build 50 reactors before 1985. This plan gave rise to much opposition, in one case leading to the 1981 abandonment of the Plogoff project in Brittany by newly elected President Mitterrand, and in others to a delay in opening (as at Superphenix, 50 kilometres from Lyon, even when after several incidents it began to work normally).

The construction of the case study power plant of Golfech was, for its part, characterized by both repeated 'violent' actions[10] – sabotage of electric pylons and attacks on the branch offices in Toulouse of EDF, France's state-owned public utility company – and more conventional protests – demonstrations, negative votes in regional institutions. This opposition combined multiple trends present in unionism (Durand and Harff, 1984, pp. 188–91). It was not systematically all anti-nuclear: its concerns ranged from the danger of the nuclear industry and its negative ecological impacts (waste, radioactivity) to a refutation of the 'nuclear political order' and criticism of the secrecy surrounding the functioning of power plants, and to the mode of decision making regarding energy policy and the choice of location for nuclear plants.

The trade unions were divided both nationally and locally about Golfech. Some were involved in the opposition, and others were in favour. There was no clear dividing line between the different French trade union confederations. Some local sections of the CGT, the main national union that supported the nuclear programme, joined in the anti-nuclear criticisms.[11]

However, locally, trade union opposition to the power plant mostly arose from within the structures of the CFDT[12] (the second largest French union). This position built upon arguments put forward by the CFDT leadership in a union book (CFDT, 1980) that included all the drawbacks of civil nuclear energy whilst not being formally anti-nuclear. As a result, the local structures of CFDT were relatively close to the anti-nuclear movement, to which, until the beginning of the 1980s at least, they also supplied material help.[13]

Nevertheless, this union opposition to the power plant arose out of the same variety of reasons as indicated above. Most of the CFDT unionists followed the radical anti-nuclear movement without really fitting in there. In fact, the appointment of a regional leader who is 'personally' anti-nuclear does not inevitably commit the regional structure to a permanent and radical opposition,[14] in particular because the 'violent' modes of protest introduced some distance between the union and the anti-nuclear committees.[15] The CFDT's demands for a moratorium on the nuclear programme also reflected the development of internal tensions, in particular within EDF. The CFDT's electricity workers were far from being unanimous concerning their opposition to the development of the civil nuclear energy, with professional engineers often being in favour of the programme (Groux and Mouriaux, 1989, pp. 167–9).

The CGT's national policy supported the principle of development of the nuclear power even after the abandonment of French technology (graphite–gas) in favour of an American pressurized water technology. It did so through arguing that the technology had been 'Frenchified' and that it created jobs. With respect to the Golfech site, the CGT sought, at first, the setting up of a coal power plant, linked to production from mines situated not far from Golfech. In this way, the CGT position was first of all concerned with the survival of the coalmining industry. However, when the government decided to establish a nuclear power plant, the CGT's approval of the decision came up against the hostility of a wide part of the population and of the elected representatives of the towns surrounding the proposed site. Thus, a referendum on the establishment of a nuclear installation in Golfech, organized in 1975 by the elected representatives of the districts of Tarn-et-Garonne, led to a clear 'no' (80 per cent) from a huge turnout (60 per cent of voters). This majority refusal by the population and the local elected representatives influenced the French Communist Party (PCF), which had close links with the CGT since many union leaders and activists were also members of the party,[16] to pronounce against the installation. In 1976 the PCF set out a national policy of opposition to the nuclear programme,[17] basing this on its rejection of a perceived tendency to privatize nuclear energy.[18] It then reconsidered its position at the end of 1979. The tension between the CGT and PCF at the end of 1970s, often ignored or hidden thirty years later, was not, however, about an ideological debate within the leadership of the CGT about nuclear power (a 'necessary evil or technological progress').[19] Instead it resulted primarily from the regional dimensions of the Communist movement, caught between immense local opposition to the nuclear plant and a fundamentally pronuclear policy that led the Communist Party (and the CGT) to be a pillar of the French nuclear programme.

Faced with these difficulties, the CGT departmental unions of Tarn-et-Garonne and Lot-et-Garonne agreed to avoid the development of internal debates, either because they hesitated to show a stance which would divide the organization,[20] or because these internal debates might generate a cleavage that would be hard to overcome as it did not correspond to the usual tensions created by the activism of extreme left-wing activists.[21] If, at first, the CGT did not particularly support the establishment of a power plant, at least before it was under construction, the very temporary freezing of construction works by the new Mitterrand Socialist government of 1981 facilitated the emergence of a movement calling for the resumption of the work. This involved sections of the CGT and FO,[22] but not the CFDT, which was still opposed to the nuclear plant. This movement was not so much pro-nuclear as pro-employment, because it concerned only the construction stage of the installation. The defence of the construction of the nuclear site temporarily eclipsed traditional divisions between employers and employees by bringing together particular interests.

In this way, the issue of employment proved a catalyst of industrial interests, combining in practice employers and some labour unions. However, even when they were based on a demand for a public service satisfying energy needs and national independence and for more transparency on how power plants are operated, locally trade union practices did not embody this approach. In other words, when there was trade union *promotion* of nuclear power, it used arguments from a multitude of references inherited from the traditional labour movement. When there was trade union *opposition* to the development of nuclear power, its premises came from a multitude of references arising from the new social protests of the 1970s. Thus, through these multiple points of view trade unionism at the end of the 1970s and in the early 1980s reflected both roles of worker and citizen. More recently, it has emphasized the first role and distanced itself from the second one.

A SHOPFLOOR-LEVEL APPROACH TO NUCLEAR SAFETY

Some decades later, after the effective implementation of the nuclear programme in the 1970s, another configuration emerged. The local anti-nuclear campaign had switched to 'standby mode', despite some spectacular demonstrations, such as the climbing of a cooling tower at the end of the 1980s. As a result, trade union policies became increasingly focused no longer on a public debate questioning the existence of nuclear power, but on coverage of the classic issues: employment, wages, duration of work and working conditions, including health and safety at work.

In a nuclear plant, beyond the customary health and safety issues, radioactive risks affect employees directly, through either accidents or so-called 'acceptable' doses. However, radioactivity may 'overflow' the physical limits of the power plant, thus constituting nuclear power as the archetypal technological risk. The question then arises of how trade unions deal with a characteristic which tends to blur the boundaries of the factory, since external protests also exercise a form of surveillance on the operation of the plant itself.

However, far from using this blurring as a means to support demands about nuclear safety, trade union practices continued to focus on classic work problems, and to neglect local regional ones. They thus also neglected citizenship in the form of taking into account and getting in touch with the local residents.[23] This focus of interest on work problems was particularly explicit in the safety area. Within the Golfech nuclear power station, the demands and mobilizations of the union on nuclear safety were less significant than those concerned with privatization or in defence of basic union rights. Yet the campaigns tended to refer to health and safety *at work* rather than evoke *nuclear safety* as any kind of threat for the environment. Where nuclear safety issues were regularly and collectively considered by the local and national trade union structures, the discussions were founded on narrow work-related approaches, offering criticism only in relation to management's search for 'productivity at any price'.

In the field of health and safety at work, the nuclear division of EDF and the unions have without any doubt a stronger tradition than in the other constituents of the company (Tixier and Mauchamp, 2000, p. 82), even if subcontracted workers appear to be much less protected than EDF workers (Thébaud-Mony, 2000). On the other hand, this tradition must be clarified: it focused on the radio-protection of employees, certainly specific to the nuclear plants, but which is only one aspect among others of nuclear danger. The essential safety of nuclear power was not a direct trade union theme, and was not raised either in the local Health and Safety Committee (CHSCT[24]) or in EDF's national Health and Safety Council,[25] which disappeared at the end of the 2000s.[26] Where periodic meetings took place between the trade unions and EDF's Nuclear Production Division, in the case study power plant the issue was not taken into account by the trade unions. A line was drawn between the so-called 'human factors', amply handled in as far as they directly affected the employees, and the technical and even organizational factors. These were considered essentially from the perspective of hierarchical relationships and productivity gains, but not in terms of the general functioning of the power plant.

From this union perspective, the safety issue refers essentially to the principle of a safety culture promoted by the company. Even if demands were renewed about training,[27] necessary to replace numerous retiring employees, or about the hierarchical rigidities obstructing feedback to management,[28] union demands were mainly focused on the capacity of employees to intervene in the functioning of shops or in maintenance work. At the same time, the trade unions intervened little in the central aspects of the nuclear process, failing to mobilize the necessary skills on a complex issue, despite including among their members a number of engineers (often having worked their way up from the shop floor) and even some directors of power plants. A study of the multiplicity of questions raised and the length of treatment given to them in the CHSCT and

Production Committees (CMP) revealed not only the predominant place of the issue of health and safety at work but also the weak place of nuclear safety.[29]

Indeed the problem of nuclear safety was not viewed as falling within the competence of the CHSCT, in the sense that this latter was not supposed to deal with this aspect. This characteristic can be attributed to the will of management, itself subjected to a policy decided by the Nuclear Production Division (DPN) of EDF. Yet requests to include the theme of nuclear safety as a public problem on the agenda did not emerge in the CHSCT meetings.[30] On this subject, it was rather management-speak that was regularly repeated: references to the idea that the viability of nuclear power is based on 'public confidence' and 'communication' with the surrounding population.[31] Thus management put pressure on workers through raising the issue of a possible closing of nuclear plants because of ecological protests.

While in voicing these views management effectively introduced 'public opinion' and the nuclear debate into the plant, the union activists did not respond by using this public dimension of nuclear power to support their own demands. At another level, it was the EDF management which used the machinery of collective agreements to raise the issue of 'corporate social responsibility',[32] without trade union requests for negotiations on the topic. Thus, management, national and local, when confronted with awareness that the safety issue is a determining factor in the societal acceptability of nuclear power, on the one hand publicly involve trade unions and, on the other one, determine that the issue is a kind of reserved area from which trade union voice is excluded.

For a long time, the processing of incidents or accidents was differentiated in three ways: whether they involved employees or not, whether they stemmed from an operational mistake and whether they resulted from hardware failures.[33] The control assured by the Nuclear Safety Authority (ASN) was itself ambiguous. There was a distinction between a 'health and safety inspection' by external labour inspectors and a 'work inspection' (which does not come under the remit of the Ministry of Labour and its inspectorate). Additionally, the variable of 'work inspection' depended on different administrative divisions. Thus an ASN representative within the Golfech power plant fulfilled the function of 'work inspector' exclusively dealing with working issues unrelated to safety, but did not have any responsibility as a nuclear safety inspector.[34] As a result, the unions saw the function of 'work inspector' as a management responsibility but did not view the function of nuclear safety in the same way.[35] This approach consequently creates an interpretative model of safety, as the activities are controllable or not only at workshop level: the basis of union intervention is the specific workshop, except for maintenance, where more and more of the work is being subcontracted.

An annual report on safety was given to the site Production Committee, yet the trade unions barely intervened at these meetings. It was as if the unions accepted that the management indicators, particularly their descriptions of specific events where operating rules had been broken and their reports of the significance of the incidents, were sufficient to monitor changes in the level of nuclear safety fully. The trade unions only intervened if the incidents directly concerned workers. Their interventions on safety issues were limited to work and labour relations issues or to the restructuring of the company.

This historic situation was disrupted not only by greater questioning with respect to the existence of high-risk activities, but also by the evolution of regulations reflecting such questioning. For example, the Nuclear Safety Transparency Act of June 2006 made it possible for health and safety issues to be placed before a Commission Locale d'Information (Area Information Committee, or CLI). The CLIs, the first of which was created at the Fessenheim[36] nuclear plant in 1977, include regional and area representatives, government representatives, trade unions and nuclear experts, and deal directly with the issues raised in protests against civilian nuclear energy. Although the unions put forward the principle of defending public services, including nuclear safety, the plant-level trade union involvement in this CLI was quite limited.

It was the same limited involvement for the area trade unions, whose representation is generally from the regional union federations. Both the trade union federations and the regional structures were divided, depending on whether they were about technical or political issues.[37] None the less, their divisions were not decisive because in practice the trade union presence was very uneven. In the CLI of Golfech (and it is similar to other cases that emerged during interviews), the regular attendance of the trade unions in the meetings was an exception: only the CFDT representative of the union's Tarn-et-Garonne Regional Committee, who was a former employee of the power plant, attended the sessions regularly.

If part of the explanation for this poor attendance can be understood in the context of the decline of active trade unionism, this cannot be viewed as decisive. For example, if former nuclear industry engineers wanted to establish closer relations with the CGT, they were not likely to wish to participate in the CLI as union delegates.[38] And, from a different angle, conscientious participation in the CLI does not imply close links with the inter-industrial structure that delegated the trade unionist.[39] It does not ensure that demands are raised or that there are regular discussions of reports. Furthermore, raising 'criticisms' of the functioning of the power plant in public meetings was not something that many union activists could easily envisage.[40]

This low level of union involvement in these public dialogue committees is not comparable to the refusal of anti-nuclear activists to legitimize what they call a 'sham consultation'. Rather it shows the relative isolation of the unions within one single big company (EDF) and the setting aside of atypical subjects as too touchy to be handled. Where regional inter-industrial structures question the autonomous approach of EDF's trade unions, they do not raise concerns about nuclear safety. Such a situation suggests the unions are making no connection between the concept of public service and the idea of *transparency*, and are not attempting to use the CLI as a lever in relation to the company's new status as an independent, publicly owned firm – despite the fact that this new status is opposed by the CGT and CFDT and only accepted with reservations by FO. This failure reveals the tension between trade union positions in the field of wage relations (defending workers as consumers) and their positions in the civic sphere (where citizenship questions about the dangers of nuclear power are raised). In other words, it reveals trade union difficulties in overcoming its worker/consumer role, a difficulty largely confirmed when a new public debate started on a programme to revive the nuclear power industry.

THE SEPARATION OF LABOUR AND CITIZENSHIP

In the 2000s, at the instigation of the French government, a programme to establish (European pressurized reactors) (EPR) was launched, aiming to replace the tens of ageing reactors built in the period 1960–80. The scale of this programme was not explicitly defined when it was formally decided in 2005, but it seems to be smaller than that of the 1970s: one reactor per year (compared with 50 reactors in 10 years in the 1970s programme). This EPR programme appeared as a cheap energy project (to supply electricity at a 'good price'), as an industrial strategy (to develop a new type of reactor and retain a major sector of French industry), and as an ecological solution (to facilitate quasi-neutral energy in global warming terms), despite offering no solutions to the nuclear waste problem. It thus integrated, upside down, the debates about environmental degradation while valuing highly the arguments about low-cost production and the retention of a French industry.

The launch of this new programme and the public debate which it aroused imply that trade unionism should extend itself beyond the labour issue and approach the civil nuclear energy question as a general societal problem. If we set aside a certain reluctance to participate in most public debates, most prominently characteristic of FO, new tensions appear that are not rooted in the debates of the 1970s. As described above, the intra-trade union divisions at that time concerned the economic and political legitimacy of the nuclear power sector. The trade union movement as a whole thus occupied both the wage relations sphere *and* the citizenship space, combining their roles as representatives of the worker-consumer and of the worker-citizen. However, in the 2000s another situation arose.

Trade unionism is not really divided any more about the existence of the nuclear sector, even if recently created unions such as SUD support a range of positions including some that are very critical.[41] The public debate has moved on: it is now between those who make severe criticisms of the social and economic aspects of nuclear power in relation to safety (including the deterioration of maintenance and the growth of subcontracting) and the rising risks for employees and the public, and those who argue there is a strong social, economic and environmental case (employment, energy needs, and countering fossil-fuel based dangers of global warming) for developing a new nuclear programme (at the very least to replace old reactors).

During the public debate dedicated to the EPR in 2005 the CGT national leadership[42] presented initial texts[43] and, finally, an activists' policy pamphlet,[44] around two main subjects: energy as having a vital stake in economic development, and the construction of the EPR reactor as the answer to the need for jobs. Addressing the issue of safety, the activist pamphlet referred to the capacity of public services to fulfil the missions of safety and to the need to reject the financial profitability criteria as a way to manage electricity production.[45] Its way forward on this was to sound 'the alarm to encourage the government to convene . . . a Round Table . . . *to discuss the economic and social challenges posed* by the EPR . . . *For the CGT, the stakes are huge, in particular regarding employment and the energy independence of our country*'.[46] It was evident that the nuclear safety problem did not appear at the same level as did employment or independence.[47]

However, some local CGT leaders[48] differed from the CGT national leadership's position. Certain leaders, although welcoming the revival of the nuclear programme of the 2000s, asserted nevertheless that 'the prevention of risk of climatic change associated with greenhouse effects should not be offset by an increased risk due to financial decisions made on nuclear installations'.[49] This statement actually challenged that of the CGT national leadership[50] because it proposed that an economic/industrial project should be based on a social project, which should deal both with health and safety at work and with nuclear safety as a precondition of any new programme.[51] This critical position on the EPR programme has been used by the opponents of the nuclear industry.[52] It reflected an interrogation not so much of the value of civil nuclear energy as of its reliability in relation to EDF restructuring and privatization. More generally, local leaders are very critical about the cost-reduction policy of EDF and its effects on workers' health and safety, as well as wider nuclear safety, because of the lack of maintenance and the poor quality of the subcontracted work. Thus in such conditions they express hesitations about the EPR programme.

The position of the CFDT was also a critical one but in a different way. On the one hand, CFDT suggested skipping the intermediate level represented by EPR (a third-generation reactor) and waiting for the development of reactors of the fourth generation. But, in CFDT history, the Superphenix fast-breeder reactor of this fourth generation had previously been opposed and it had provoked an internal conflict. The stopping of Superphenix, a major symbol of the anti-nuclear movement, had revealed a conflict between the CFDT confederation's national leadership, the leadership of the chemical energy national union and the CFDT union of the Isère region, where the Superphenix was established in the village of Creys-Malville with local members inside the power plant. All of the wider structures had accepted the closure decided by the Socialist government in 1997, but the local section of CFDT inside the power plant continued to argue for its staying open through defending its technological dimensions.[53] The same internal difficulties emerged again during the presidential elections of 2007 when the CFDT's electricity union rejected the Socialist Party candidate's proposal to close the Fessenheim nuclear power station in Alsace, arguing that it 'is unacceptable that a second Creys-Malville will serve as a means of attracting the Greens' voters'.[54] From this point of view, the technical debate on EPR reflects, in a certain way, the difficulty for the unions of holding to a position in a simple debate: for *or* against nuclear energy.

The evidence suggests that the national trade union leaders saw the economic and technical aspects of the EPR programme as the main issues in the debate, even if some local leaders were more cautious in their support of EPR. Consequently it was the environmental movement and not trade unionism that acted on behalf of citizens generally, through raising critical questions about the dangers of nuclear energy and about energy saving as a way to decrease electricity consumption.

CONCLUSION

Trade unionism is facing a problem which is not specific to civilian nuclear energy and which has become widespread in industrial nations: how to keep a perspective representing the voice of the employees of an industry, based on labour traditions and the employment relations history, when the public is protesting against the developments happening in this very same industry. We can, in fact, observe that there is a distance between both characteristics of trade unionism: as a social partner and as a creator of societal values (Hyman, 2001, pp. 38–64). The question is how far societal values are susceptible to coverage by unionism, in particular since workers' trade unions have become the residual shape of the labour movement with the general weakening of strongly rooted labour parties.

In this respect, a tension has developed between the role of worker and that of citizen. From this point of view, the historic social dynamic which presided over industrialization is not extinct, but it is significantly challenged by an environmental dynamic that goes beyond trade unionism and which extends at the global level, even while trade unionism remains based essentially in the nation state. To this extent, it is possible to speak of a new challenge to trade unionism.

NOTES

1. After the AZF disaster in Toulouse in September 2001 it appeared this was the reason it was not possible to relocate the manufacturing of a special fuel for rocket motors that took place in a nearby factory either to the United States or to China (conversations with employees and industrialists).
2. The location of chemical plants in Asia responds to local market needs, but local companies often make close copies of the design and technologies used in 'Western' plants.
3. Conversations with industrialists.
4. One Paris-region chemical factory founded at the end of the nineteenth century was 'reconverted' (exiting the chemical sector and joining the biotechnology industry, with several hundred job losses) because of a negative estimation by the executive management regarding the possibility of reducing pollutants which widely exceeded statutory thresholds (conversations with industrialists).
5. In the sense of Habermassian social theory. Habermas (1997) distinguishes *systemic integration* regulated by money and state-administrative power on one side and, on the other side, *social integration* through discussions building solidarities and, thus, public opinion.
6. France has the highest proportion of any country's electricity supplied by nuclear energy (80 per cent is nuclear).
7. This research was financed by the Foundation for a Culture of Industrial Safety (FONCSI) and by the Ministry of Ecology, Energy, Sustainable Development and Land Settlement (MEEDAT, 'Risks, Decisions, Territories' plan).
8. This plant was and is still opposed by activists, partly initiators of the national network 'Out of Nuclear', including approximately 800 voluntary political and labour union organizations.
9. Called 'Plan Messmer', from the name of the prime minister initiating it.
10. Most of the episodes are reported in Comité de Recherche pour une Alternative Sociale (CRAS) (1999).
11. Interviews with MM. S., CGT activist, Syndicat des Cheminots d'Agen.
12. In particular the Syndicat Général de l'Education Nationale.

13. Interview with Mrs G., anti-nuclear activist.
14. Interview with M. F., former union area CFDT leader, Tarn-et-Garonne.
15. Interviews with MM., A. and F., former union area leaders, Tarn-et-Garonne.
16. The PCF was very influential until the 1980s. In national elections it had reached almost 30 per cent at the end of the 1940s and still had around 20 per cent of the national vote at the end of the 1970s.
17. See Gaston Plissonnier's letter dated 15 July 1976. As Secretary of the Central Committee in the national leadership of the PCF he wrote: 'Everything confirms our orientation, to reject this programme [state nuclear power] and to say no to the setting up of power plants which ensue from it, without entailing us in a systematic opposition to any electricity production of nuclear origin.'
18. Interviews with M. R., former federal secretary of PCF Tarn-et-Garonne.
19. Interview with M. D., former confederate CGT leader and the former General Secretary of the Mines-Energie Federation.
20. Interviews with MM. G. and M., former departmental union (UD) CGT leaders of Tarn-et-Garonne.
21. Interview with M. M., former-UD-CGT leader of Lot-et-Garonne.
22. Born of an anti-Communist split within the CGT, in 1947.
23. In a seminar 'The Nuclear Power and the Man', on 9–10 October, 2002, introduced by labour unions under the aegis of the Conseil Supérieur des Comités Consultatifs des Comités Mixtes à la Production, the issue of the relationship with the local population was very, very marginal.
24. Comité d'Hygiène, Sécurité et des Conditions de Travail (Committee on Health, Safety and Working Conditions).
25. An examination of minutes of CHSCT meetings is used as a basis for this assertion.
26. Because of a privatization process in the company.
27. Minutes of a union member of the Fédération Chimie-Energie CFDT meeting on the general inspection of the nuclear safety of EDF, 4 December 2006.
28. Recurring demand within the CHSCT (source: minutes).
29. However, a new orientation can be observed at the end of the 2000s, which has a consideration of these subjects long left aside. Interview with M. D., Secretary of the labour union CGT, and M.L., member of the leadership of the National Federation of Mines and Energy.
30. We base this on an analysis of the CHSCT minutes between 2001 and 2007.
31. Speech of a power plant manager in February 2001.
32. Interviews with MM. P., Secretary of the European group committee of EDF, and T., member of the committee of group for the CGT-FO.
33. Interviews with activists.
34. Unlike the situation in several other power plants, where both skills can be combined.
35. Interview with ASN inspectors.
36. Very close to the German border.
37. Interview with MM. D. and G., respectively Secretary of the CGT labour union of Golfech and former UD CGT leader, Tarn-et-Garonne.
38. Interviews with federal leaders.
39. Interview with M. G, CFDT representative in the Golfech CLI.
40. Interviews with CGT activists from Golfech.
41. The union SUD, largely stemming from a left-wing split from the CFDT, is not represented in the case study power plant. The positions of SUD-Energie (opposed to the EPR but without formally expressing its opposition to civil nuclear energy) and those, for example, of SUD-Education and SUD-Rail ('out of nuclear power') are not expressed in an identical way.
42. CGT Federation Mines-Energie, Construction, Metallurgy, CGT Region of Normandy, Union Départementale CGT Manche and Confédération CGT.
43. Various texts, slide shows and internal mails, from the Federation Mines-Energie of CGT, were consulted.

44. A document giving the official position of an organization in an institutional public debate.
45. CGT, activists' booklet on the EPR Tête de Série project.
46. Internal e-mail, 6 October 2004.
47. In the four-page activists' booklet, the nuclear safety issue covers four lines.
48. Federal Union of Engineers, Executives, Technicians.
49. CGT Federation Mines-Energie, 'The necessary guarantees for a safe, transparent and democratic nuclear power', Lyon, 29 October 2004.
50. Interview with M. D., Secretary of the CGT of Golfech.
51. Interview with M. L., originator of CGT local leaders' statement of October 2004.
52. Interview with Mrs G., member of the board of the 'Way out of Nuclear Power' network.
53. Interview with M. M., former Secretary of the CFDT section of the Creys-Malville power plant (Superphenix).
54. CFDT, IEG branch, Direction Production-Ingénierie: minutes of the meeting between the CFDT and the Socialist party, 6 February 2007.

REFERENCES

CFDT (1980), *Le dossier électronucléaire*, Paris: Seuil.
Chaskiel, Patrick (2007), 'Syndicalisme et risques industriels: avant et après la catastrophe d'AZF', *Sociologie du Travail*, **49**, 180–94.
CRAS (1999), *Golfech: implantation et résistances*, Toulouse: La Rotonde.
Durand, Michelle and Yvette Harff (1984), 'Les syndicates face aux problèmes d'environnement et de qualité de la vie', in Mark Kesselman (ed.), *Le mouvement ouvrier français: crise économique et changement politique*, Paris: Les Editions Ouvrières, pp. 179–201.
Groux, Guy and René Mouriaux (1989), *La CFDT*, Paris: Economica.
Habermas, Jürgen (1997), *Droit et démocratie: entre faits et normes*, Paris: Gallimard.
Hyman, Richard (2001), *Understanding European Trade Unionism: Between Market, Class and Society*, London: Sage.
Jasper, James M. (1990), *Nuclear Politics: Energy and the State in the United States, Sweden and France*, Princeton: Princeton University Press.
Luhmann, Niklas (1993), *Risk: A Sociological Theory*, Berlin: de Gruyter.
Meynaud, Hélène Yvonne and Marc Xavier (2002), *Entreprise et société: dialogue de chercheur-e-s à EDF*, Paris: L'Harmattan.
Offe, Claus (1984), *Contradictions of the Welfare State*, Cambridge: MIT Press.
Suraud, Marie-Gabrielle (2007), *AZF: de la concertation à la contestation*, Paris: La Documentation Française.
Thébaud-Mony, Annie (2000), *L'industrie nucléaire: sous-traitance et servitude*, Paris: INSERM-EDK.
Tixier, Pierre-Eric and Nelly Mauchamp (2000), *EDF-GDF: une entreprise publique en mutation*, Paris: La Découverte.
Touraine, Alain, Zsuzsa Hegedus, François Dubet and Michel Wieviorka (1980), *La prophétie antinucléaire*, Paris: Seuil.

Index